History of the Town of

Manchester, Essex County,

Massachusetts, 1645-1895

D. F. Lamson

Alpha Editions

This edition published in 2020

ISBN : 9789354013737

Design and Setting By
Alpha Editions
email - alphaedis@gmail.com

. HISTORY .

OF THE

TOWN OF MANCHESTER

ESSEX COUNTY, MASSACHUSETTS

1645=1895

By Rev. D. F. LAMSON

"Historie is the memorie of time, the life of the dead, and the happinesse of the lyvinge." — CAPTAINE JOHN SMITH.

"A people which takes no pride in the achievements of remote ancestors, will never achieve anything worthy to be remembered with pride by remote descendants." — MACAULAY.

PUBLISHED BY THE TOWN

HISTORICAL STATEMENT.

THE interest on the part of the people in the Two Hundred and Fiftieth Anniversary is due in large measure to the Historical Society, which was formed in 1886, and which has made its object the awakening of interest in the history of the town, and the collecting of materials in view of the approaching Quarter-Millennial. Regular meetings of the Society have been held, and papers read by the members on various matters of interest connected with the town's earlier or later history. These papers, after being discussed, have in some instances been deposited in the archives of the Society. A few donations have been received from members and others of old books, records, manuscripts, etc., as the nucleus of a Historical Collection. Above all, a stimulus has been given to antiquarian interest and historical research, dusty cobwebs have been brushed from the walls of memory, fading recollections and dim traditions have received new freshness and life, and some things of value to the historian have been rescued from the oblivion into which they were fast passing.

The initiatory steps towards a celebration of the Two Hundred and Fiftieth Anniversary and the preparation of a History of the Town, were taken by the Historical Society in the appointment of a committee to bring the matter before the town at the annual meeting, March 20, 1894. At that meeting a large committee was

chosen to report at the next annual meeting a plan for
the suitable celebration of the event, and to publish in
connection with it a History of the Town. A Committee on Publication was subsequently appointed by
the General Committee, consisting of W. H. Tappan,
R. C. Lincoln, D. F. Lamson, D. L. Bingham and A. S.
Jewett.

The work of preparing the History was placed in the
hands of Rev. D. F. Lamson, and commenced in July,
1894.

The History is published by the Town, and the elec-
trotype plates are in the possession of the Town, for its
subsequent use.

The publication of the History has been delayed, in
order to include a record of the celebration.

PREFACE.

IN undertaking this work, the author was aware that it imposed upon him a difficult and responsible task — that of presenting within the compass of a moderate-sized volume, in a readable manner and yet with scrupulous regard to historical accuracy, the life of this ancient town through a quarter of a millennium. There was needed something more than a narration of events. Independent or slightly related and widely separated incidents — incidents in themselves often trivial — were to be brought together and grouped according to the laws of historical perspective, and invested with living interest.

Not the least of the difficulties met with has been to give a proportionate view of the many interests and industries of the community during this extended period. The author cannot hope that the work will altogether escape criticism in this particular. Men will estimate things very much according to their point of view, and their individual training, tastes and dispositions. The claim can only be made that there has been an attempt to hold the balance in a judicial and even hand. For the sake of presenting a consecutive and readable narrative, much valuable matter has been thrown into foot-notes, while other matter finds place in Appendixes.

A difficulty has been found, it should perhaps be said, in the scarcity of material at some points for anything

like a complete narrative. There are picturesque incidents and quaint *asides*, often, where there is little from
which to construct a reliable and consecutive history.

Contemporaneous events and events of very recent
occurrence have been, in general, very lightly touched
upon, or omitted altogether; for the reason that it is
difficult in some instances to treat such events fairly, and
in others there is often a doubt whether they will attain
the dignity of history or are simply passing shadows
flitting across the stage.[1]

The life of a small community is of interest especially
as it is seen to be a part of the larger life of the times.
The author has accordingly sought to connect the narrative with what was taking place upon a wider theatre.
It is thought that the picture will not be less attractive
because of its framing in the events of the time.

It is well that attention should be called to the fact
that there was no standard of orthography in the English language in the seventeenth and eighteenth centuries. Special confusion exists in the spelling of
proper names, the use of abbreviations, capitals and
marks of punctuation. It is hardly to be expected that
errors have been wholly avoided; but it is hoped that
they are but few, and that they do not impair the value
of the work.

Due acknowledgment has been made, it is believed,
of all sources which have been relied upon for information. For the rest, the author desires once for all to
express his thanks to all who have kindly aided him by
their suggestions and reminiscences, which have helped
to give the work a local coloring and make the features
of actors in the history more lifelike.

It is hoped that the book, upon which much labor has

[1] Other omissions may be accounted for by the fact that the work is a
History, and not a Business Directory or Advertising Medium.

been expended for many months, will prove of permanent value as a contribution to the literature of town history in Massachusetts. The author, who has been for some years a resident of Manchester, though not " to the manor born," has found his work a pleasant and congenial one, and in taking leave of it commends it to the kind regard of its reader

D. F. Lamson

Manchester, July 4, 1895.

TABLE OF CONTENTS.

APPENDIXES.

SUPPLEMENT.

ILLUSTRATIONS.

PORTRAITS.

NOTES.

ILLUSTRATIONS.

The illustrations are by Kilburn & Cross, Boston, with the exception of the Map of the Town, which was lithographed by A. W. Moore & Co., Boston.

OLD AND NEW STYLE.

In 1751, an Act of Parliament ordered that the new year begin with Jan. 1, 1752. Before this, the year had commenced March 25. It was also ordered that eleven days be dropped, September 3 being reckoned September 14. This attempt to rectify the calendar must be borne in mind in connection with dates previous to March 25, 1752, unless it is stated that they are given in New Style.

A CORRECTION.

In a quotation on page 87, is a statement which should be corrected. The exploit of Capt. Pert, which belongs to the war of 1812, and not to the Revolution, was brought to a successful termination by the aid of Manchester fishermen with whom he managed to get into communication, near the entrance to Gloucester harbor, and not " under the guns " of the forts at Boston. Manchester deserves the full credit of this remarkable feat in the history of naval tactics.

GENEALOGIES.

In the circular issued Dec. 20, 1894, it was stated that genealogies of the earlier families would be published, so far as they were furnished for that purpose, and as there should be space for them. To the disappointment of the committee, there have been but nine genealogies sent in, in time for publication, and of these five were more or less defective, one being a mere fragment. The other four have already appeared in print. In these circumstances, the committee deemed it advisable to omit the publication of genealogies altogether. The MSS. have been deposited in the archives of the Historical Society.

HISTORY OF MANCHESTER.

CHAPTER I.

INTRODUCTORY.

" Shooting round the winding shores
Of narrow capes, and isles which lie
Slumbering to ocean's lullaby,—
With birchen boat and glancing oars,
The red men to their fishing go."

Whittier.

CHAPTER I.

INTRODUCTORY.

INDIAN OCCUPANCY — MASCONOMO — RELATIONS BETWEEN
WHITES AND INDIANS — GEOGRAPHY — CLIMATE — SOIL —
PRODUCTIONS — OLD AND NEW.

THE history of America begins with the advent
of Europeans in the New World. The Red
Men in small and scattered bands[1] roamed
the stately forests and interminable prairies, hunted
the bison and the deer, fished the lakes and streams,
gathered around the council-fire and danced the
war-dance; but they planted no states, founded no
cities, established no manufactures, engaged in no
commerce, cultivated no arts, built up no civiliza-
tions. They left their names upon mountains and
rivers from lordly Agiochook to the mighty Mississippi; but they made no other impress upon
the continent which from time immemorial had
been their dwelling-place. The record of their past
vanishes like one of their own forays in the wilderness. Their shell-heaps[2] and their graves are the

[1] Of course, all estimates of the numbers of the Aborigines are conjectural; but they were probably fewer than is popularly supposed. "The
pre-Columbian population was astonishingly small as compared with the
enormous extent of territory." *The United States of America*, Prof. N. S.
Shaler, vol. I, p. 224.

[2] "On the shores of some of the lagoons, or forming small conical
islands in their midst, were white heaps of broken clam-shells. . . .
When these shell heaps were first explored they contained bones of many
kinds of fish and birds, including fragments of that extinct bird, the
great auk. They also yielded broken pieces of roughly ornamented pot-
tery, bits of copper, and stone implements of the Indians who had made
the Ipswich River and its sand-hills one of their principal camping-
grounds." *Land of the Lingering Snow*, Frank Bolles, Boston, 1893, p. 64.

5

only remains that are left to show that they once called these lands their own.[1] *They made no history.*

The country was practically unoccupied, when the white man first set foot upon its shores. The vast wilderness, stretching westward for league upon league toward the setting sun, and teeming with waste fertility, was but a hunting-ground and a battle-field to a few fierce hordes of savages.[2]

Unless, therefore, the imagination be drawn upon for facts, the Indian Period, except so far as Europeans became actors upon the stage, presents almost no material for the historian. It is known that the whole of the eastern part of Massachusetts that is now included in Essex County was inhabited, on the arrival of the first colonists, by the Agawams, a tribe of the Algonquins. They are described by Gosnold, who appears to have touched at Cape Anne in 1602, as " a people tall of stature, broad and grym visaged; their eye browes paynted white."[3] There is evidence that the Aborigines of this part of New England had been greatly diminished in numbers, not long before the arrival of the colonists. Mention is made of " a three yeeres Plague, which swept away most of the inhabitants

[1] Indian graves have been discovered in several places in town, but reverently filled up again without disturbing the skeleton remains. Mr. John Lee has left a carefully written account of one of these "finds." *Vide* p. 345.

[2] "One might sometimes journey for days together through the twilight forest, and meet no human form. Broad tracts were left in solitude. All Kentucky was a vacant waste, a mere skirmishing-ground for the hostile war-parties of the north and south. A great part of Upper Canada, of Michigan and of Illinois, besides other portions of the West, were tenanted by wild beasts alone." Parkman, *History of Pontiac,* 148.

[3] Strachey's *Historie of Travaile into Virginie.*

all along the Sea coast, and in some places utterly consumed man, woman and childe, so that there is no person left to lay clame to the soyle. . . . In most of the rest, the Contagion hath scarce left alive one person of an hundred." [1] Hutchinson (I, 38 *n.*) says that " Some tribes were in a manner extinct "; " the Massachusetts particularly said by some to have been reduced from 30,000 to 300 fighting men." Morton, speaking of the epidemic, says, " The hand of God fell heavily upon them, with such a mortal stroake, that they died on heapes." [2] No doubt the spirit as well as the power of the tribes was greatly broken.

The chief, or Sagamore, who ruled in a patriarchal sort of way in this region, was named Masconomo.[3] His chief camping place seems to have been at what is now Ipswich,—

" large limbed *Ipswich* brought to eye 'mongst woods and waters cleer." [4]

He seems to have been a kindly disposed and peaceable neighbor to the whites, rather than a war-like foe.[5] It was owing, no doubt, largely to his friendly disposition that no bloody conflicts with the original possessors of the soil stain the early

[1] *Planter's Plea*, London, 1630.   [2] *New English Canaan*, ch. iii.

[3] Hubbard, 130. Hutchinson calls him *Masconomeo* (I, 25, *n.*). In the deed given by his grandsons (1700), he is called *Masconomo* and *Masque-nomenit*. He received the name from the settlers of Sagamore John. He died in 1658.

[4] *Good News from New England*, 1648.

[5] *Maskonomett*, with four other sachems, signed an agreement, Mar. 7, 1644, " to bee true & faithfull to the government, ayding to the main-tenance thereof . . . . & to bee willing from time to time to bee instructed in the knowledge and worship of God." *Massachusetts Colonial Records*, vol. II, p. 55.

records. No colonists were waylaid and shot in
ambush; no glare of burning dwellings, no savage
war-whoop, terrified the infant settlement. The new
comers planted and builded, went to church and
mill, in safety.

Lands were gained by purchase,[1] or by peaceful
possession, and not by the sword. More honor is
due to the first settlers of Cape Anne in this respect, from the fact that this principle was not
held to by the colonists generally. One thing that
made Roger Williams unpopular at Salem, and that
led to his banishment, in addition to his claim that
magistrates had no authority in matters of conscience, was his position that "the land belonged to
the Indians. and title thereto could be acquired only
from them, and not by virtue of the king's grant."
The final payment for the land, however, was not
made until 1700, when the town paid the grandsons
of Masconomo. £3, 19s., for relinquishing all right,
title and interest in the land then comprising the
township.[2]

[1] This indeed was but following the instructions given to Endicott:
"If any of the salvages pretend right of inheritance to all or any part of
the lands granted in our patent, we pray you endeavor to purchase their
tytle, that we may avoid the least scruple of intrusion." Hazard, 1, 263.
On the other hand, Winthrop had written before he left England: "That
wch lies comon & hath never been replenished or subdued, is free to any
that will possesse and improve it . . . And for the Natives in New
England they inclose noe land neither have any settled habitation nor any
tame cattle to improve the land by, & soe have noe other but a naturall
right to those countries Soe as if wee leave them sufficient for their use
wee may lawfully take the rest, there being more then enough for them &
us." Conclusions, etc.

[2] For a copy of the Deed, see p.345. It was not until half a century
after the occupation of Boston peninsula, that the citizens troubled themselves to obtain a deed of the land from the grandson of Chickatanbut.
This was in 1708. Memorial History of Boston, vol. 1, p. 249.

An ancient record is not without a touch of pathos, as showing how early this once independent chief lost every vestige of his power; the date is Oct. 7, 1646. "Upon ye petition of ye sagam^r of Aagawam, for lib^{r}ty for one of o^r smiths to amend his gun, it is ord^{r}ed y^t warrant shalbe granted." [1] The Indians in this vicinity, it would seem, were soon reduced to a condition of weakness and vassalage, similar to that of the Israelites in the time of Saul. [2]

The suggestion has been made, and it is to be hoped that it may sometime be acted upon, that a native boulder marked with the simple inscription

MASCONOMO,

be placed in some suitable spot, as a memento of the chief who first welcomed the white man to these shores, and of a once numerous but now vanishing race. [3]

One other influence, besides the plague already mentioned, no doubt had an effect in cowing the spirit of the Indians, and rendering the work of settlement an easier and less hazardous one. Humphry Woodberye, of Beverly, aged about 72 years, testified upon oath, 16 February, 1680, "When wee setled the Indians neuer then molested vs in our improvemen^t or sitting downe, either on Salem or Beuerly sides of the ferry, but shewed themselues very glad of our company, & came &

---

[1] *Massachusetts Colonial Records*, Vol. II, p. 163.

[2] 1 *Sam.* xiii, 19, 20.

[3] Schoolcraft estimates their number at the beginning of the settlement of the country by Europeans as 1,000,000. It is supposed there are now in the United States, including Alaska, about 280,000.

planted by vs, & oftentimes came to vs for shelter,
saying they were afraid of their enemy Indians vp
in the contry, &c.," i. e., the Tarratines,[1] who had
terrorized eastern Massachusetts before the arrival
of the English. In this our devout forefathers
saw a fulfilment of the ancient scripture, " He cast
out the heathen before them, and divided them an
inheritance by line, and made the tribes of Israel to
dwell in their tents."[2]

MANCHESTER is one of the smaller Essex County
towns; its length on the seacoast being about four
and one-half miles and its breadth about two and
one-quarter miles; and containing something over
five thousand acres of land. Its soil is rocky and
its surface uneven, especially near the coast. Some
moderate elevations rise in the north and west.
Without any high hills, its general appearance is
picturesque, much of it being well wooded, with
fertile fields and rich meadows intermingled with
precipitous ledges and bold escarpments. A striking peculiarity of the scenery is the close proximity
of verdant foliage and grassy slopes, and the "stern
and rock-bound coast." In many places the green-
est of fields and woods approach almost to the ocean
itself.[3] The shore is composed of rugged cliffs and

[1] Johnson speaks of this tribe as "a barbarous and cruell people," and
mentions a belief that they were cannibals. *Wonder-working Providence*,
ch. 25. Some descendants of this once powerful and warlike tribe encamp
every summer on Ipswich River, and gather in money from the whites
by the sale of baskets, berries, etc.

[2] *Psalm* lxxviii, 55.

[3] "It sounds like a paradox to state that you may look out from
rugged cliffs over a summer sea and inhale its salt fragrance, and yet by a
turn of your heel find yourself face to face with a landscape of rustic
meadows and stately woods." Scribner's Magazine, article, *The North
Shore*, July, 1894.

boulders of sienite, Eagle Head being a particularly noble and commanding point, and of deeply indented coves and inlets; several small islands, Kettle, Crow, Graves, Great and Little Ram, and House, lie at a short distance from the shore:

> "a rude and broken coast-line . . . .
> Wood and rock and gleaming sand-drift, jagged capes,
>   with bush and tree,
> Leaning inland from the smiting of the wild and gusty sea."

"Singing Beach"[1] is widely celebrated as a natural curiosity, as is "Agassiz' Rock"[2] in the depths of the "Essex woods."

The climate is variable, but the nearness of the ocean tempers both summer's heat and winter's cold. The prevailing winds in the warm season, being from the sea, render the summer and autumn weather often delightful.

The soil is chiefly diluvial, and in some places well fitted for cultivation; there is not, however, very much farming carried on, owing in part to the limited areas of arable land, in part to the adoption of other pursuits, as fishing, seafaring and cabinet-making, and in part, latterly, to the high value which land has acquired in many localities since the incoming of the summer population.

There are many wild flowers and ferns in the

---

[1] Hugh Miller describes a phenomenon similar to the "Musical sands" of Manchester in "the loose Oölitic sand of the Bay of Laig" on the island of Eigg, Scotland. *Cruise of the Betsey; or a Summer Ramble among the Hebrides*, p. 75.

[2] A boulder on the east side of the Essex road, measuring about 6,000 square feet. From its top quite a view may be obtained. There is a very much larger boulder in the valley to the north. "It has the body of an aged and much twisted birch tree embedded in a cleft on its side, and a fifty-year-old cedar tree on its top." W. B. in *Manchester Cricket*, Sept. 1, 1894.

fields and woods, and near the Gloucester line, in a swamp not far from the road,

"The white magnolia-blossoms star the twilight of the pines." [1]

Some small manufactures are carried on, and a few of the inhabitants subsist by fishing. The town has of late years become a noted resort of summer visitors and residents, and has lost much of its individuality, greatly to the regret of its older inhabitants who remember it as a place which had life in itself.

" The old order changeth, yielding place to the new," and man's wisdom is seen in adjusting himself as best he can to new conditions and environments.

The town has the reputation of being a healthy one, and there is no reason in its location why it should not stand among the foremost in this respect. In former years there have been a large number of aged persons; there are living at present, eighteen between the ages of eighty and ninety, and two between ninety and one hundred. If the present generation is less robust than former ones, the explanation may be found perhaps in the hardships, privations and excessive labors of the earlier inhabitants being transmitted in their effects to descendants to the third and fourth generation. The law of heredity is an inexorable one. If nature is overburdened, or strained beyond its power of recuperation, the result is sure to appear, if not in the present, in some future age.

[1] " Manchester woods are celebrated for producing the magnolia; it is a low tree, with deep green leaves, and is rarely found at any other place in this region; the flowers are white, and possess a most delicious fragrance; the scent is so powerful that a small grove of them will perfume the air for miles." (!) *Essex Memorial*, Salem, 1836, p. 162.

CHAPTER II.

BEGINNINGS

" Small things in the beginning of natural or political bodies
are as remarkable as greater in bodies full grown."   Governor
Dudley's *Letter to the Countess of Lincoln*, March 12, 1631.

———————

" On yonder rocky cape, which braves
    The stormy challenge of the waves,
    Midst tangled vine and dwarfish wood,
    The hardy Anglo-Saxon stood."

                                 Whittier.

CHAPTER II.

BEGINNINGS.

CONANT'S COLONY — MASSACHUSETTS BAY COMPANY — ARRI-
VAL OF WINTHROP — "COMMON LANDS" — JEFFREY'S
CREEK — "ERECTING A VILLIAGE" — MAN-
CHESTER — TOWN GOVERNMENT.

WE have now reached the period where the authentic history of Manchester begins, and we have the comparatively clear light of contemporary records to guide us. Conant's[1] colony was established at Cape Anne[2] in 1624, but the "ill carriage" of some of the first settlers led to the abandonment of the colony by the "adventurers," and the company at Cape Anne was finally "purged of all but a brave and resolute few." Finding the location not all that they desired, and that the fishing "sped very ill,"[3] these men removed to "a more commodious place four or five leagues distant to the south-west, on the other side of a creek called Nahum-keike, or Naumkeag,[4] better adapted

[1] Roger Conant, whom White styles "a pious, sober, and prudent gentleman."

[2] This is the spelling in all the older documents and maps, and in the Charter.

[3] Captain John Smith attributes the failure in certain fishing voyages which he mentions to "sending opinionated, unskilfull men that had not experienced diligence to save that they tooke nor take that there was."

[4] Naumkeag retained its Indian name until about July, 1629, when it was called Salem, a name said to have "been given in remembrance of a peace settled upon conference at a generall meeting betweene [the inhabitants] and their neighbours, after expectance of some dangerous jarre." *Planter's Plea*, London, 1630.

to the purpose." From this movement resulted the
settlement of Manchester, of which Hubbard quaintly
says, " A door was opened for them at Cape Anne, a
place on the other side of the bay more convenient
for them that belong to the tribe of Zebulon than
for them that chose to dwell in the tents of Is-
sachar."

In March, 1629, Charles I, " By the grace of God,
Kinge of England, Scotland, Fraunce, and Ireland,
Defendor of the Fayth, &c.," granted the Charter of
the " Governor and Company of the Mattachusetts
Bay in Newe-England." This Charter granted to the
" Councell established at Plymouth, in the County
of Devon, for the planting, ruling, ordering and gov-
erning of Newe England in America, and to their
Successors and Assignes forever, all that Parte of
America, lyeing and being in Bredth, from Forty
Degrees of Northerly Latitude from the Equinoctiall
Lyne, to forty eight Degrees of the saide Northerly
Latitude inclusively, and in Length, of and within
all the Breadth aforesaid, throughout the Maine
Landes from Sea to Sea,[1] together also with all Firme
Landes, Soyles, Groundes, Havens, Portes, Rivers,
Waters, Fishing, Mynes, and Myneralls, aswell
Royall Mynes of Gould and Silver, as other Mynes
and Myneralls, precious Stones, Quarries, and all
and singular other Comodities, Jurisdiccons, Royal-
ties, Privileges, Franchesies, and Prehemynences,
both within the said Tract of Land vpon the Mayne,
and also within the Islandes and Seas adioining."

[1] The early explorers and geographers were ignorant of the widening
of the continent north of Mexico; they supposed the *South* [Pacific] Sea
to be only a few hundred miles west of the Atlantic coast.

In the following month (April), three ships sailed for Massachusetts Bay with supplies and a number of "planters." One of these ships, the "Talbot," was probably the first that ever entered Manchester harbor, dropping anchor here June 27, 1629. Rev. Francis Higginson, one of the ministers sent out by the Company to superintend the spiritual affairs of the settlement, wrote in his journal :

June 27, 1629. — Saturday evening we had a westerly wind, which brought us, between five and six o'clock, to a fyne and sweet harbor, seven miles from the head of Cape Ann (in this harbor twentie ships may lie and easily ride therein), where there was an island near, wither 4 of our men went with a boat, and brought back ripe strawberries, gooseberries, and sweet single roses. Monday, 29th, as we passed along to Naim Keake, it was wonderful to behold so many islands replenished with thicke wood and high trees, and many fayere green pastures.

The government by agents residing in England proving unsatisfactory, on the following October, the government and patent were transferred to New England, and John Winthrop, the "Founder of Massachusetts," and ancestor of a distinguished family, was chosen Governor.[1] Winthrop sailed in the "Arbella,"[2] a vessel of 350 or 400 tons, and six other ships, with three hundred settlers, for Salem. On June 11, 1630, the "Arbella" seems to have come to anchor nearly opposite "Gale's

[1] Winthrop was at this time forty-one years of age. "He was a man of remarkable strength and beauty of character, grave and modest, intelligent and scholarlike, intensely religious, yet liberal withal in his opinions and charitable in disposition." John Fiske, *The Beginnings of New England*, p. 102.

[2] Not "Arabella," as often printed; the flag ship, or "admiral," as Winthrop calls her. She was named for Lady Arbella Johnson.

Point." The following extract from Winthrop's *Journal* gives an account of the arrival :

Tuesday, 10th June, the wind continued all day a gale from the south, and yet we bore all sail and at four o'clock, P. M., made land, called " The Three Turks Heads." To-night we could see the trees very plainly, and had a fine fresh smell from the shore. The next day we stood too, and as the wind would bear, on Saturday we stood in towards the harbor, and by the aid of some shallops we passed through the narrow strait between Baker's Island and another little island,[1] and came to anchor within the harbor. Our friends came down from Salem, and many of our Gentlemen returned with them at night, where they supped on good venison and beer; but most of them, dis-liking their lodgings, returned to the ship. In the mean-time most of the people went on shore on the other side of the harbor,[2] where they were feasted with Strawberries, and were like as merry as the Gentlefolks at their venison and beer. Sunday Masconomo, the sagamore of the tribe, with another Indian, came on board and bade us welcome, tarrying with us all day. On Monday, the wind coming fair, the ships proceeded to Salem, where the planters landed. Here they found about ten houses and some indian corn planted, which was good and well liking.

Capt. John Smith had previously described the natural advantages of the region. He speaks of " many rivers and fresh springs, an incredible num-ber of fish, fowle, wilde fruits, and good timber, much corne, many good harbours, a temperate aire."[3] Governor Dudley, writing about a year later than Winthrop, thus sums up the resources of the colo-

[1] House Island (?).

[2] I. e., on the Manchester side.

[3] *New England's Trials and Present State.* Captain Smith, as " Ad-miral of New England," made a careful survey of the coast from Penobscot to Cape Cod in the summer of 1614.

nists : " Materials to build, fewell to burn, ground
to plant, seas and rivers to ffish in, a pure ayer to
breathe in, good water to drinke till wine or beare
can be made, which together with the cowes, hoggs,
and goates brought hither allready may suffice for
food, for as for foule and venison, they are dainties
here as well as in England."

Nearly all the settlers were " freemen," [1] and as
such had a right in the " common lands." They
were afterwards known as " Proprietors," and the
" common lands " were otherwise known as " the 400
acres grant," comprising what is now the centre of
the town. [2] About 1692 an Act was passed for the
" Regulating of Townships, Choice of Town Officers,
and setting forth their Power." This Act was virtually the incorporation of the " Proprietors " as a
body politic, defining their duties and responsibilities. It appears that the Proprietors of Manchester
did not organize under this Act until Aug. 26, 1718.
From that time until Feb. 28, 1769, their doings
were recorded in what is known as the " Commoners

[1] No one could be admitted a " freeman " unless he was a member of
the church. *Massachusetts Colonial Records*, vol. I, 87. Besides the
" freemen," were " residents," who were not allowed, or had declined, the
privilege of becoming " freemen," who were required to take the oath of
fidelity when they had attained the age of sixteen. (*Qu.* Were these the
" half-polls" mentioned in the early Assessors' lists ?) Every male, whether
freeman, resident or inhabitant, child, servant or slave, was required to
pay 1s. 8d. per head as poll tax, and 1s. for every 20s. in value of real or
personal estate.

[2] These " common lands " were probably held by intention in trust, but
in many instances, as Mr. Harrison's inquiries into the history of public
holdings in the Commonwealth show, common grounds have been absorbed, little by little, by private ownership. " Land-hunger " is nothing
new under the sun. The early land grants were based on a similar principle in New England townships generally. It was no doubt a survival of
the feudal system. See Weeden, *Economic and Social History of New
England*, vol. 1, ch. 3; also 1 *Johns Hopkins University Studies*, ix., x.

Records." The relation of these "Proprietors" to
the town has been a matter of question. They seem
to have constituted a kind of "landed gentry," and
virtually controlled town affairs, for our fathers had
little idea of democracy, *pur et simple.* There is no
evidence, however, that they abused their privileges,
setting themselves up as feudatory lords and treating
the rest of the inhabitants as vassals, but rather that
they used their power in a wise and liberal manner,
coming to the relief of the town from time to time
in assisting it to bear the burdens of taxation.[1] The
Salem records show that the land at "Jeffrey's
Creek "[2] was ordered to be divided, February, 1636,
as follows :

Tho: mores widow 10 Acres at Jeffrys creek

Samuell Archer	60	Srgt Dixy 50
Wm Allen	50	
Jo: Sibley	50	Att Jefferys Creek
Geo: Wms	40	
Jo: Moor	40	
Jo: Black	30	
Srgt Wolfe	50	

Subsequent grants were made to Jnº Pikwod, Jnº
Gally, Jnº Norman, Wm Benitt, Robert Allyn,

[1] See *Town Records of Manchester*, vol. 11, iii-v; to the editor, Mr.
A. S. Jewett, credit is due for light thrown upon this obscure subject connected with the early town affairs.

[2] Almost nothing is known of William Jeffrey, or Jeffreys, who gave
his name to the little plantation. He seems to have left the place early,
and is afterwards heard from at Ipswich ; but his later history seems now
beyond recovery. Hutchinson gives a letter (*History of Massachusetts*, vol.
1, 35, n.) written from England, May 1, 1634, by Thomas Morton to "one
Jeffries in New England." Whether this is our William Jeffreys, we have
no means of determining ; but if he was a confederate of Morton's, he may
have been a similar restless spirit, and this may account for his early disappearance from our view.

James Standish, Beniamin Parminster and Richard Gardner.

At a general towne meeting held the 26th day of the 8th moneth 1646 [it was] Ordered that William Woodburie and Richard Brackenburie Ensigne Dixy Mr. Conant & Lieutenut Lothrop & Lawrence Leech shall forthwth lay out a way betweene the fferry at Salem & the head of Jeffryes Creeke & that it be such a way as men may travell on horseback & drive cattle & if such a way may not be found then to take speedy Course to sett vp a footebridge at Mackrell Coue.

The last division of " the 400 acres " was in 1711. In this year the Proprietors made a final settlement. " In bounding the land to each Proprietor, those who had their divisions by the beach were bounded by the bank; while at Graves, the Proprietor was limited by the sea." In 1704, " the Land lying to the Eastward of Eagle Head was bounded by the sea to the Proprietors ";[1] the plain meaning of which would seem to be, that west of Graves' Beach and Eagle Head, the bank was recognized as the boundary.[2]

The first settlers landed, it is supposed, at Kettle Cove,[3] in 1626 or 1627.[4] These were of Conant's company; the later emigration probably chose the

[1] Dr. Leach's MS. *Town Records*, vol. I, pp. 121-128, 109-114.

[2] A contest dragging its slow length along in the courts, between the town and some owners of " Shore Acres," may throw new light, and may not, on the obscure subject of " Proprietors' Rights." The distinction between *law* and *equity* may also receive new emphasis.

[3] Named probably, as has always been supposed, from John Kettle. It is a little singular that weirs are called " kettles " in Kent and Cornwall, England ; " Kydells " in *Magna Charta* (33).

[4] The first house may have been built on the estate of T. Jefferson Coolidge, Esq., by John Kettle. The earliest *frame* house was no doubt that of William Allen.

Town Landing.[1]   Both of these locations presented
the promise of a safe harbor, and with the streams
of water, the sheltering hills and the abundant opportunity for building fish-weirs, offered an almost
ideal spot for the planting of a new settlement.

The little hamlet, clinging to the shore, grew
slowly and by cautious advances into the interior.
The country even a few miles back from the sea
was a *terra incognita*, covered with "infinite thick
Woods," a land of darkness and dread, the lurking-
place of savage beasts and of still more savage men.
Gradually, however, the land was taken up, divided
into farms, the bounds of which were carefully recorded,[2] and the limits of the settlement pushed
farther and farther into the primeval forest.   That
no successful effort was made, for at least the first
decade, to "boom" real estate, appears from a record
in 1651, to the effect that "Robert Isabell of Manchester, carpenter, for £15 sold his dwelling house
& 49 acres of land, with his partition of meadow
which is ½ acre allotted to him in 1638 by Richard
Norman."   As early, however, as 1640, when there
were but sixty-three people in all living at "Jeffrys
Creeke," we find these sturdy and independent
pioneers "jointly & humbly" requesting the Hon-

[1] "The place picked out by this people to settle themselves in, was in
the bosome of the outstretched arme of Cape Anne." Johnson, *Wonder-
Working Providence*, ch. ix.

[2] The simple and homely ways of the fathers is illustrated by the manner in which the bounds of the lands allotted by the Proprietors are described in the early records. Some of these are "a black burtch, pichpine,
grate hemlock, white oke, Litel black oak tree, a stump of fower mapls,
wortle bush, bunch of oalders, a white pritty bigg pine tree, and standing
upon a grate high Rock which is Almost to the Admiration of them that
doe behold it."

orable Court to give them "power to erect a Villiage." [1] This petition was granted. In 1645, the
inhabitants petitioned for a change of name, and on
June 18, the settlement received the name of Manchester. Although the name of Jeffrey disappears
from this time as the name of the little settlement,
it lingers still in the neighborhood. Stretching
northeastward from Cape Ann is a bank marked as
" Jeffreys " on the charts, and which is named in a
map in Blome's *Amerique*, 1688,[2] *Iefferey's Lodg*.
One of the oldest inhabitants says that he used to
" go fishing on Jeffreys'." Certain names often live
with a strange persistency when those more worthy
of perpetuation are forgotten.

There seems to have been no formal Act of Incorporation. This, however, was something not peculiar to the history of Manchester. Previous to 1655,
" the Governor and Company of Massachusetts Bay "
made grants of land to companies and individuals
for towns and plantations, usually annexing certain
conditions to their grants ; such as " that a certain
number of settlers or families should within a stated
time build and settle upon the same; or that the
gospel should be regularly preached, or a church
gathered upon the granted premises." [3]

The first book of Town Records, from 1645 to
1658, is lost ; the gap cannot now be supplied. The
first town meeting of which a record is extant was
held Feb. 25, 1657 (O. S.). The town meeting has
often been considered the unit of a democratic form

---

[1] See p. 26.   [2] Reproduced in *Cartier to Frontenac*, 1894, p. 346.
[3] *History of Groton, Mass.*, Caleb Butler, pp. 10, 11.

of government — "a government of the people, for
the people, by the people." In his *History of the
English People*, John Richard Green has traced the
origin of town-meeting government to a remote
period and a distant region — to the fifth century,
and to the little district of Sleswick in the heart of
the peninsula that parts the Baltic from the Northern Sea. It is in the village " moots " of Friesland
that we find the germ of that most primitive form of
government, the town meeting; the germ of all that
is best in our municipal, state and federal institutions.[1]

The town meeting has been of great value as an
educator, and a conservative force, in New England
life. The annual meeting was always opened with
prayer,[2] and was governed by the rules common to
parliamentary bodies. Each " freeman " had an
equal voice in its deliberations and an equal vote in
its action. It admitted of the utmost freedom
within certain well-defined limits. The moderator
was chosen by a majority vote, and his decisions were
final, though subject to an appeal to the house.
The town meeting was the town itself, acting in
both a legislative and an executive capacity. The
" select-men " were simply the agents employed by
the town, and chosen by popular suffrage, to carry
out its will. In municipal affairs the town was an
autonomy ; only in state and national concerns did

---

[1] See Howard, *Local Constitutional History*, vol. I, ch. ii, for a detailed
account of the town of New England as a political factor.

[2] This ancient custom was revived at the suggestion of the Moderator,
Mr. Henry T. Bingham, and by vote of the town, at the annual meeting,
March 18, 1895.

it acknowledge any higher power. It was the *fons et origo* of all earthly governmental authority. The town meeting shares with the church and the common school the honor of shaping and controlling New England civic and social life. Attendance upon town meetings, and taking part in them, if only to the extent of voting, unconsciously moulded the minds and formed the habits of men. The "March meeting" has for generations occupied a foremost place among the agencies that have helped to form the character of the rural community. An advantage which the town has over the city is the training which it affords in self-government, and the opportunity which it gives for its exercise. And if majorities are sometimes unwise and infatuated, and minorities sometimes obstructive, if the weakness of universal suffrage sometimes makes itself prominent, the government of the town is on the whole as safe and just as any which human wisdom has yet devised. It will be a dark day if it ever utterly fails and breaks down, if the "common sense of most" becomes a fiction and a dream.

PETITION FOR POWER TO ERECT A VILLAGE.

The petition of the inhabitants of Salem for some of their church to have Jeffryes Creeke, & land to erect a village there for Mr Willi: Walton, John Blacke, Willi: Allen, Sam: Orchard, Geo: Norton, &c., comp^a; what land & inlargement may bee convenient, & is not granted to any other plantation, is granted them: & it is referred to Mr John Winthrope, Iunior, and Mr Symon Bradstreete, to settle the bounds of said village. *Massachusetts Colonial Records*, vol. I, 30; *Town Records*, vol. I, 13.

[The following copy of the Petition is from the *N. E. Genealogical Register*, vol. VII. It is believed by the Editor, in whose possession the MS. was at that time (1853), never before to have appeared in print.]

We whose names are subscribed belonging to the church and Towne of Salem (being straitened in our accomidations, soe that we are not ably comfortably to subsist, haveing advised and taken counsell about our present state and condition, it being Judged full and free liberty being granted us to remove, and noe place being soe convenient, for our Easye removeall as Jefferyes Creeke lying soe neare us and most of us haveing some small quantity of ground allotted to us there already) doe therefore Jointly and Humbly request the Hon[bl] Court to give us power to erect a Villiage there, and to alow us Such Inlargement there abouts as is not granted to any other plantation thus leaveing our request to your wisdomes Consideration, With our prayers for a blessing from heaven on your psons and proceedings we rest

Your Humble petitioners.

William Walton	John Sibley	Robert Allen
John Black	James Standish	Jo[n] Norman
Wm Allen	John ffriend	Edmond Grover
Sam[ll] Archard	John Pickwith	Pasco ffoote
Geo Norton	John Gally	Wm Bennett
Wm Dixy	Ben: Parmenter	
1640		

14th: 3 mo

The petition is granted & referred to M[r] John Winthrop & M[r] Symond Bradstreet to settle the bounds.

p. curiam Increase Nowell, Secrety.
vera copia atest Hilliard veren cler.
vera copia of that coppie, attest, Robert Lord, cler.

NAMES OF PLACES.

This List of "Names of Places in Town" is from Dr. Leach's "Collections," 1836. Most of them date back to the earliest times.

HILLS. — Image, Moses, Eagle, Bennett's, Mill Stone. Jacks, Shingle Place, Town, Flagstaff, Great Powder House, Waterman's Rocks.

PLAINS. — Briery or Bushie, Poplar.

MEADOWS. — Fresh meadow, Cranberry, Beaver Dam, Cold Spring.

SWAMPS. — Cedar, Millett's.

MARSHES. — Norman's, Bishop's, Cheever's, Barberry.

CREEKS. — Jeffreys, Chubbs, Days.

COVES. — Kettle, Black, Lobster, Pebble, Pitts.

POINTS. — Pickworth, Gale's, Smith's, Goldsmith's, Marsters, Glasses, Bishop's, Cheever's, Tuck's.

NECKS. — Great or Old, Norton's.

BROOKS. — Wolf Trap, Clay, Cheever's, Saw Mill, Foster's Mill.

BEACHES. — Neck, Graves, Gray's, Black Cove, Lobster Cove.

ISLANDS. — Great and Little Crow, Kettle, Egg, Ram Great and Little, Howes, Chubbs, Friends or Island Wharf.

SPRINGS. — Cold, North Yarmouth, Kettle Cove, Newport, Plains, Row, Great Neck, Smith's Farm, Town Landing, Great Pasture, Norton's Neck, Nicholas Commons, Graves.

LANDINGS. — Smith's, Marsters, Black Cove, Church Lane, Town Landing, Kettle Cove, White Head Landing.

BRIDGES. — Jabez, near Bear's house, Jones below Capt Knights, Town Bridge, Centre Bridge built 1828, Chubbs built 1835.

It may interest some of the present generation to locate some of these places, that are no longer familiarly known by the above names: e. g., Waterman's Rocks, Clay Brook, Nicholas Commons.

CHAPTER III.

THE FIRST COMERS: WHO AND WHAT WERE THEY?

" Let us thank God for having given us such ancestors;
and let each successive generation thank Him not less fervently
for being one step further from them in the march of ages."

CHAPTER III.

THE HOME OF THE EARLY SETTLERS — THEIR ESTATE — AB-
SENCE OF THE ARISTOCRATIC ELEMENT — MORALS —
LAWS — FAILURE OF THE "THEOCRACY" —
A TRUE NOBILITY — "GROOVES OF
CHANGE."

WHAT manner of men were they who first
settled these shores, who sowed the seed
whose harvests we now reap, who laid the
foundations of church and state on which we now
build?

From its name, Manchester, it has been thought
that the town was settled by people from the vicinity
of Manchester, England.[1] Another supposition has
been that the town received its name from the Earl
of Manchester, a warm friend of the American colonies, an associate of Cromwell, Hampden and Pym.[2]
Without any definite knowledge or even tradition
on this point, it is more than likely that the men
who planted Manchester in Massachusetts were
mostly from the Eastern shires, which furnished so
much of the bone and muscle both of Old and New
England : they were the friends and neighbors of

[1] William Allen is said to have been from that place; but of this there
is no proof.

[2] Macaulay speaks of his " humanity and moderation." *John Hampden*, Edinburgh Review.

31

Cromwell's Ironsides and of the men and women who were the originals of Bunyan's immortal characters.

The founders of New England belonged mainly to the middle ranks of life. There were among them a few of greater social position — as the Winslows, the Carvers, the Brewsters, the Winthrops, the Saltonstalls, the Endicotts — but they were largely descendants of the liberty-loving weavers of Flanders who had fled to England in the previous century from the persecutions in the Low Countries, and the small farmers of the southern and eastern counties.[1] They were of the best stock of English Puritanism. They were not broken-down gamblers and *roués*. They were of the stuff of which commonwealths are made. They knew that public prosperity must rest on the foundations of intelligence and morality. They did not thank God, like Governor Berkely of Virginia, " that there are no free schools, nor printing." They were men who prized education, virtue and religion, and they gladly made great sacrifices to secure for themselves and their posterity these inestimable blessings. Their character was of such a strain that it has transmitted its traits through centuries, and has made all succeeding generations its debtors.

The migration had become a serious matter to England, where there was then no surplus population. Lord Maynard wrote to Archbishop Laud of the " danger of divers parishes being depopulated."

[1] Many names of towns in New England, especially upon the seaboard, as also the counties, Suffolk, Norfolk, Essex, Plymouth, are from these parts of England.

Green says, " The Third Parliament of Charles was hardly dissolved when 'conclusions' for the establishment of a great colony on the other side of the Atlantic were circulating among gentry and traders, and descriptions of the new country of Massachusetts were talked over in every Puritan household." In 1637, King Charles endeavored by royal proclamation to prevent " men of substance " from emigrating to New England.[1] But if this had any effect in deterring the more wealthy and aristocratic from leaving the Kingdom, it resulted in New England being settled by the most substantial of emigrants, sifted out of the mother country by royal and prelatical proscription.

The growth of the settlement was slow — it was "the day of small things "; but there were planted in a few years on these rugged and storm-swept shores by these plain, brave yeomen the seeds which in a century bore fruit in varied industries ; the forests slowly gave way, boat-building and the taking and curing of fish afforded employment to a frugal community, axes swung and anvils rang, and the little hamlet showed unmistakable signs of enterprise and thrift. True to their instincts and their training, the settlers soon began to exercise a care for the higher nature ; a place of worship was built, around which the village gathered, thus fixing the site of the centre of the town for generations to come ; for

---

[1] " The officers and Ministers of his severall Ports in England, Wales and Barwick " were commanded that " they doe not hereafter permit or suffer any persons, being Subsidie men or of the value of Subsidie men, to embarque themselves " . . . etc. *A Proclamation against the Disorderly Transporting of His Maiesties Subiects, etc.*

where the Puritan meeting-house was reared, there
was the nucleus of social and civic life.[1]

It is difficult, after the lapse of two centuries and
more, with the slight materials at our command, to
draw a full-length portrait of a Manchester man of
the seventeenth century. But from what we can
gather from brief records and occasional letters that
have come down to us, and from the few traditions
that still linger, we shall not be far wrong if we
conceive of him as in the main a religious and God-
fearing man, one who ruled his own household well,
a faithful husband and true friend, honest in all his
business transactions, strenuous in his attachment to
his religious and political beliefs, somewhat narrow
and wholly uncultivated, but possessed of strong
native character, and not ill-fitted by heredity and
training to act his part in life.

From a general knowledge of the men and women
of the time, we may fairly judge what Manchester
men and women — *cœteris paribus*—must have been.
They were of the average material of which the early
New England colonists were made. They were neither
great-minded founders of empire nor mere commercial
adventurers. They were not religious separatists like
the men of Plymouth, nor revellers like the men of
Merry Mount. No doubt there were differences among
them, as there are among their descendants; and,
perhaps, whether conscious of it or not, most of them
were actuated by somewhat mixed motives. There
was on the part of many, no doubt, the desire to seek

[1] For a time it might have seemed as if the *eastern* part of the town
would be the " West End," the " Cove " having the start and for some
years keeping the lead.

"a faith's pure shrine "; but there was as certainly,
on the part of many, the desire to better the conditions of living. It is always safe, however, to estimate men by their works; and, judging the tree
planted on " Cape Anne in Newe Englande " by its
fruit, it must have been of sound, sturdy stock, its
juices nourished by the best soil of English Noncon-
formity in the times of the Stuarts.

There was, at the first, a high state of public morals. The slave-trade was prohibited; even cruelty
to animals was a civil offence. Imprisonment for
debt was forbidden by law, except there was suspicion of fraud.[1] The first settlers were almost without exception industrious, enterprising and frugal.
The consequence was a thrifty, healthy, happy community. Even Lechford, who was no friend to the
civil or ecclesiastical government of the colony,
frankly says, " Profane swearing, drunkenness, and
beggars are but rare in the compass of this patent."[2]
There was respect for age and deference to authority; the time had not come when " the child [should]
behave himself proudly against the ancient, and the
base against the honorable."

There were laws against lying, as well as stealing;
against " meeting with corrupt company," against
" tipling in ordinaries," against " contumacy and diso-
bedience to parents " : the court endeavored even to
regulate the matter of courtship.[3] The law made
itself felt everywhere; one could hardly get away

[1] *Massachusetts Colonial Records*, vol. II. p. 48.

[2] In 3 *Massachusetts Historical Collections*, vol. III. p. 86.

[3] *Massachusetts Colonial Records*, vol. II. p. 207.

from it, even if he took to the woods; in **1750**, ox-
sleds were ordered to be four feet wide, and all over
were to be " cut off by any who shall meet them,"
which looks much like legislation run into the
ground. There were laws that went to an extreme
in the line of sumptuary legislation, as regarded dress
and personal adornment, " excesse in apparrell,"
" new, strainge fashions," " superstitious ribbons,"
" immodest laying out theire haire," etc.[1] But that
many of the stories popularly current are untrue and
a libel upon the Puritan legislation is abundantly
proved.[2] It is easy to laugh at such absurdities and
trivialities as appear in our early legislation. But it
was the very earnestness of our fathers, and their intense desire to found a " godly " community, that
led to these blunders. They made the mistake of
endeavoring to found a New England Theocracy,
and incorporated into the statute-book the Old
Testament code of legislation. But they had a high
ideal, and strove nobly to attain it ; that they failed
was due more to the imperfection of human nature
than to their special lack of wisdom. They were
beclouded in their judgment by their training in the
school of ecclesiastical controversy. They were mis-

[1] *Massachusetts Colonial Records*, vol. III, p. 243.

[2] Trumbull, *Blue Laws True and False*, 1876. The famous " Blue
Laws " of which so much ridicule has been made are contained in a " History of Connecticut," published anonymously in London, and ascribed to
Rev. Samuel Peters, an Episcopal clergyman and Tory, who had been sent
back to England ; a disappointed and malicious enemy of the colony,
whose mixture of truth and fable made his work a mischievous one, and
whose Munchausen-like tales of the " Windham frogs," the nondescript
" Cuba " and " Whapperknocker," stamp his work as that of a mendacious
story-teller. Peters admits that the " Blue Laws " were " never suffered
to be printed." A copy of his book is in the Library of the Essex Institute, Salem.

led by the common habit of the time of taking precedents of action from the stories of a repealed economy and examples of living from the heroes of a dispensation that had vanished away. As it was, however, with all its mistakes and failings, this must be
said, the Puritan commonwealth was a great advance
upon anything that had preceded it, unless it was
Calvin's autocracy at Geneva; it was a long step
from the despotism of the Stuarts in the direction of
light and liberty.[1] It is not too high praise to give
to the men who founded Massachusetts, the class to
which our own forefathers belonged, to say that they
made grand material for the foundations of the
future state.

It has well been said by a former chief executive
of this state [2] : " We owe it to them that Massachusetts to-day is a state with such a form of government that she really governs herself — a commonwealth with a people so brave, so educated, so
founded on principle and character, that they govern
themselves. And so, while we do not forget the
great advantage we possess, and the great gain we
have made, we shall also do well if we maintain our
ancestors' standard of high principle."

They cared little for patents of nobility or ecclesiastical preferment. They were " nobles by the right
of an earlier creation and priests by the imposition

---

[1] Even the Episcopal lawyer, Lechford, unwelcome and obnoxious as
he was to the fathers of the colony, and retiring disaffected from their
discipline, wrote of them in 1642, " I think that wiser men than they,
going into a wilderness to set up a strange government differing from the
settled government in England, might have fallen into greater errors than
they have done." *Plain Dealing* (To the Reader).

[2] Hon. John D. Long.

of a mightier hand." They looked with contempt
upon the claims of long descent. They knew
that

> " Kind hearts are more than coronets,
> And simple faith than Norman blood."

They revered conscience as king. They feared no
evil and they thought none. Men like George William Curtis,[1] Macaulay and Froude, who are not
overfond of the Puritans, are compelled to admit
that the social and civic virtues which they eulogize
are the lineal and logical offspring of Puritanism.

The intelligence of the Puritans was in strong
contrast with the ignorance and superstition — the
fear of ghosts and fairies, the prayers to tutelar
saints and the worship of images — that still prevailed in many parts of England as in the time of
the Tudors.[2]

It is easy for us in our comfortable homes, surrounded by all the appliances and arts of civilization,
to laugh at the foibles, the mistakes, the often crude
ways of the pioneers. But if we rightly consider
the circumstances in which their lives were lived,
beset with difficulties and dangers behind and before, with the perils of the wilderness on the one
hand and opposition from over seas on the other, we
shall be ready to accord to our forefathers no common meed of praise [3]

[1] *Literary and Social Essays*, New York, 1895.

[2] Sanford's *Studies of the Great Rebellion*. Orme's *Life of Baxter*.
Fuller's *Church History*. Rushworth's *Collections*, etc.

[3] " Patient, frugal, God-fearing and industrious . . . obeying the word
of God in the spirit and the letter, but erring sometimes in the interpretation thereof — surely they had no traits to shame us, to keep us from thrilling with pride at the drop of their blood which runs n our backsliding
veins." *Alice M. Earle.*

" Homage, affection, we gratefully cherish;
  Peerless their fortitude; faith unsurpassed
Wrought in them character, lustrous in virtues,
  Masterful, rhythmical, while time shall last."

Our forefathers were far from being perfect; they
had about the average assortment of human failings.
When we get near enough to them, we find that
they were made of the same clay as ourselves.
There is no need to idealize or apotheosize them.
We may well be thankful that we had such ancestors, and we may well be thankful, also, that in
many respects we have been able, while imitating
their excellences, to avoid their mistakes. With the
advantage of their knowledge and experience, we
may see farther and more clearly than our fathers,
though less mighty men than they. They were explorers who laid down on the chart many a rock and
shoal on which they narrowly escaped making ship-
wreck, that we coming after them might sail over
smooth and pleasant seas.

To inquire whether " the former days were better
than these " has been pronounced unwise, by one
who had a large experience of mankind. And it is
certainly hazardous to make sweeping generaliza-
tions. In some respects, Manchester has witnessed
a great advance; but some very desirable things
have been wellnigh " improved " off the face of the
earth. There was a manly self-reliance, a spirit of
independence, a faithfulness to trust, a cheerfulness
under the pressure of poverty and in the midst of
discouragement, that put to the blush the fastidious
and pretentious ways of a "gilded age." On the

other hand, there has been a gain in breadth, in intelligence, in refinement, in the conveniences and comforts of life. The past teaches us that "the secret of true living" is not the monopoly of any one age.

"New occasions teach new duties; Time makes ancient
    good uncouth;
They must upward still and onward, who would keep
    abreast of Truth.
Lo, before us gleam her watchfires; we ourselves must
    Pilgrims be,
Launch our Mayflower, and steer boldly through the des-
    perate winter sea."

The following graceful and noble tribute to the "Pilgrim Fathers," from the *Boston Daily Advertiser*, Dec. 22, 1894, will serve, in the main, for the Puritans of Massachusetts Bay:

They believed that the invisible things of this world are greater that the things which are seen. They believed that eternity is of more consequence than time. They believed that he who should lose his own soul to gain the whole world would make a bad bargain. They believed that plain living is none too dear a price to pay for the privilege of high thinking. They believed that he to whom any precious and pregnant truth has been revealed must utter it, or else stand condemned of high treason at the judgment bar of the King of heaven. They believed that a true church may be instituted by the voluntary act of a body of Christian disciples organizing themselves into a communion, and a lawful state by the consent and coöperation of self-governing citizens. They believed these things practically as well as theoretically. They had the courage of their convictions. They dared to do. They feared nothing else so much as sin, and they counted no other shame so great as recreancy to their loftiest ideals. They said what they meant and meant what they said. For truth as they saw it, for duty as it was revealed to them, they braved the stormy, lonely ocean, endured poverty and exile, hunger, cold and death, a savage wilderness peopled by savage men. In thus believing, they set an unsurpassed example of faith. In thus choosing the better part, as between flesh and spirit, they made a like choice easier for all coming generations of the children of men in all the earth.

CHAPTER IV.

THE EARLY LIFE OF THE TOWN.

" The great eventful Present hides the Past, but through the
        din
Of its loud life hints and echoes from the life behind steal in;
And the love of home and fireside, and the legendary rhyme,
Make the task of duty lighter which the true man owes his
        time."

                                                    Whittier.

CHAPTER IV.

THE EARLY LIFE OF THE TOWN.

SEA AND FOREST — "LIGHTS AND SHADOWS" — PLAIN LIVING
— MUTTERINGS OF STORM — INDIAN TERRORS —
"DEVOURING WOLVES" — STURDY
GROWTH — LOUISBURG —
BRIGHTER DAYS.

THE smoke from the " catted chimnies "[1] of the
log-huts that here and there broke the forest,[2]
arose in the air. A " fishing-stage " was set
up, Sabbath worship was maintained, town meetings
were called, the community took on outward shape
and life. The beginnings of life are in all cases
hard to describe. It is often impossible to trace,
step by step, their slow evolution. In this, as in
other instances, there was an almost imperceptible
advance. The winters were severe, the soil was
rock-bound, means of communication with the outside world were of the most primitive kind, a cordon
of dark and impenetrable woods hemmed in the little
settlement, the ocean had its dangers and terrors —
sometimes smooth in its treacherous calm, sometimes
lashed with fearful tempests. The daily work was
carried on with something of military precaution.

[1] A term applied to chimneys built of wood, "cob-house" fashion, with
the spaces filled with clay.

[2] Ancient cellar-holes are still visible at " North Yarmouth." Where
or by whom the first house was built is unknown; probably several arose
almost simultaneously.

45

Muskets were constant companions, and unrelaxing
vigilance was the price of safety. The maps of the
period, as those of Champlain (1613, 1632), of Alexander (1624), of Sanson (1656), of Heylyn (1662),
show that the knowledge of the interior was meagre
in the extreme. Less was known of New England
a little more than two centuries ago, than is known
of equatorial Africa to-day. Life was a stern reality,
and partook of the solemnity of the mysterious sea
and the pathless forests. It is no wonder that the
character of the early settlers took on a serious, not
to say a sombre, coloring. The graces invoked by
Milton in *L'Allegro* had small place in New England
life or thought. What had men who faced the soul-
depressing solitude of the wilderness, to do with
"soft Lydian airs," or with

> "many a winding bout
> Of linkéd sweetness long drawn out"?

The needs of the people were simple and easily
supplied. The woods furnished game, the sea and
shore yielded a supply of fish ; [1] wild fruits and berries were abundant in their season, and potatoes,
beans, corn and pumpkins were grown with little
labor.[2] The implements of the farm, the fishery and
the household were of the most primitive kind.
There were few conveniences and no luxuries. The
inventories left to us of household goods, of farm

[1] "Some one boat with three men would take in a week ten hundreds [of
exceeding large and fat mackerel] which was sold in Connecticut for £3,12
the hundred." Winthrop's *Journal*, 1639. But this was apparently an exceptional season.

[2] Francis Higginson gives a most glowing account of the fertility, climate and natural productions of Massachusetts Bay. *New England's
Plantation*, ch. xii.

implements, and of apparel are often amusing illustrations of the frugality, paucity and rudeness of
their furnishings, which still were of such relative
value as to be carefully appraised. Settles stood in
the fire-place, box-beds occupied one end of the
kitchen, great logs blazed on the irons, a huge crane
hung in the enormous chimney ; a noon-mark served
the purposes of a time-piece.

There was small variety in the way of literature.
A few households might have a copy of the " Simple Cobler of Agawam," " A Glasse for New England," " Meat for the Eater," " A Posie from Old
Mr. Dod's Garden," or Michael Wigglesworth's
" Day of Doom," which was printed on broadsides
and hawked over the country. But they were
hardly better off in the mother Isle.[1] But if books
and newspapers were " few and far between," the
Bible [2] had been brought with the household stuff
from England, and was the " present angel of the
dwelling " ; learning was as yet but little prized,
many of the chief men of the town being unable to
write their names ;[3] the language spoken was the
racy, idiomatic English of Ben Jonson and Shake-
peare, many so-called Americanisms being survivals
of a usage current in the time of Queen Elizabeth.[4]
It was the " age of homespun."

[1] Macaulay, *History of England*, ch. iii.

[2] The Geneva Bible was generally preferred by the Puritans, as giving
less sanction to prelatical and kingly assumptions than the version of King
James (1611). See Appendix 1.

[3] This was the case as late as 1716. See *Town Records*, vol. 1, 52, 133,
135, etc. Five, out of the thirteen original settlers of Rhode Island, in
signing the contract under which Providence was governed, " made their
mark." The settlers of Manchester were not unlettered above other men
of their time.

[4] J. R. Lowell, *The Biglow Papers*. *Harper's Magazine*, January,
1895.

The first road (one of the indexes of civilization)
is said to have followed the sea-beaches as far as
practicable, as a sort of natural highway. Afterwards the laying out of roads was determined partly
by private or local convenience. If something more
elaborate than a cart-way was attempted, the surface
soil was removed and some of the larger stones were
dug up. Rocks too large for the crowbar were left
in situ, and the road obligingly went round them.
Such highways as that which caused a good deal of
dispute between Manchester and Beverly, would
hardly be accepted by County Commissioners at the
present day ; but they answered for " the time then
present."   They were not built for " rustlers " or
for skeleton gigs, but they could be made to do for
ox-carts and for " the deacon's one-hoss shay."   Our
fathers had almost a contempt for material ease and
comfort ; they sometimes preferred to go over a hill,
when they might without increasing the number of
rods travelled have gone round it.   They learned
not only to " *endure* hardness," but, it would seem,
to *enjoy* it.   What, indeed, was a little temporary
inconvenience to men whose life was one long, toil-
some journey, not to the New England, but the
Heavenly Canaan ?   The way tô the Celestial City,
as Bunyan had pictured it, was rough and difficult ;
should the way to the next parish be made easy to
the flesh?   The world was not made for Sybarites.[1]

[1] This was good reasoning from the Puritan standpoint; as Whittier
well puts it,
　　" Heaven was so vast, and earth so small,
　　And man was nothing since God was all."
Have we gained anything by overturning the pyramid? We have better
roads, but have we more conscience? have we a higher sense of duty? do
we hold a more sensitive balance of right and wrong?

LOW HOUSE.

BAKER HOUSE.

About 1690, the first mention is found of a "slay"; carriages appeared a little earlier, but they were very rare. "Chairs" — two-wheeled vehicles without a top — and chaises, were the earliest style of carriages, next to the farm carts and wagons. Riding was almost entirely on horseback, by saddle and pillion, until near the close of the seventeenth century : the roads, indeed, except in the vicinity of Boston, would hardly have permitted any more luxurious mode of travel.

About 1690, John Knight built a house at the " Cove " which was taken down in September, 1890, thus witnessing two hundred years of the town's life. It is thus decribed by Dea. A. E. Low :

The house was of one story, 18 feet long on the front, and 27 feet on the end. The front roof set on a plate three feet above the attic floor, with a long roof on the back coming down to the first story. The frame was of oak, covered with one and a half inch plank; the posts and beams were finished into the rooms. The lower part was divided into a living-room in the front, and kitchen and small living-room in the rear. This house had a cellar and represented the better dwellings of that date.

Until a few years ago it was occupied as a dwelling-house, and was apparently comfortable, though with " a general flavor of mild decay."

The house of Mrs. Abby Baker, on Pine street, built before 1690, and which is in good preservation, is another specimen of a class of houses which must have been rare at that time. The old chimney was taken down a few years ago; it gave the house a much more antique appearance.

The discomfort of the old houses in winter, even
the best of them, was doubtless great. Judge Sewall wrote in 1717: "an Extraordinary Cold Storm
of Wind and Snow. . . . at six o'clock my ink
freezes so that I can hardly write by a good fire in
my Wives Chamber." And Cotton Mather writes
in 1721, in his usual pompous fashion : " Tis Dreadful cold, my ink glass in my standish is froze and
splitt in my very stove. My ink in my pen suffers
a congelation." There were "Dutch stoves" as
early as 1700, but we know nothing of their construction, and they were probably in use only in the
larger towns, as Boston and Salem, and among the
wealthier people. Huge fireplaces which consumed
an enormous quantity of wood,[1] but allowed most of
the heat to pass up the chimney, were the usual
means of warmth, and this at a period when, according to all accounts. the winters were far more severe
than in recent times.[2]

As to the Puritan table, the fare was coarse often,
but in general, plentiful. Higginson speaks of lobsters weighing twenty-five pounds, and says that " the
abundance of other fish was beyond believing."
Oysters and clams were to be had for the trouble of
digging. There were fruits and vegetables, and a
good supply of game. Wild turkeys sometimes
weighed forty pounds apiece, and Morton says they
came in flocks of a hundred. A dozen wild pigeons
sold dressed for threepence. In 1684, beef, mutton

[1] Ministers had sometimes sixty cords of wood given them annually
by the parish.

[2] We must all agree with Hosea Biglow, that

"Our Pilgrim stock wuz pethed with hardihood."

and pork were but twopence a pound in Boston. By Johnson's time, the New Englanders had "Apple, Pear and Quince tarts." Judge Sewall speaks in his Diary of "boil'd Pork, boil'd Bacon and boil'd Venison; rost Beef, rost Fowls, pork and beans; conners, hogs Cheek and souett; Minc'd Pye, Aplepy, chockolett, figgs," etc. The fare of the common people was, however, very simple. Fresh meat was rarely seen, but a hog or a quarter of beef was often salted down in the autumn, bits of which later on were boiled in the Indian porridge. The bread was Indian or Indian and rye, and the common drinks at meals milk and cider, very rarely tea.

People were much crowded in the habitations of those days. An old MS. of 1675 [1] gives the size of families as 9.02 persons; this included, of course, servants and dependents; but families of ten or twelve children were not uncommon. The smallness of the houses, and the number that often found shelter under one roof, even down to quite recent times, is matter of surprise. The increase in the number and size of houses in Manchester within two hundred years, has been out of all proportion to the increase of population.

The people were content with their simple, homely ways; if they sometimes suffered privation they made the best of it; and they appear to have found comfort in circumstances that seem to have been entirely destitute of it. And so the life of the little town went on, generation after generation, with little

[1] *New England Historical and Genealogical Register,* vol. xxxix, p. 33.

change and with little desire for change. To use
Burke's happy phrase, it was the existence of a people "still, as it were, in the gristle, and not yet
hardened into the bone."

The town records give us glimpses of a very primitive mode of life. In 1686, "Rates" were made
for the "use and support of his maiesties government
in new england," levied upon thirty-one taxpayers,
in sums varying from 6d. to 1s. 6d. A large part of
the town's doings related to the allotment of the
"coman land"; then there was the "suport of a
Gospill menestery," which was an ever present and
pressing source of solicitude; "Howards and feild
Drivers" were to be chosen; penalties were enforced
for "swyne fownd without the youke"; provision
was made for a "Scoolmaster," for "seaviers of high
wayes," for "fence vewers," and for "seateing the
meting hous"; a vote was taken to "chuse a man to
saveus in the Juri of triAles at salam," or to "send
to the Jennerel Cort."

The life of the town was chequered with light
and shade; it was sometimes sombre and sometimes
glad; but it was never humdrum. The glint upon
the sunlit waves and the boom of the ocean surge,
the roar of the wind in the rocking pines and the
weird sounds of the forest depths, the voice of prayer
and psalm, the mysteries of birth and death, the influences of a deep, all-pervading, awe-inspiring faith,
invested the homely and prosaic with wonderful
pathos and sublimity.

One of our oldest citizens, Dea. A. E. Low, well
remembers the stories told around his father's fire-

side in his childhood and youth, by those whose
memory went back to the time of the French war,
of "the toils and privations endured, the care, skill
and rigid economy brought into requisition to supply the wants of the family, the clearing away the
forests, erecting houses and building vessels, work
that involved a great amount of labor." The men
and women of that time were hard toilers, rising
early, "eating the bread of carefulness," accustomed
to privation and hardship, knowing nothing of the
luxuries and little of what we consider the comforts
of life. "The story of their rugged lives would fill
volumes." [1]

It is not without a feeling of respect almost akin
to reverence, that we think of those brave, indomitable pioneers. Barren as their lives seem to us of
cheer and brightness, almost as barren as the rocks
among which they dwelt ; lonely as were their lives,
like the shore visited only by the sea-fowl : limited
as were their intellectual and social resources ; we
must award them a high meed of praise for their
patience, their piety, their pluck, their perseverance.

The rude and hard conditions of life which surrounded the earlier generations from the cradle to
the grave left little room for the amenities and
graces ; they repressed and dwarfed the sentiments ;
but they furnished a ground in which the hardier
virtues grew. A church dignitary has recently
said, " A young man can do better work on $4,000 a
year than on $2,000, because he will not have to

[1] The condition of the people, however, was better than that of the
common ranks in England and France at this period. See Green, Jessop,
Macaulay, Lecky, etc.

look so sharply after the dimes and nickels." The
Bishop uttered a half truth ; the self-denial, frugality and bravery, often necessitated by what Jeremy
Taylor calls " a small economy," make up with many
a component part of a noble character.   It is at least
open to question, whether a condition of comparative
privation is not quite as favorable to sturdy and self-
reliant growth as a condition of ease and opulence.
Manchester has had some experience of both extremes.

This infantile age of the settlement was not without its dread alarms.   As early as 1637 the Indians
began to show signs of hostility to the new-comers,
and the Pequot War for a few years spread dismay
and terror through the little settlements.   In 1643,
the colonies of Massachusetts Bay, Plymouth, Connecticut and New Haven formed themselves into a
union, under written articles of confederation, " for
mutual help and strength in all future concernment,"
a confederation which may be called the prototype
of " the larger union of the colonies which conducted
the War of the Revolution." [1]

Although, from its location on the seaboard, Manchester did not suffer directly from Indian attacks
as did many settlements in the interior — as Haverhill, Medfield, Sudbury, Marlborough, Groton,
Brookfield and Deerfield [2] — a constant apprehension .

[1] Justin Winsor, article on *Massachusetts*, Encyclopedia Brittanica,
ninth edition.

[2] The same spirit of enterprise and love of adventure which peopled
the Great West and the Pacific Coast, and in an earlier day overflowed the
Alleghanies into " the Ohio," had sent out not only its scouts but its *bona
fide* settlers into the Connecticut Valley before the last of the men who
came over with Winthrop and Endicott had passed to their graves.

of danger and false alarms made the life of the community for many years one of disquiet and trouble. The frontiers of New England were struck with fire and slaughter ; rapine and death fell upon peaceful settlements ; the outposts of civilization were driven in, and the very life of the English colonies in the New World was seriously menaced.

It is impossible, on account of the loss of early records, to discover with accuracy what part the town had in the early Indian wars. But among the " flower of Essex " who served in the company of Captain Lothrop of Beverly at Bloody Brook,[1] the following Manchester men were slain : Samuel Pickworth, John Allen, Joshua Carter, John Bennett.[2] Seventy men were later drafted for the Essex County Regiment, to fight the French and Indians. This Essex Regiment consisted of thirteen companies of foot and one of cavalry.

The pay of soldiers was 6s. per week, and 5s. for " dyet." Prices of clothing were, " Wastcoats," 6s. ; "Stockens," 2s. ; Shirts, 6s. ; Shoes, 4s. The old " Matchlock " musket was the regulation weapon of

[1] " On the 18th of September (O. S.), 1675, a large number of men who were spoken of by Colonel Winters as " the Flower of Essex," were ambushed and killed at Bloody Brook, South Deerfield, Mass. The circumstances were as follows. These men were doing garrison and patrol duty along the Connecticut River in the fall of 1675. On the morning of September 18 they started from Deerfield to relieve the inhabitants of Hadley, who were threatened by the savages. Some four miles south of Deerfield, at the crossing of a brook, they were taken in an ambuscade and were all destroyed. This has been called ' that most fatal day, the saddest that ever befell New England.' The brook by which they fought, and on whose bank they were buried in a common grave, took from that day and from that incident the name of Bloody Brook." *The Spirit of '76*, November, 1894.

[2] Dr. J. B. Felt, followed by Dr. Leach, gives the name *Samuel* Bennett.

the time ; it was an exceedingly cumbrous affair, and was so long and heavy as to require a "rest." The other equipments of a foot-soldier were a "Snap-sack," six feet of match or fuse, a Bandolier — a leathern belt passing over the right shoulder and under the left arm — containing a dozen or more boxes each holding one charge of powder ; a bag of bullets and a horn of priming powder were also attached to this belt.[1]

The Indian uprising left its blood-stained mark upon our early history. But out of it came a brighter day for the colonists. At its close, the power of the red man was effectually broken. Men breathed more freely when they were no longer obliged to carry arms to church and field, and to watch every thicket for a lurking foe. The death of Philip, and the breaking up of the confederacy of which he was the head, marked the commencement of a new era of peace and prosperity for the English settlements. It was, however, a costly victory. In the loss of property, and the increased burdens of taxation, it was felt in the community for many years.[2] Of the ninety towns in the colonies " twelve were utterly destroyed, while more than forty others were the scene of fire and slaughter."[3] Taxes increased from ten to fifteen fold; the debt incurred by the Indian wars has been estimated as high as fifty thousand pounds.[4]

1 *Soldiers in King Philip's War*, George M. Bodge, Boston, 1891.

2 "It was years before some towns recovered" from the blow. Barry, *History of Massachusetts*, vol. I, p. 447.

3 *The Beginnings of New England*, John Fiske, 249.

4 Barry, *History of Massachusetts*, vol. II, p. 8.

Perils and fears from wild beasts, also, were added
to those from wild men. There were hypothetical
" lyons " at Cape Anne, and veritable bears and
wolves.[1] On one occasion, the people at the " Cove "
were alarmed by the sound of distant firing, and ap-
prehended an Indian raid, but as nothing came of it,
it was afterward supposed that some settlers were endeavoring to frighten the wolves from their sheep-
pens and barnyards. The town voted, July 8, 1754,
that " the present Selectmen shall Draw From the
Town Treasurer What Money they shall think ned-
ful to Joyn with other Towns and Lay it out in such
a way and manner as they shall think most Likely
to Destroy those Devouring Wolves which are in
or may be found in the Woods between Ipswich
Gloucester Manchester Beverly and Whenham." If
the wolves were such a trouble in the middle of the
eighteenth century, what must they have been a
hundred years earlier? A letter from Governor
Dudley to the Countess of Lincoln, written in 1631,
shows to what annoyance the first settlers were subject:

" Uppon the 25 of this March one of Waterton having
lost a calfe, and about 10 of the clock at night hearinge the
howlinge of some wolves not farr off, raised many of his
neighbours out of thir bedds, that by dischardginge their
muskeets neere about the place, where he heard the wolves,
hee might soe putt the wolves to flight, and save his calfe:
the wind serveing fitt to carry the report of the musketts to
Rocksbury, 3 miles of at such a time, the inhabitants there

[1] The wolves must have been particularly aggravating; as one chroni-
cler relates, " They sat on their tayles and grinned at us." The wolves
have long since disappeared, and it is many years since the last family of
Bears lived in Manchester.

took an alarme, beate upp their drume, armed themselves
and sent in post to us in Boston to raise us allsoe. Soe in
the morning the calfe being found safe, the wolves af-
frighted, and our danger past, wee went merrily to breake-
fast."

After more than half a century of struggle between the colonies and the crown, the King an-
nulled the charter in 1685, and Sir Edmund Andros
was sent out to govern New England and New
York. His administration proved so arbitrary and
oppressive that the inhabitants of Boston rose in
revolution in 1689, deposed and imprisoned Andros,
and reëstablished the colonial form of government.
Manchester, it appears, was true to the interests of
the colony, and put on record its determined action
in this critical state of political affairs.

May 17, 1689.

We the inhabitants of the town of Manchester being met
together on the day aforesaid to consider and advise about
the present exigency, being very sensible and thankful to
God for his great mercy in giving us such a wonderful deliverance out of the hand of tyranny and oppression, and
rendering our hearty thanks to those gentlemen who have
been engaged in so good a work as the conserving of our
peace and safety and likewise very sensible of the present
unsettlement of our affairs do hereby declare that we expect our honored Governor,[1] deputy governor and assistants
elected by the freemen of this colony in May 1686, together
with the deputies sent down by the respective towns to the
Court then holden, shall convene, reassume and exercise
the government as a general court according to our charter
forthwith, for and in submission to the crown of England.
We do hereby promise our assistance in persons and estates.

By me Thos. Tewksbury, Ck.

in behalf of the Town.

[1] Simon Bradstreet, who was elected in 1679, and, with the exception of
the administration of Sir Edmund Andros, continued in office until 1692.

It is evident that our forefathers were men of intelligence, public spirit and patriotism; they kept
rank with the brave and devoted leaders of those
heroic times. The moral and civic virtues were
being nursed in every little village and hamlet
which were afterwards embodied in such men as the
Adamses, James Otis and John Hancock, and resulted in the independence of these United States.

With the relief that was experienced after the cessation of Indian hostilities and the high-handed acts
of Andros, the colonists entered upon a more prosperous career. Manchester shared in the general
activity. New enterprises were undertaken, measures of public utility were set on foot, and the community emerged from the torpid condition in which
nearly half a century of poverty and general disturbance had left it. About this time, a new road was
laid out from Manchester to Gloucester. This began
at the Common, went up Union to Washington
street, thence through the burial ground, down Summer street, to near the " Row " schoolhouse, and
thence by what is now known as the " old road " it
crossed the railroad track and connected with the
road as now travelled near the top of the " great
hill." Before this time the road was by Sea street,
through the Towne and Dana estates, and crossed
the present county road near the entrance to the
most western of the " Dana Avenues."

At this period also, the first store was opened in
town in the house now owned by Mr. Joseph Proctor
on Sea street. The first tavern was built " for the
entertainment of man and beast," on North street.

This old house was originally two stories in front, with a long sloping roof to the rear. The whole structure was remodelled about sixty years ago. It is now owned by Mr. Alexander Kerr. The second tavern was the old "Joe Babcock house," at the head of Beach street; and the third stood nearly in front of the Priest Schoolhouse, and was kept by Dea. John Allen, "innkeeper," and afterwards known as the "Murray house." It formerly had over its door a gilt ball from which it received the name of the "Golden Ball."

But little is known of the first taverns or their keepers. No doubt these ancient hostelries bore an important part in the early life of the town. The tavern was "the secular meeting-house of the community." In it affairs of moment were planned and discussed. It was the scene of many a warm debate, and of many an encounter between village wits. It held a position of influence and importance, which it lost with the passing away of the stage-coach and the advent of railroads.

In 1691, the old church was found too small, and the town voted to build a new one. The second schoolhouse, also, now appeared, with its "School dam" and "horn-book." [1] A tide-mill had been built as early as 1644, "upon the river near the meeting-house"; it was a one-story log structure.[2]

[1]   "books of stature small
                    Which with pellucid horn secured are
                    To save from fingers wet the letters fair."
These horn-books were studied by the children of the Puritans as late as 1715. They are referred to in Judge Sewall's Diary, and appear in the booksellers' lists in the early part of the eighteenth century. It is not known that one is now in existence.   [2] It stood until 1826.

In 1705, a small mill was built upon the site of the " old Baker mill," on what was then called " Brushie plain."

About the year 1700 the "Cove " had grown to be " quite the largest precinct in the town." Joseph Knight then owned there three hundred acres of land, on which were a saw-mill and blacksmith shop. Asa Kitfield built a large number of vessels, and was engaged in the fishing business and in the lumber trade. Capt. Nehemiah Ingersoll, a retired Boston merchant, owned " a nice hip-roofed house, handsomely furnished," just beyond Wolf Trap Brook, where he resided with his daughters after the death of his wife. Here came Dr. Manasseh Cutler of Hamilton, one of the most accomplished men of his time, and a great factor in the settlement of Ohio, to talk botany with Miss Mary. It was here that Gifford Goldsmith lived, who held most persistently that the sun travelled around the earth, and that its distance as calculated by the shadow cast by his walking-stick was four thousand miles, and whose conclusive answer to all who questioned his cosmogony was, " Let God be true, and every man a liar."

The first half of the eighteenth century is generally considered an uneventful one. The colonies grew and strengthened themselves, men planted and builded, married and were given in marriage, the seasons came and went in all their pomp. The people were mostly too busy in subduing the wilderness and reaping the harvest of the sea to trouble themselves with the great conflict between England and

France, or with the great political movements that were taking place in Europe.

There were still many drawbacks. Great inconvenience, if not suffering, was caused by the unsettled financial condition. According to the Suffolk Probate Records, the price of silver rose between 1720 and 1745, from 10s. to 36s. per oz., and gold from £8 to £24. The money market was in a constant state of disturbance, owing to the irredeemable "fiat" currency. But there was peace if not prosperity. "Fear of change" might perplex monarchs and statesmen, but the lot of the people of Manchester was a comparatively quiet one. The rumored massacre of some of their number by the savage Indians at Pemaquid, or a large haul of cod on the Banks, excited more interest than the great Marlborough's victories. The community lived largely within itself. At last, however, an event occurred which stirred to life the English colonists, especially those of the seaboard towns.

In 1745, the far-famed fortress of Louisburg, on Cape Breton, a strategic position of such importance that it had received the name of "the French Dunkirk in America," was besieged by a combined British and American force under the immediate command of Sir William Pepperell. After a vigorous siege and assault, the stronghold surrendered, June 17, and the English became masters of the whole North American coast. The roster of the men who served from Manchester has not been preserved. But it is known that Lieut. Samuel May was in the engagement : Jacob Morgan and John Hassam were killed; William Tuck was a sailor on a British frigate; Jacob Foster was at the siege and not heard from afterwards; Benjamin Craft was attached to the Commissary Department, kept a journal, and wrote beautiful, Christian letters home to his wife;[1] and David Allen kept a journal of the expedition, of which unhappily nothing remains.[2]

The expedition to Cape Breton and the siege and capture of Louisburg has well been considered the most daring and marvellous feat in all our naval history. "The New England sailors had no fear to anchor on the open coast, close in shore, and they landed their guns, and by their handy use of ropes and tackles, transported them over creeks, swamps and morasses, and mounted them on platforms and opened fire."[3]

The great thunder-peal to the eastward was followed by an after-clap which echoed on our own shores. On Sept. 26, 1746, we are told, there was great alarm in town, lest an attack should be made by a French fleet; a company was raised at Cape Ann, a watch-house was built, people were in great fear, and many secreted their effects. The storm-cloud, however, passed off to sea, and its mutterings subsided into calm. The fishing-boats pushed out from the inlets, the brown sails slipped over the horizon's rim, blanched cheeks took on color again, and the grim sentinels went back to the caulker's shops and shipyards.

[1] Appendix K.

[2] Dr. Leach gives the names also of Daniel Foster and Thomas Jones at Louisburg.

[3] Admiral F. A. Roe, *Wooden Walls and American Seamen*, The Spirit of '76, March, 1895.

In his "Oration on the History of Liberty," at
Charlestown, July 4, 1838, Edward Everett made
mention of "a citizen of Manchester" as then living,
who was at Braddock's Defeat, July 9, 1755, and
who well remembered Washington's appearance and
almost miraculous escape, at that disastrous rout.
But as eighty-three years had elapsed since that
date, any one present at the battle must have been
one hundred years old or more, in 1838. There
were no soldiers living at this time in Manchester,
as Mr. W. H. Tappan has ascertained, over ninety
years of age. The distinguished orator had evidently
been misinformed, and Manchester loses the honor
of having been represented, so far as is known, in
the ill-starred expedition to Fort Duquesne.

With the fall of Louisburg, followed by that of
Quebec (1759), the supremacy of France in the New
World passed into the hands of her great rival, and
the colonies were freed from a constant menace.
The overthrow of the French arms meant also the
weakening of the strength and courage of the Aborigines to such an extent, that they gave little
trouble in future to the whites. The peace of
Aix-la-Chapelle left many things still unsettled —
questions as to boundaries and the possession of
islands off the coast of North America — but the
struggle which from the first had kept the colonies
in an almost continual state of excitement and perturbation was transferred from New England soil.
The imagination no longer saw in the sunset glow
the glare of burning villages, or heard in the cry of
the screech-owl the dreaded war-whoop. With the

brightening of the horizon after the capture of
Louisburg, came a general advance, improvement in
the style of living, increase of towns, better buildings, larger trade and more prosperous times.

" Over the roofs of the pioneers
Gathers the moss of a hundred years;
On man and his works has passed the change
Which needs must be in a century's range;
The land lies open and warm to the sun;
Anvils clamor and mill-wheels run;
Flocks on the hillsides, herds on the plain,
The wilderness gladdened with fruit and grain !"

Below is a list of the early residents, as near as
can now be ascertained, with the date of their connection with the settlement.

1626.
William Allen.
Richard Norman.
John Norman.
William Jeffrey.

1629.
John Black.

1636.
Robert Leach.
Samuel Archer.
Seargent Wolf.
John More.
George Norton.
John Sibley.

1637.
John Pickworth.
John Galley.
William Bennet.
Pasco Foote.
Thomas Chubbs.

1640.
John Friend.
William Walton.
James Standish.
Benjamin Parmiter.

Robert Allen.
Edmond Grover.
Rev. Ralph Smith.

1650.
Henry Lee.
William Everton.
—— Graves.
Joseph Pickworth.
Nicholas Vincent.
John Kettle.
Robert Knight.

1651.
Robert Isabell.
Nath'l Marsterson.
Richard Norman.

1654.
Thomas Millett.

1660.
Moses Maverick.
Samuel Allen.
John Blackleeche.

1662.
—— Pitts.
John Elithope.

1664.
John Crowell.

1665.
John West.

1666.
Richard Glass.
Rev. John Winborn.

1667.
Thomas Bishop.
Jenkins Williams.

1668.
Oneciphorus Allen.

1670.
William Hooper.
Nich. Woodberry.

1674.
Ambrose Gale.
Commit Marston.
Elodius Raynolds.
John Mason.
James Pittman.

1680.	1684.	1687.
John Lee.	William Hosham.	John Norton.
Samuel Lee.	John Foster.	William Allen.
Isaac Whitcher.	Mark Tucker.	Thomas Ayhairse.
John Gardner.	John Knowlton.	Eliab Littlefield.
Robert Leach.	Emanuel Day.	Richard Leatherer.
John Marston.	Elisha Reynolds.	John Bishop.
Thos. Tewkesbury.	Joseph Woodberry.	Samuel Crowell.
Thomas Ross.	James Pitman.	Rev. John Everleth.
Samuel Allen.	Robert Knight, Jr.	Rev. John Emerson.
Manassa Marston.	Epharam Jones.	John Burt.
Walter Parmiter.	John Allen.	Jonas Smith.
James Rivers.	Aaron Bennett.	
	Felix Monroe.	

TABLE OF PRICES.

1657 — 1661.

Negro Boy	. . . . . £20.	Swine	. . . . . .	20s.
Cow	. . . . 3.	Cord of Wood	. . .	1s.
Horse	. . . . 10.	Yoke of steers	. . .	£10.
Ox	. . . . 5.	Otter skin	. . . .	10s.

1755 — 1760.

Indian Corn,	6s. per bu.	Wood, £4 to £4, 15s.[1] per cord.
Rye,	6s. per bu.	Cider, £1, 10s. to £2[1] per bbl.
Wheat,	10s. per bu.	Eggs, 3s. 6d. per doz.
Pork,	7d. per lb.	Cheese. 4s. per lb.
Beef,	3d. per lb.	Chocolate, 11s. per lb.
Potatoes, 5s. to 17s. per bu.		Wool, 1s. per lb.
Hemp & Flax,	1s. per lb.	Salt, £1, 17s.[1] per bu.
Sugar,	5s.[1] per lb.	Bread, 19s. per cwt.
Codfish, £1, 10s. to £2, 10s.[1] per quintal.,		Iron, £4 per cwt.
		Turpentine, £2 per bbl.
Laborers, 7s. to 15s. per day.		

[1] Old Tenor.

MURRAY HOUSE.

CHAPTER V.

THE REVOLUTIONARY EPOCH.

" Wise, and brave, and virtuous men are always friends to
liberty."

A THANKSGIVING DISCOURSE, *Dr. Jona. Mayhew*, Boston, 1766.

" What constitutes a State ?
Not high-raised battlement or labor'd mound,
    Thick wall or moated gate ;
   *   *   *   *   *

  No : — Men, high-minded Men,
   *   *   *   *   *

Men who their *duties* know,
But know their *rights*, and knowing, dare maintain ;
   *   *   *   *   *

  These constitute a State."

Sir William Jones.

CHAPTER V.

THE REVOLUTIONARY EPOCH.

GATHERING CLOUDS — THE STORM — "FAINT YET PURSUING"
— DAYS OF DARKNESS — INVENTORIES — ROMANTIC
GLEAMS — THE INSURGENTS — "THE GREAT
SICKNESS" — BELIEFS AND MISBELIEFS
— "HEROES OF '76."

THE period which now passes under review includes the War of the Revolution with the causes which more immediately led up to it, and the more immediate results of that struggle for independence. It may be said to begin about the year 1760, and to close about 1800. These four decades were a time of momentous and stirring interest. The period of repose which followed the peace of Aix-la-Chapelle was not long to continue. The memories of the French war were still fresh in the mind : the men who fought with Amherst and Abercrombie had hardly beaten their swords into ploughshares and their spears into pruning-hooks ; the exploits of the "Rangers" still formed the theme of many an evening gathering around the wide-mouthed chimney-place, — when ominous signs of an approaching conflict with England appeared in the horizon.

It were a weary and profitless task to trace all
the causes which led up to the War of the Revolution. Successive acts of oppression on the part of
the British ministry, matched by a growing spirit of
independence on the part of the Colonists, prepared
the way for the open rupture. Had Lord North's
administration been more politic, had the elder Pitt's
counsels been heeded, America might have remained
a loyal dependence of the British crown. But with
an infatuation that seems difficult of explanation,
the whole legislation of the mother country seemed
contrived to alienate the affections of her children,
and to drive them from her side. The iron hand
was not covered with the velvet glove. Gradually
at first, and then more swiftly, complications multiplied. Troops sent to enforce the decrees of the
King in Council and to support arbitrary Provincial
Governors were quartered upon the people; exaction
after exaction strained to the utmost tension the
relations between the two parties,[1] until it was evident that a conflict was inevitable. The *jus divinum*
of kingship had never been an article of the Puritan
creed. The men who had settled America were
acute, inquisitive, dexterous, prompt in action, full of
resources ; they could " augur misgovernment at a
distance, and snuff the approach of tyranny in every
tainted breeze." [2]   It has been said of them that they
had a " high constructive *instinct*, raising them above

[1] The feeling towards England felt by many at this time is illustrated
by a story told by Capt. Thomas Leach of his grandfather, Ezekiel Leach,
who told his children one day as they were going to school, if the teacher
asked them to spell " England," not to do it.

[2] Burke's *Speech on Conciliation with America*, 1775.

their age, and above themselves." John Adams gave
utterance to a general conviction, when he declared
in the Congress of 1775 : " No assembly ever had a
greater number of great objects before them ; provinces, nations, empires are small things before us." [1]

In all the hitherto passive resistance to British
oppression, Massachusetts had taken the lead ; her
position as a champion of liberty had been recognized. Even three-quarters of a century before a
contemporary writer had said, " All the frame of
heaven moves upon one axis, and the whole of New
England's interest seems designed to be loaded on
one bottom ; and the particular motions to be con-
centric to the Massachusetts tropic. You know who
are wont to trot after the Bay horse." [2]

When things had come to such a pass that it was
felt that forbearance was no longer a virtue, the colonies began to appoint Committees of Safety and
Correspondence, and to unite for consultation and
mutual assistance. The year 1775 dawned with a
dark and troubled sky ; the spirit of resistance was
fairly aroused ; no one could foretell just where or
how the crisis would come, but men " stood still
with awful eye," and in the silence that precedes
the storm watched to see the curtain rise.

Our interest is in the humble part which Manchester played in this great drama. Year after year
the records are chiefly occupied with local municipal

---

[1] *Life and Works of John Adams*, vol. I, p. 170.

[2] *Letter* of Mr. Wiswall to Governor Hinckley, Nov. 5, 1691. Instances
of punning like this are exceedingly rare in the writings of the Puritan
age. Our fathers were not without their humor, grim as it sometimes
was, but it found expression in other ways.

matters, as the "asessing of Rates," "Releife of The
Poor," settling of Bounds, raising money to "suport
the Hy Ways," voting of appropriations for a
"Gramer Choole," directing the selectmen to "Care
for those who should Behave themselves disorderly
in ye Meeting-house by leaving their Seats and taking others," electing "Haywards and Deer Reaves,"
and such other business as came "Legaly before the
Meeting." But with the historic year, 1775, matters
of wider and more public concernment began to find
place in the records. Among these are the appointment of Committees of Correspondence, establishment of "watches," voting of bounties, and various
acts respecting requisitions for the Army, which
were sometimes granted and sometimes refused,
raising of quotas, appeals to the General Court for
abatement of taxes, and dealing with "Internal
Enemies."

It was a "storm and stress" period, and not all
who were of Puritan ancestry, whose progenitors had
fought at Naseby and Marston Moor, were of the
stuff to stand the strain. Besides the Tories who
openly espoused the royal cause, there were others
like the men of Meroz, who "came not up to the help
of the Lord," to the weakening and discouragement
of the patriots of Israel.[1] The disturbed condition
of the seaboard during the years immediately preceding the Revolution may be inferred from the
emigration which took place to Nova Scotia and

[1] One patriotic family — so at least tradition has it — retired from their
home to live for a time in the Gloucester woods; anxious probably, in case
of an invasion, to support their friends and neighbors as a sort of rear-
guard.

New Brunswick from the eastern towns of Essex County.[1] There is a tradition that many of these emigrants before leaving painted the chimneys of their houses *white*, with the understanding that they would be respected by the British in case of hostilities.

The following extracts from warrants and records of town meetings will show something of the temper and condition of the town during these " times that tried men's souls " :

Jan. 8, 1775.   To Choose a Committee to agree upon a Certain sum of Money to be raised for the support of the Minute men so-called.

Mar. 20.   Voted to keep four Watches : one at Glasses head or Black Cove : to Rang from Chubs Creek to Marsters Point one in the Center of the Town to Range from Bennetts Hill to Edward Hoopers Corner : one at the old-Neck to Rang from the Northern End of Glasses Beach to Thunder-Bolt Hill : and one at Kettle-Cove on Great Crow-Island.

May 23.   Voted that if Mr Daniel Presson shall refuse to watch or do his turn in Watching that He will greatly Incur the displeasure of the Town.

July 17.   Voted to Choose a Committee of Correspondence to consist of Nine Men.

The committee of correspondence were, John Lee, Jonathan Herrick, Samuel Forster, Jacob Hooper, Aaron Lee, John Edwards, Isaac Lee, Isaac Proctor, Eleazer Crafts.

Dr. Joseph Whipple, the first physician in Manchester, was made captain of the Coast Guards ; the following is a copy of his orders.

[1] *Life of William Lloyd Garrison*, vol. I. p. 2.

"At a meeting of the Committee of Correspondence on Monday, the 25th of September, 1775.

"Captain Joseph Whipple. — As you and the half company of soldiers stationed in the town of Manchester and under the care of the Committee of Correspondence, we order you to proceed as followeth : —

"*Firstly.* We order you and your enlisted soldiers to meet on the Town Landing, complete in arms, as directed by the Congress, at two o'clock every day except Sunday, and to discipline your soldiers two hours and a half, and them that don't appear by half after two o'clock shall pay a fine for each default of eight pence to be taken out of their wages.

"*Secondly.* We order you and your soldiers to carry your arms to meeting every meeting day, according to the resolves of the Congress.

"*Thirdly.* We order you to keep three watches in town, two in each watch by night, and one by day. One watch on Glasshead, and one watch on Image Hill, and one on Crow Island.

"*Fourthly.* We order you to go the rounds two nights in each week, to see that there is a good watch kept, and in case any of them should be found deficient that they may be tried by the articles of war, as they are in the army at Cambridge.

"*Fifthly.* We order you to see that no night-watch leaves the watch till he is relieved by the day-watch, and no day-watch till relieved by the night-watch, and see that the watch-houses are not left destitute the day or night.

"*Sixthly.* We order that the Town Landing be the Laram port at all times, that in case of any alarm that the soldiers make the best of their way to the Laram port to receive orders ; except as is for Article Eighthly.

"*Seventhly.* We order that if any shall leave the body and not appear on parade without leave of the officers, they shall pay a fine of six shillings, to be taken out of their wages for each default.

" *Eighthly*. We order that if any alarm should be at Kettle Cove that the men that are there shall keep there, and the rest to appear at the alarm post, and in case the alarm should be at Newport the men that are there shall keep there, and the rest to appear as above."

Jan. 22, 1776. Voted, Firstly to throw up Some Intrenchments In sum Convenent Place In the Town. . . . Forthly voted that the People of Town should work Two Days If they Please on said Intrenchments.

Mar. 18. To see if the town will Choos a Standing Committee of Correspondence and also To see if the Town will Choos a Committee to Petition the house of Representatives for this Colony to obtain Pay for the Town watching.

Feb. 13, 1777.[1] Voted to give to Each Person that will Inlist into the Contenental servise Fowerteen Pound Besides the Bountys Given by the Continent and Provinces.

Jan. 9, 1778. To Consider or Determin what Efectual meathod shall be Taken towords assesing Leveing and Colecting the money Paid as an Extra Bounty to those Solders who Inlisted in to the Continentel service for the terme of three years for the town of Manchester ware as some of the famelys of the solders of the Continentale Service are in a Suffering Condition and for their Emediate Releave.

Att a Town Meeting Leaguly worned for the Porpose mentinoid in the foregoing worant Voated for the Committee of Supplyes to settle with the solders namely that their husbands are in the Continentale Service so Far half of their wages will go agreaible to the Price acct and Refund the over and above Surpresage.[2]

---

[1] In 1777 the warrant for the town meeting began with: " In the name of the government and people of this colony" instead of " In the name of his Majesty George the Third, etc.," as before.

[2] What questions of construction, interpretation and intention might arise, to the delight of lawyers, were acts so expressed in our modern legislation. But want of legal phraseology is a small affliction compared with a " government of lawyers."

April 13.   Att a Town Meeting Leagully assembled In
order to Consider of the forme of the Government Constitution and Proceeded as folloeth. . . . adjourned the Meeting Tell Monday 18 Day of May at 8 In the Morning and
Then Meet 1ly Voted by the whole body at the meeting
which was 23 In Number that they Disaprove of the
meathod of the Constatutiant.

May 17.   Voted Not to send a Representative Judging
the Town as a Town Not able to Pay the charge.

[No date] 1779.   Att a Towne Meeting Leagully assembled to Geather to see if the Town would Proceed to rais six
men to Joyne the Continentall Army Voted after Long Debate Weather The Selectmen should rais ye whole of the six
men or Not it passed in the Negitive Voted Not to Rais
more than two out of the six [1] Voted to Perfer a Pertishon
to Generall Tidcolme [2] to Git of the men To be Raised on
the Town Voted that ye Select should try to Hyer two men
in the Best manner they Can.

Att a Town Meeting Leagully Assembled on ye Third
Day of Janary 1780 To Petishion ye Court for an Abatment
of ye Late Tax Layed on this Town.   2ly Voted to Chuse
an agent to Represent ye town at Court with a Memorall or
a Petishion as the Assessors shall think proper.   3ly Voted
that Eleaser Craft for their agent to attend the Court for
the Above Purpos. [3]

[19 June 1780] Voted to Give Twelve Pounds in addition to their wages in Hard Mony Sartan or if the Mediam
is More puting the Towns To gather than our Solders is to
Receive as Much more as the Mediam amounts To Puting
all the Towns To geather.

[26 June 1780] Voted Not to Give more Bounty than the
Towns give In Generall Voted to Give 120 Hard Dollars as
a Bounty to each solder that shall Enlist To serve for the
terme of six Months & No More.

---

[1] No wonder that the raising of six men was opposed, as only twenty-
three voters mustered at an important meeting a few months before.

[2] Brigadier Benjamin Titcomb.

[3] *Vide* NOTE A at end of chapter.

Oct. 9. Voted to Rais Seven Thousand Pounds [1] To Purches ye Beef [2] Voted to Reconsider ye Vote Voted Not to Comply with The Orders from the Court sent to this Town Let the Consequance Be what it will. [The town was subsequently fined for this recusancy.]

Nov. 21, 1781. Voted to Lay out 1000 Hard Dollers In Hyering Men for three years or During the War as far as that will go.[3]

[May 7, 1782.] Voted Sam^ll Foster & Elez^r Craft be a Commett to see if the Two men that was Engaged for the service would Release ther Engagments the Answer Returned Yes.

In April, 1775, came the call to arms, on the occasion of the attempt of the British to seize the military stores at Concord. The following men responded and marched for the scene of conflict, but receiving at Medford tidings of the retreat of the British, they returned home. Their names deserve being put on record : —

Andrew Marsters, Captain ; Sam. W. Forster, First Lieutenant ; Eleaser Crafts, Second Lieutenant ; Andrew Lee, John A. Brown, Benj. Crafts, Jona. Herrick, William Brown, Sergeants ; John Baker, Jos. Killam, Daniel Obier, Corporals ; Jacob

---

[1] This must have been in paper, or " Continental " currency.

[2] In the Schedule appended to Resolves passed by the House of Representatives, Dec. 4, 1780, Manchester is assessed 8,626 " weight of beef," or " money sufficient to purchase the same."

[3] The original draft of a letter, dated Boston, Oct. 10, 1781, from Israel Hutchinson to " Col. Eleazer Crafts manchister," is on file in the Town Archives, in which the town is warned against men from the " Eastern Contry " who were offering themselves for the army and in some instances proving deserters, and saying that if the town can " Rease the money," " men anuff " can be found who "Stands fare " ; the explanation of which is, there were men ready to take advantage of the dire necessities of the time, who after letting themselves to the towns to make up their quotas, were sometimes not to be found. All rascality and meanness do not belong to the last part of the nineteenth century.

Allen, Ezekiel Allen, John Allen, Samuel Ayers,
Zachari Brown, Wm. Badcock, Sam. Bennett, Simon
Baker, Aaron Bray, John Cheever, Thomas Cheever,
Thomas Colony, David Carter, Jesse Dodge, Moses
Dodge, Joseph Eveleth, Thomas Grant, Nath. Has-
kell, Benj. Haskell, John Knowlton, John Knights,
Wm. Knights, Edward Kitfield, Aaron Lee, Nath.
Lee, Simeon Low, Joseph Lee, James Lee, Aaron
Lewis, Israel May, Azariah Norton, Wm. Stone,
John Tewksbury, Privates: John Bailey, Drum-
mer. [1]

Twenty-one of these men enlisted in the Continental Army. Samuel Ayres was discharged in 1771
from H. M. 64th Regt., in which he had served
nineteen years. He served through the war, making in all twenty-eight years of military service.

Manchester bore her part in the historic conflict
by sea and land, from the opening action to the final
victory; her sons fought, and bled, and died, sinking
often into unknown graves, and leaving their only
memorial in the hearts of mourning friends. [2]

It is easy to see, as we read "between the lines"
of the almost illegible records with their quaint
spelling and phraseology, that our fathers of the Revolution, with all their hardships and poverty and
illiteracy, were in the main brave, loyal, determined
men, men with whom the liberties of the nation
could be safely trusted. These "village Hampdens"
made a bold stand when they voted "that Constable

[1] "The colors of this company were preserved for many years by Major
Forster, and at his death passed into the hands of his grandson, James
Knight, a soldier in the War of the Rebellion." W. H. T.

[2] A list of the Revolutionary soldiers is given in Appendix F.

Brown shall not pay Treasurer Gray [Harrison Gray,
Esq., Treasurer of the Province] what of the
Province Money he has in his hands," and " that
Constable Jonathan Brown pay what of the publick
Money he has in his hands forthwith to Henry
Gardner, Esqr of Stow." [1]   Such were the men who
in their humble seaside homes in New England
shared the spirit of Cromwell and Pym, " daring to
feel the majesty of Right," and loving the liberties
of mankind.   It is not so easy to realize the " straitness and scarcity " which these men and their families suffered.   It is said that there were times when
all the men capable of bearing arms were either in
the army, or manning the little earth-works dignified
by the name of " forts," or serving on board privateers,[2] leaving women and children and old men to
till the land and to eke out their subsistence from
the sea.   Added to all other difficulties the Continental money had so depreciated that in 1780, £75
was the common exchange for £1 in silver.[3]   At
this time " four months' pay of a private soldier
would not purchase for his family a single bushel

[1] *Town Records*, Nov. 21, Dec. 27, 1774.

[2] There was but little objection felt at this time to the profession of
privateering. Franklin had not yet published his protest against it.
Privateering afforded a vent for the active and restless spirits of the
time ; it was not without some creditable associations, and the life of a
privateersman was full of the charms of novelty, adventure and risk.

[3] In 1781, there " had been issued by Congress a total of about $350,000,-
000 in paper," and this volume had been augmented by various and excessive
issues of paper money by the States. These unsecured " promises to pay "
were quoted at one time " at the rate of 64½ to 1 of gold, and soon after ceased
to be quoted at all and were considered entirely worthless." *The Spirit of
'76*, New York. Bancroft (*History of the United States*, ed. 1885, v, 440)
gives the value of the dollar " buoyed up by the French alliance," in 1778,
at 20 cents ; it fell to 5 cents the next April, and to 2½ cents in December.

of wheat; the pay of a colonel would not purchase oats for his horse"; [1] a leg of mutton was cheap at $1,000.

These inconveniences and sufferings may not have been so great as those experienced in the Jerseys and on the so-called *Neutral Ground*, in the vicinity of New York, during the occupation of that city by the British : but they were sufficient to put the patience and patriotism of the inhabitants to a severe strain.

The fear of a descent upon the coast by some of the enemy's cruisers was one that was always felt ; people lived in almost constant dread.   Persons still living remember " The Old Garden," as it was called, a locality near the present Magnolia station, where families in the easterly part of the town made for themselves a temporary settlement in times of threatened danger.[2]   The comparative poverty of the people, the almost total destruction of the maritime and fishing interests, and the demand of the war for men and money, made the years from 1774 to 1784 a decade of almost unparalleled trial and suffering.   " The Declaration of Independence was entered in full on the Records of the Town of Manchester at the time it was made, and throughout the war every nerve was strained and every resource was nearly exhausted in its support.   The town called in, and spent in the war, all the money which was at interest for the support of the ministry, and

[1] Irving, *Life of Washington*, iv, 31.

[2] The apple-trees were in " a state of decay " in 1816; the wall is still standing.

all that could be collected from taxation, and then gave their notes for means to pay the Government drafts and to support the soldiers and their families, in the defence of that Declaration." [1]

The spirit of our fathers, their love of freedom and their unselfish devotion to the principles for which the "embattled farmers" stood on Lexington Green and at Concord, were worthy the memories of Thermopylæ, of Marathon, of Runnymede, of the Dutch war for independence.

It will add to our admiration of these men if we remember that the country had not recovered from the strain of the French war, when the Revolution began. Franklin said that the colonies had "raised, paid and clothed nearly twenty-five thousand men during the last war — a number equal to those sent from Great Britain, and far beyond their proportion. They went deeply into debt in doing this, and all their estates and taxes are mortgaged for many years to come for discharging that debt." And nowhere did the burden of the public charges rest upon the people more heavily than in New England. Owing in part to the location of the colonies on the seacoast, they suffered, both directly and indirectly, to an extent which only the most unflinching devotion and heroic endurance could have enabled them to bear.

We are to make some allowance, no doubt, for the strong language used by John Adams, who was a born aristocrat, in the Debates on the Declaration of Independence, " the condition of the fishermen of

[1] *Paper* read at celebration in Salem (Monday), July 5, 1852, by John Lee.

the Northern States is as abject as that of slaves ": [1]
but no doubt it was one of great poverty and hardship; so much the more credit is due to them for the
many noble and manly qualities which they developed. They were men, at all events, in whom was
an inextinguishable love of freedom; they believed,
" Better is a dinner of herbs where *liberty* is, than a
stalled ox and *slavery* therewith." [2]

The following extracts from an Assessors' Book,
preserved in the Town Treasurer's Office (supposed
date about 1760), a little pamphlet of 32 pages, note
size, date and names of Assessors wanting, give an
idea of the taxable property of that time:

Dea. Jon[a] Herrick: Polls rateable 3. Dwelling Home 1.
Annual worth £28. Money at Interest £20. 2 Horses.
6 Oxen. 6 Cows. 5 Sheep. 2 Hogs. 100 acres Pasturing.
10 acres Tillage, 150 bushels Grain, 10 barrels Cyder, etc.
The Hon[ble] Daniel Edwards Esq[r]. 2 Polls. 1 Dwelling
Home & Shop. 1 Warehouse. 2 Fish houses. 165 ton of
Vessels. Trading Stock £146.13.4, 2 horses, 4 oxen, 5
cows, 70 acres of pasture, 10 acres Eng[h] mowing, 25 B:
grain, etc: John Lee Esq[r]. 1 Poll Rateable. 1 dwelling
home. 2 warehouses. 5 Fish houses. 130 Feet wharf.
Annual worth £30. 3 Servants for Life.[3] 261 Ton Vessels.
£130 Trading Stock. Interest money £53.13.4. 52 acres
pasture, 4 acres Marsh, 9 acres English mowing, 100 B:
Grain, 3 Barrels Cyder, 5 Tons produce, etc. Richard Day
½ Poll not Rateable. 1 Servant Negroe. 1 Mare. 1 Cow.
2 acres Tillage. 2½ acres English mowg. 25 B: of grain,
1½ Barrel Cyder 1½ Ton hay; etc.

[1] Papers of James Madison, Mobile, 1842, vol. 1, p. 29.

[2] Prov. xv, 17.

[3] Samuel Lee was also an owner of slaves, one of whom, a waiting maid,
he bequeathed to his wife "and her heirs *forever*."

These were among the largest taxpayers. The majority of the inventories show very modest incomes and estates. In many instances, one-half, one-third, or one-fourth of a dwelling-house is assessed. The "annual worth" is rated in some cases as low as 20 shillings. Here were certainly no bloated bond holders or millionaire overlords; there was a comparative equality, presenting few temptations to anarchistic uprisings and few opportunities of avaricious and domineering oppression. There was no impassable gulf between the lowest and the highest. There was no severe strain upon the relations between employer and employed. And yet there were distinctions, and no doubt some complained of the inequalities of rank and wealth, and declared that the rich were becoming richer and the poor becoming poorer. Each century and generation fancies that the golden age was in the past; if we take heed to the voice of history and experience, we shall "seek one to come."

The War, as it dragged its slow length along, had its stirring and romantic incidents. The situation of Manchester on the seaboard, and the employment of many of its men in the naval service and in coast defence, gave to its history its full share of the adventurous and sometimes tragic element. Some of these incidents have been preserved and make a part of the history of the period. A bit of local color is thrown upon the dark background of the first years of the War, by an incident related by Mr. D. L. Bingham, who heard it when a boy from his grandmother who was a witness of the event. When the

Continental Army was at Cambridge, recruits were sometimes landed at Cape Ann and marched through the town to camp. On one occasion, three hundred Virginians, on their way to join Washington's command, passed through Manchester, encamping near the site of the present Parsonage. They were supplied with food by the people, and for their amusement displayed their skill with the tomahawk. Their soldierly appearance, their green frocks, their rifles and their general bearing, representing as they did the patrician blood of the South, were well fitted to impress a young girl of sixteen, accustomed to the plain accoutrements, motley arms and untrained step of the farmers and fisher-folk who had rallied at the sound of war. The stay of these gallant Southrons appears to have been too short, however, for them to win the hearts of any of Manchester's fair daughters.

Among the most serious disasters to the town during the War was the loss of the privateer " Gloucester," a new brig from the port for which she was named, which put to sea in July, 1776, with a crew of one hundred and thirty men. Shortly after sailing she captured and sent in two prizes; after that nothing was heard of her; perfect mystery shrouds her fate.

"The loss of this vessel cast a deep gloom over Manchester, and made widows and orphans in many homes. The surgeon was Dr. Joseph Whipple, who had won an enviable reputation as a physician in the town. He left a widow and seven children. He was an ardent patriot, a safe counselor, and greatly beloved by his fellow-citizens, eighteen of whom shipped with him, and with him sank to their eternal rest." Among them were Daniel Morgan, Daniel Ober, Nicholas Babcock, James Pittman, John Allen, John Carter, ———— Tucker, Amos Allen, David Brown, Andrew Brown, Jacob Lendall, Simeon Webber, Azariah Allen and James Morgan.

Andrew Leach and ten others belonging to the town, were also lost in the privateer "Barrington," of Newburyport.

As illustrating the spirit and readiness in meeting an emergency of many of the hardy sons of the ocean of this period, the following incidents in the lives of Manchester men, gathered from different sources, may here find place.

"It is related of Captain Daniel Leach who was a mate under Captain Tuck: their vessel was captured, and a prize crew placed on board to take her to Halifax. While on her way they put into a small harbor on the Nova Scotia coast. Captain Tuck was a fine conversationalist and of most excellent address, and he so ingratiated himself into the good graces of the prize captain, that he was invited to accompany that officer to visit some of his British friends on shore.

"During their absence, Leach, who was on deck, was watching the doings of the prize crew, who were all in the rigging, making some repairs and shaking out the sails, that they might dry. In this, Leach thought he saw his opportunity, and with him to see was to act. Some of the prisoners were on deck, and soon comprehended the plan. Leach loitered towards the arm-chest, and, seizing an axe, burst the cover open; and this being the signal agreed upon, the Americans were quickly armed, and the crew in the rigging were at their mercy. Leach and his former crew were in charge, and the English crew were his prisoners.

"After a pleasant visit on shore, the prize captain and his polite friend were rowed alongside. Leach received them courteously, and surprised the English captain by ordering him below as his prisoner, and Captain Tuck was informed that the ship was his again, and his old crew were awaiting his orders. Under his direction the vessel was taken safely to Boston."

From the *Salem Register* of July 30, 1838, we copy the following:

"At an early period in the great struggle for Independence, Mr. William Kitfield, when only 21 years of age, with John Girdler, of this town, and a young man by the name of Lawrence, of Gloucester, shipped at Boston with Captain Smith, of Salem, on a voyage to Bilboa. On their return voyage they were taken by a British ship of war, and carried to England and thrown into prison, from which they managed to escape and find their way to a sea port, where, as Englishmen, they shipped on a vessel bound to Jamaica and Halifax. While at the former place Kitfield proposed to the other two a plan for taking the vessel while on her way to Halifax. They agreed to it, and the next day, while on shore, each bought a sword. When they were well to the northward, about midnight, when all three were in the same watch, Girdler, armed, was placed at the cabin-door; Kitfield went to the second mate, who was at the helm, and told him the anchor was off the bow. Thus they got charge of the deck, and the officers were prisoners below. The crew, being promised a share of the prize, readily joined them and assisted in working the vessel. The next day they ran alongside an American privateer, and were taken into Salem, where the vessel was given up to the three daring youngsters. The Captain cried bitterly, and said he would not care so much about it if it were not the first time he had been Captain."

"Captain William Pert was so unfortunate as to have his ship captured by an English cruiser when he was quite near Boston. A prize crew was put on board and she was headed for Halifax.

"Among the cargo of the captured vessel was a large amount of provisions and excellent liquors. For the first day the wind was very light, and but very little progress was made. The English officers had already discovered the merits of the food, and they very frequently refreshed themselves with the liquors. As the sun was setting there were indications of more wind. The prize officers, not feeling sufficiently familiar with the difficult navigation of this part of Massachusetts Bay, asked Captain Pert to work the ship, to which he very cheerfully agreed. But occasionally he found time to go below, and added zest to the festivities by bringing to their notice some untried varieties of brandies and wines, which were greatly relished.

"The night set in very dark with a strong breeze. Captain Pert being pilot, managed to gradually change the course of the ship, and by daylight the following morning, the bewildered officers found themselves, with bad headaches, under the guns of the fort in Boston Harbor, and that they were prisoners."

The return of peace brought great relief to the distressed and impoverished people. The little hamlet

by the sea shared to the full in the general joy.
The old cannon that had stood in front of the
church was taken in charge by two war-worn veterans, Benjamin Leach and Joseph Kelham, and
taken to every part of the town, followed no doubt
by the inevitable crowd of jubilant youngsters, and
fired off again and again as an expression of the
popular rejoicing ; powder and refreshments were
everywhere furnished, and the town "rested from
war."

As a few men from Manchester were engaged in
putting down what is known as "Shay's Rebellion,"
a famous *emeute* in its day, and bearing some resemblance to the labor uprisings and anarchical demon-
strations of the present time, a brief account of it is
here subjoined :

Following the War of the Revolution, scarcity of
money and a derangement of the business of the
country resulted in a very widespread disaffection,
which assumed the form in Massachusetts of an
insurrection called "Shay's Rebellion." A body of
about 1,500 insurgents, led by Daniel Shay, assembled at Northampton, and prevented the sitting of
the courts. In December, 1786, they took possession of the court-house at Springfield. In January,
1787, an army of 4,000 men was raised by the State
to suppress the insurrection. The mob of insurgents,
for it was nothing more, was dispersed on its retreat
at Petersham, 150 were taken prisoners and the rest
fled. Among the men who were called into service
to put down this insurrection, which threatened to
become serious, were eleven men from Manchester.

They were enlisted January 17, 1787, in "Capt. John Rowes' Company, Col° Wades Regt."[1] They were discharged Feb. 23, 1787, their whole time of service being one month and fifteen days ; distance marched from home, 173 miles ; pay, Sergeant, £3, 12s. ; Corporal, £3, 6s. ; Privates, £3 each. The original Roll contains the names of 61 men ; the following men are credited to Manchester : Sam. Ayrs, Serg^t, Joseph Badcock, Corp., Samuel Tuck, Jacob Dowe, Benjn Craft, Pharoch Miller, Emkins Woodbery, Eben^r Phelps, William Osbon, Eben^r Craft, William Dowe, Privates.

The condition of things in Manchester at the close of the War, as in the country generally, was dispiriting. The fishing interest had been almost destroyed, the people were poor and embarrassed by debt, and the general outlook was far from cheering. But the native pluck, energy and self-reliance, nurtured by a century and more of hardship and toil, soon helped them to rally from the depressing influences of the long and wasting contest. With the improving condition of the country, the revival of maritime interests, the opening of new markets, the increase of trade, and the hopeful feeling that began to prevail, the town entered upon a new era. New fishing stations sprang up, new vessels were built, new warehouses, wharves and " flakes " appeared where the old had fallen into decay, and the stir of prosperity took the place of idleness. The state of things resembled on a small scale that which

[1] *Original Roll*, signed by Captain Rowe and sworn to by him before Peter Coffin, Just. Peace, July 9, 1787. *Attest*, Daniel W. Low, Gloucester.

marked the close of the English Revolution in 1688, and the accession of the Prince of Orange, as William the Third, to the throne. "The cheerful bustle in every seaport and every market-town indicated, not obscurely, the commencement of a happier age."[1]

One more cause of local trial and sorrow remained to throw a pall over the closing years of the century. In the year 1794, an epidemic, probably a severe type of typhus fever, swept off about seventy persons in a few months. Great want and suffering ensued. The heart of one of Salem's honored merchants responded to the cry of distress, as shown by the following letter, preserved in the town archives.

SALEM, 15 April, 1795.

Gentlemen : Considering the great calamity your town has suffered by sickness and death. I think you must have many who are objects of charity, which has induced me to ask your acceptance of the inclosed, which request you will please distribute to such deserving objects as have claims to the sympathy of the Humane. I request no publick notice to be taken of this.

Cash $100.

Order for 100 bush. corn.

I am gentlemen, with respect,
your most obedient servant,
William Gray, Jr.[2]

To the Selectmen of the Town of Manchester.

[1] Macaulay, *History of England*, cxxii.

[2] Beginning at the lowest round of the ladder, at the time of his death in 1825 Mr. Gray was the largest ship-owner in America. At one time he owned 60 square-rigged vessels, whose sails whitened every sea. He is said to have been an early riser, performing much of his work before breakfast. He was affable in intercourse, unostentatious in manner, and a man of practical benevolence. He was elected lieutenant-governor with Elbridge Gerry, in 1810. Mr. Gray's old homestead in Salem afterwards became the Essex Coffee House, now the Essex House. (*Old Landmarks of Boston*, p 201.)

A picture of the time would not be complete without some notice of its superstitions and beliefs. In addition to the real causes of fear and suffering, were others which were no less potent because they were imaginary. Our forefathers believed in an all-surrounding atmosphere of mystery, and lived in a kind of border-land of vagueness and fear. It was easy on a dark and stormy night to hear the death groan of a murdered mariner in the creaking of the giant trees of the forest,[1] and the cry of a belated and waylaid traveller in the lone wolf's howl or the trumpet of the loon. Wood declares, "Some being lost in the woods [at Cape Ann] have heard such terrible roarings as have made them much aghast, which must be either *lyons* or *devils*, there being no other creatures which used to *roar*." It required little stretch of the imagination to see in the morning mirage ships in the clouds sailing against the wind, or dropping to pieces in the air. Such portents were familiar in the daily life of our ancestors, and were seriously chronicled. Among the alarming occurrences which are recorded are comets,[2] electric storms, earthquakes, and especially mysterious, the "dark day,"[3] when there fell "over the bloom and sweet life of the Spring a horror of great darkness," when lamps were lighted at noon-day, and cattle came home to the barnyard and

[1] *History of Essex County*, vol. II, 1259.

[2] People are still living among us who remember hearing old people speak of comets with fear and dread, as presaging war or other calamities; and no wonder, for it was not so many years before that they were the terror of governments, "with fear of change perplexing monarchs."

[3] May 19, 1780.

fowls went to roost :[1] a phenomenon which has never been satisfactorily accounted for,[2] although it has been partially repeated as in the "yellow day" of 1881. It is a matter of interest that we have a reference to this occurrence in the life of an inhabitant of Manchester, Edward Lee; it is said that "when the darkness came on, the neighbors all flocked around [him] begging his prayers. While every face but his was pale with fear, he was as happy and joyful as ever." A nephew, who was then a little boy, said "he got as near his good uncle as he could, and then thought, if the judgment day had come, he was safe."[3]

The town, like most other towns, had its "witch" in the last century, a poor, harmless imbecile, named Molly Sennitt, who lived in a little house, still remembered by some of the older inhabitants, near the site of Mr. W. H. Tappan's house, on North Street. The story is told of the boys of the period playing a practical joke on the poor old creature one night by slyly depositing a bag full of felines inside her door and "letting the cat out of the bag," in a wholesale manner, in her domicile. As no cruelty was intended or inflicted, it may be supposed that the juvenile prank was

[1] "We were obliged to have a candle to eat dinner by ; it lookt very melloncaly indeed." *Diary of Col. Samuel Pierce*, Dorchester, Mass. See Whittier, *Abraham Davenport*.

[2] Elizabeth Crafts White, of Brookline, Mass., who died Oct. 7, 1839, a woman of remarkable character, familiarly known as "Aunt White," wrote an account of the "Dark Day," in which she gives "various opinions of the darkness" prevalent at the time. *The Crafts Family*, p. 168.

[3] *The Apostolic Fisherman: A Tale of the Last Century*. By an Aged Relative. Am. S. S. Union, pp. 21, 22.

OLD TOWN HOUSE.

NEW TOWN HOUSE.

winked at and hushed up by the authorities ; though
it may have brought down in private some solemn
reprimands from grave elders upon the thoughtless
offenders. Such escapades were regarded by many
as a sort of safety valve for the effervescence of
youthful spirit, although frowned on and highly
disapproved by the general moral sentiment of the
community.

The Revolutionary Period, covering the closing half
of the eighteenth century, was a period of general
upheaval. The country was poor, the finances were
almost hopelessly deranged, business was paralyzed,
families were scattered and broken up, schools closed
and meeting-houses in some instances left to decay.
The early part of the century had been one of formal-
ism, growing out of causes which lie within the province of the ecclesiastical historian to discuss ; the
"living faith of the settlers old " had almost died out,
or had been repudiated by their descendants. Then
came the " Great Awakening," under Whitefield,
Edwards and others, which passed over the churches
of New England like a thunder-storm, clearing the
air, but leaving uprooted trees and broken branches
in its track. It produced a profound and lasting
effect ; notwithstanding the fanaticism with which
it was accompanied, it broke up a reign of indiffer-
entism and left a " result of holier lives."

> " The tide of spiritual life rolled down
> From inland mountains to seaboard town."

It reached Ipswich, where Whitefield preached to
assembled thousands on the hill " before the meet-

ing-house " ; it resulted in the foundation of a
" New Light " church in Chebacco (now Essex),
but the afflatus was scarcely felt on this side of the
Cape.[1]

The events of the Revolution have been cast into
the shade by those of the later strife for Freedom.
The former conflict was " a war of skirmishes and
outposts," as compared with that which a generation
ago shook the Continent as if the Titans were at
war again. But the deeds of bravery in the War
for the Union ought not to make us forget that earlier struggle for Liberty, marked by acts of heroism
as splendid as those that have made illustrious our
later story. The spirit of the men who fought at
Ball's Bluff, and Gettysburg, and Lookout Mountain,
was but the rekindling of that which has invested the
names of Bunker Hill, and Trenton, and Yorktown
with undying glory.

Note A [p. 76 ante].

There should be something " read into " the
record. The bare statement of the town's neglect
to fill its quota needs explanation. The following
Memorial addressed to " The Honourable the Council and the House of Representatives of the State of
the Massachusetts Bay," puts the matter in quite a
different light :

The Petition of the Inhabitants of the Town of Manchester — Your Petitioners begg Leave humbly to Say —
We Think our selves hardly treated — in having a fine of
two hundred pounds Requir'd of us — as we take it — For

[1] For some account of the relations of Rev. Benj. Tappan and the Manchester church to the " Whitefield movement," see Appendixes A and B.

not Complying with an order of Court upon April 20, 1778: by which the Town was ordered to Send Five men to Serve in the Continental army for Nine Months. — For we assure your Honours that we took Unwearied Pains in Endeavours to obtain the Five: But Yet Could procure no more than three. — But though we would have furnished the five, we yet think that, If other Towns had furnished the Seventh part of their Numbers — First Called for, the three we furnished would Have been our full Proportion. for when the Continental Army was formed, Twenty Nine were a Seventh Part of our Numbers: and that number we Compleated to a Man; and all of them, Saving two, are still in the Field.

We also think ourselves hardly treated, in that so Large a Proportion has been Demanded of us by a late act of the Court — for Apportioning and Assessing a Sum and sums of Mony for Defraying publicke Charges, and satisfying Representatives for the Expences of their travell, And their attandance in the General Court, in the year 1778. For, we begg Leave to Certifie you, that, Since we furnished men for the Continental Army, our Numbers have been so Diminished, by Deaths — Captivities And Removals out of town, that we are now, at Home, But about half so many, as we were then. — *Besides*, several of those that have left the town were some of our more wealthy members of society.[1] And the Proportion Demanded of us, according to our Valuation Return is about the fifteenth Part of the Interest of the whole town. *And* our Internal Charges amount to more than our External.[2] *We* have great Numbers of Poor to relieve, *Tho'* but a Small town, yet we have four

[1] This was an evil, it appears, from which the seaboard towns specially suffered. A petition of the inhabitants of Salem, May 27, 1778, mentions among other "unnatural mischiefs," as "Vessels taken," "fishery destroyed by the Enemy," "stores, Warehouses, distilhouses, & wharves, generally unimployed and useless," — "that some inhabitants of this town who have Acquired great Riches, and who pay one sixth part of our taxes, have already removed, while others are daily removing to the Country," etc.

[2] The "Want of Tents" in the Continental Army was "help'd out by a Collection of now useless sails from the Sea Port Towns." Washington's *Letter to the President of Congress*, July 10, 1775.

Score widows in it, and far more Fatherless Children. *Our* trade & Commerce is but very inconsiderable. *And* Demands made for the Necessaries of Life, of which we are almost universally Purchasers, are high to astonishment, and Continually rising.—*In short.* *There* are many among us, who, we think, Cant be rationally thought able, at present, to Do anything more towards Defraying publick Charges. *And* others of us see not how we shall be able to do more than Provide Necessaries for our families, and releive the Distresses of the poor, widows & fatherless; if so much.

We therefore pray your Honours will please to take our Case into Consideration, and take off the fine. And abate, at Least, a part of the Sum Lately Requird of us — as our Proportion for Defraying the Publick Charges, &c. *And* we shall, as in duty bound, Ever Pray &c. —

P S   We Begg Leave to add as a Farther Plea, that we have been from the First, Zealous in the Common Cause, and have Vigorously exerted ourselves in endeavours to help in the Deliverance of our Dear Country. —

Aaron Lee   ) A Committee of
Eleaser Craft   } The Town A
John Allen Junr) fore Said.

Manchester April 12th 1779.

This petition was favorably received, the fine was remitted, and also "the sum of forty-five pounds, nineteen shillings and six pence for the travel and Attendance of their Representative more than was due from them on that account." [1]

[1] Acts and Resolves of the Province of Massachusetts Bay, vol. V, 1044,5.

CHAPTER VI.

THE FISHERIES.

"Hurrah ! the seaward breezes
  Sweep down the bay amain ;
Heave up, my lads, the anchor !
  Run up the sail again !
  *   *   *   *   *
In the darkness as in daylight,
  On the water as on land,
God's eye is looking on us,
  And beneath us is his hand !
Death will find us soon or later,
  On the deck or in the cot,
And we cannot meet him better
  Than in working out our lot."

The Fisherman, *Whittier*.

CHAPTER VI.

THE FISHERIES.

PAYING BANKS — "TO WORSHIP GOD AND CATCH FISH" —
HELPS AND HINDRANCES — SMALL SIZE OF FISHING
CRAFT — OFF FOR LABRADOR — "BISKUITT" AND
"BARBELS" — A "LOUEING HOUSEBEN"
— MISSING — INDIAN MASSACRES —
WANING DAYS — A SCHOOL
OF PROWESS.

T HE Banks of Newfoundland had been visited
long before the settlement of America. Following the mysterious Basques, the successors
of the Norsemen, came the Portuguese, the Spaniards and the English.[1] One of the prominent objects in view of the first comers from England to
these shores was the "catching and curing" of
fish, for which there was a good market in the West
Indian and European ports.[2] The fishing business
has continued to be one of the chief industries of
Eastern Massachusetts to the present. Although

[1] "It is well knowne, before our breache with Spaine, we usually sent
out to New England yearely forty or fifty saile of ships of reasonable good
burthen for fishing only." *Planter's Plea*, London, 1630.

[2] Capt. John Smith names among "Staple-fish which is transported,
from whence it is taken, many a thousand mile," *Herring, Salt-fish, poore
lohn, Sturgion, Mullit, Tunny, Pargos, Caveaire, Buttargo.* Morton adds
(*New English Canaan*, c. vii), *Codd, Basse, Mackerells, Salmon, Eeles,
Smelts, Shadds, Turbut or Hallibut, Plaice, Hakes, Pilchers, Lobsters,
Clames, Raser fish, Freeles, Cockles* and *Scallopus.* Winthrop mentions
among "grounds of settling a plantation in new England," "infinite
varietie & store of fishes."

Cape Anne was for a time abandoned as a fishing station, it soon took a prominent place in the fishing interest which it has held to the present day.

According to the latest statistical Bulletin of the U. S. Commissioner of Fish and Fisheries, there are nearly 200,000 men directly engaged in the United States fisheries, with a total tonnage of 176,783 tons, and $58,000,000 capital invested. The United States' annual harvest of the seas amounts to $45,000,000. We have 37,800 deep-sea fishermen, 17,000 of whom hail from Massachusetts. Gloucester alone has a fishing fleet of more than 400 vessels, of 30,000 tons burden, manned by 6,000 men.

In 1622, a royal proclamation gave to the Massachusetts Company the monopoly of "fishing and curing fish on the shores of New England."[1] For a century or more, the fisheries were a large means of support to the seaboard, and indirectly to the whole colony. There were good seasons and poor seasons, there were frequent losses of vessels and men, the stormy seas engulfed many a wreck, and sung their hoarse requiem above the grave of many a gallant crew. But vessels were still fitted out and manned from almost every hamlet and creek, small boats were engaged in in-shore fishing, "flakes"[2] were loaded with cod, hake and pollock, and small schooners and brigs laden to the gunwale with the spoils of the sea were despatched from Salem and Boston to Virginia, the West Indies and Southern

[1] So named in 1614, by the illustrious voyager, Capt. John Smith. It had before been called " North Virginia."

[2] The first " fish-flakes " were probably on " Gale's Point," near the remains of the old wharf, and on the opposite shore, at " Glass Head," about where Dr. Bartol's house now stands. No date can be given for the erection of these " flakes," but in 1642 Jeffrey's Creek was represented to the General Court as " much engaged in the fishery."

Europe, returning with freights of bacon, corn, salt, rum, sugar, molasses and coffee.

Our forefathers, we know, placed a high value upon fish as an article of food, assigning it a place, it has been said, next in order to their religious privileges.[1] The present fondness for fish chowders in the vicinity would seem to be an inheritance from our ancestors ; and many would feel themselves guilty of an almost unpardonable disloyalty to their memory, if they discarded this time-honored diet.

The fishing industry was always encouraged by the General Court. In 1639 it was ordered that all vessels so employed with their stock and fish should not be taxed, and their men should be exempt from military duty. The great importance attached to the fisheries has been recognized emblematically in the " sacred cod " suspended in the Hall of the House of Representatives in the State House in Boston. A communication to a Boston paper during this current year, is of special interest in this connection.[2]

The business at last increased to such an extent and became such a source of revenue, that it aroused

[1] Winslow says that when the delegates of the Dorchester Company called upon King James for a Charter, his Majesty asked, " Why do you wish to go to that far-off land ? " The answer was ready, " Sire, we desire to worship God and catch fish."

[2] The codfish now in the hall of the House of Representatives was carved by John Welch, a prominent patriot and one of the signers of the famous remonstrance against the stamp act. It was done at the instance of Mr. John Rowe, another eminent patriot, who on Mar. 17, 1784, moved the general court that such an emblem ought to be exhibited as a memorial of the importance of the fisheries to the welfare of the Commonwealth and also with the object of replacing a former codfish which was hung up in the old State House (built in 1712 and burned in 1747), as a reminder of the greatest source of colonial prosperity in those days. *H. P. Arnold*, in the *Advertiser*.

the jealousy of the home government.[1]   As early as
1670, an English writer declared :

> " New England is the most prejudicial plantation to this
> kingdom of all American plantations.   His Majesty has
> none so apt for the building of shipping as New England,
> nor any so qualified for the breeding of seamen, not only by
> reason of the natural industry of that people, but principally
> by reason of their cod and mackerel fisheries, and in my poor
> opinion there is nothing more prejudicial, and in prospect
> more dangerous, than the increase of shipping in her colo-
> nies and plantations."

It is evident that there was a fear thus early — a
fear which events proved to be well-grounded — that
the fisheries would become a breeding ground of
maritime supremacy if not of independence.   England's restrictive policy manifested itself in an Act
of Parliament in 1775, forbidding Americans from
taking fish in Canadian waters ; this act, with
others intended to cripple the marine power of the
colonies, did much to embitter the colonists and to
hasten the Revolution.

Whatever may be thought of the justice or wisdom of the policy of the mother country, no doubt
her lawmakers were right in regarding the fisheries
as a school of manliness and prowess, and a source of
growing power on the seas.   It has well been said
of the fishermen of New England :

> " During the whole period of our colonial vassalage, they
> were ever among the foremost to enter the ships and armies
> furnished by the colonies to aid England in her struggles
> with France; they were engaged in every strife in French

[1] Speaking of the codfish, John Adams said, "They were to us what
wool was to England and tobacco to Virginia, the great staple which became the basis of power and wealth."

America; they lie buried in every battle-ground in Canada and Nova Scotia, and their remains have been committed to every sea. In the Revolution, Salem and Beverly alone despatched fifty-two vessels as privateers, with seven hundred and fifty guns, and during the War they captured and destroyed British shipping to the amount of 200,000 tons." [1]

Perhaps it is not too much to say that "It is more than doubtful whether we to-day would be a nation had not Colonel Glover with his Essex County fishermen twice saved Washington's army." [2] A high authority on the second war with England (1812) says : " I regard it as strictly true that without our fishermen we could hardly have manned a frigate or captured one. From the beginning of the war to its end, the fishermen were in almost every national or private armed ship that carried our flag." [3]

Our fisheries proved a school for times of peace, too, as well as war. They trained a class of seamen and master mariners who made the name of Manchester known all over the world. [4] At one time the town is said to have had more captains in the

[1] *Hon. William Cogswell, M. C.,* in Boston *Herald,* Sept. 1, 1887.

[2] *The Fisherman,* Gloucester, January, 1895. The reference is to the retreat from Long Island, and the crossing of the Delaware on the eve of the battle of Trenton. Irving, *Life of Washington,* ii, 316, 349. "Colonel Glover, with his amphibious regiment of Marblehead fishermen was in advance, the same who had navigated the army across the Sound," etc.

[3] Quoted in article in Boston *Herald,* Sept. 1, 1887.

[4] In 1810, there were fifty masters of merchant vessels who were citizens of Manchester. See Appendix L for a list furnished by Dea. John Price of ninety-one Manchester captains of vessels employed at one time and another in the foreign trade. The seamen of that day must have had brains and daring, for they had often scanty external helps in working their observations, or in laying their course. Even after 1800, a youth of nineteen sailed a ship from Calcutta to Boston with no chart whatever except a small map of the world in Guthrie's Geography. Hunt's *American Merchant,* vol. I, 136.

merchant service than any other town in Essex
County.

A shore like that of our eastern seaboard, which
abounds in inlets or is fringed with islands, is almost
sure to develop the spirit of maritime enterprise.[1]
The coastline of our own neighborhood, with its receding coves and projecting headlands, naturally
made the ocean the home and the field of labor and sus-
tenance of many of the inhabitants. It shaped to a
large extent the daily life. They were a sort of amphibious race, as much at home on the water as on
the land. The tilling of the soil and the reaping of
the sea went on together; boats and seines found
their place in the garden-plot and on the barnyard
wall; dried fish and potatoes were a common staple
of food; the same hands that framed the humble
dwellings and held the plough and swung the scythe,
were skilled to reef the sail, to man the boats and
to haul the lines. The life of the village was largely
maritime. Few young men reached their majority,
but had stood their watch on the slippery deck, or
heard the midnight boom of the breakers on the spec-
tral cliffs of La Bradore. Some of them were remarkable men.[2]

The vessels at first employed in the fishing service were of small size and often without decks.
They were in some instances of less than twenty
tons. In 1696, Samuel Allen had one of twelve
tons; Aaron Bennett one of nine tons; William
Hassam one of thirteen tons. The diminutive size

[1] *Features of Coasts and Oceans*, Professor N. S. Shaler. *The Earth and Man*, Arnold Guyot, 244.

[2] *Vide* Appendix K.

of these vessels is less to be wondered at when we remember that the ships of the early voyagers to the New World were little more than ketches or shallops. Frobisher sailed in a vessel of twenty-five tons; Cartier made his voyage of discovery (1534) in two vessels of sixty tons each; two of the caravels of Columbus were without decks; it was in a bark of ten tons that Sir Humphrey Gilbert faced the stormy seas, to be lost on his home voyage; the "Half-Moon," in which Hendrik Hudson discovered the river which bears his name, was a "fly-boat," or yacht, of eighty tons.

As late as the close of the last century, we are told, "the average tonnage of vessels engaged in the fisheries was but twenty tons, and they were extremely uncomfortable; the fire was made on a brick hearth on the floor directly beneath the companion way, up which the smoke was expected to pass, and the only way to and from the cabin was through the smoke and fire." The "Chebacco boats" were generally of from twelve to twenty tons, and valued at from $100 to $300. They were sharp at both ends, and had two masts but no bowsprit. These were called "pinkies." Later the pointed bow was shaved off and a bowsprit and jib were added, and the vessel, retaining its pink stern, was then called a "jigger."

In 1718, Capt. Andrew Robinson launched a vessel at Gloucester, whose rig was that which now belongs to a schooner. The "Grand Bankers" were schooner-rigged, with square bows and high stern. They sailed well before the wind, but they were awkward vessels to handle.[1] They could hardly have competed with "Ailsa" and Valkyrie III, but they were safe sea-boats and of large carrying capacity for their water displacement; they were built to ride the waves, rather than like a modern "clipper" or "ocean greyhound," to cut their way through them. They required skill for their management in a September gale, when the jagged reefs showed their teeth on the lee bow.

It was in such vessels, presenting almost the greatest possible contrast to the beautiful, shapely, clipper-like craft launched to-day in the Essex ship-yards, that our forefathers sailed for "Georges," Meccatina, Red Island and Brador, the home of the murre and gannet, daring the unknown currents, the sunken reefs, the white squall and the frozen mist, when spring gales and autumn tempests lashed the sea into wild and terrific billows, that with wet hands they might light the hearth and spread the board at home.[2]

One of the famous vessels of the day was the schooner "Manchester," Allen, master, which was used in the Virginia trade. A model of this vessel was on exhibition at the Centennial Exposition, and is now in the possession of Mr. Geo. J. Marsh of the Cape Ann Savings Bank, Gloucester. She was of

[1] The origin of the name has been thus explained: "Oh, how she scoons," said a bystander, as she slipped down the ways; "a *schooner* let her be," replied the builder. *Harper's Magazine*, September, 1875, p. 469.

[2] "Wild are the waves which lash the reefs along St. George's bank —
Cold on the shore of Labrador, the fog lies white and dank;
Through storm, and wave, and blinding mist, stout are the hearts which man
The fishing-smacks of Marblehead, the sea-boats of Cape Ann."

sixty-five tons, and was built in Duxbury, Mass., in
1784; she was afloat nearly a hundred years, having
been in the port of Gloucester in 1878. There was
another schooner "Manchester" built in Essex in
1845, of sixty-four tons; her first master was Benjamin Morgan.

A survivor [1] of the time when the fishing business
was the business of the town thus narrates some incidents of his early experience.

"When thirteen years of age I was put into the business; two years later I sailed on the "Richmond," Abram
Stone, master, bound for the "Straits." " [There follows
an account of several weeks' fishing on the coast of
Labrador.] "September began with stormy weather. On
the 15th we sailed for home, encountering the line gale off
Cape Breton. The strong current rushing from the gulf
raised a sharp and dangerous sea. At the height of the
gale the wind would lull suddenly, the vessel falling into
the trough of the sea, the waves breaking twenty feet
above the deck. When the gale subsided, one boat with
the davits had gone from the stern, and three boats stowed
on deck were stove. Cape Ray was sighted, and stretching
out to clear the land, the night being cloudy and dark, a
timber-ship crashed upon us, striking abaft the main chains,
knocking down the mainsail and knocking the captain
overboard, who was saved by the sail hanging from the
side. By running up the rigging, three of the crew boarded
the ship before the vessels separated. The next day we
were in tow for Miramichi. The schooner was cast off outside the bar. We landed at a small village with a tavern,
and walked down the river bank to join the schooner.
Needed repairs being made, we were again on our passage.
Beating around the eastern point of Prince Edward Island,
the vessel struck on a reef. The tide was at ebb; as the
tide went down, the decks went up, which looked much like

[1] Dea. A. E. Low.

the end of the voyage; but when the tide turned the wind changed with a strong breeze off the shore. Again afloat, we passed through the Straits of Canso with a fine leading breeze, under the foretopsail. Clearing the Straits we made sail and were six days to Cape Ann."

The following from an old record will give an idea of a fisherman's fare of the middle of the eighteenth century.

In an " agrement maid the Second Day of May anno Domi 1767, between Nath'l Allen Esq. of Gloucester and John Tuck Sen. of Manchester, Housewright," the party of the first part covenanted and promised to find for John Tuck, a " miner." for a fishing voyage. " Boots, Barbel,[1] Hooker, Leads, Lines; sixty pound good Porke a faire, and three gallons Rum, three gallons Molasses, seven pounds Shugar, eighty four pounds of Biskuitt, twenty eight pounds Flower, one bushell of Indian Meele, six pounds of Butter, share of wood a faire, and small jenerail."[2]

Josselyn gives the following list of " vtensils of the sea " — " quoils of rope and cable, rondes of twine, herring nets, seans, cod-lines and cod-hookes, mackrill-lines, drails, spiller hooks, mussel-hooks, barbels, splitting knives, basse-nettes, pues and gaffs, squid lines, yeele pots," etc.

The following letter, an exact transcript of the original in the possession of Benjamin Hilton Russell of Haverhill, a descendant of the writer, will serve as a sample of the epistolary style of the period. The autograph copy is written in a large, round hand on heavy paper, bearing the " Pine Tree " watermark, and with ink which still retains its color.

St. Eustatia[3] Januery 18 Day 1770.

Kind and Louing Weif I embreass this optunety to Rit to you to Let you know of my halth and I hoop these few

[1] Apron.   [2] Stores.

[3] St. Eustatius, one of the smaller islands of the Lesser Antilles.

Lines will find you in as Good halth as tha Leue me in att this pressent tim thanks be to god for it we are all will on Bord and after a pessage of 22 Days we arifed Safe to the Island of Berbadous [1] and Landed our Cargo In Six Days time and then Set Sail for this pleas called St. Eustatia and our Captin tokes of meaking sail of the Shooner But wear[2] he will or not I Can't tell But if he Dount Sill her we Shall Sail for St Meartins [3] and Lod with Salt and then meak the Beast of our weay houm and I am in hopes to Be atouem by the first of march if Nothing hapenes to us more than we know of but if he selles the Shooner I Dont know wear we Shall be atouem So Soun or No and So No more at preasent but I remain your Loueing houseben till Death pearts [4] Benjamin Hilton.

Remember my kind Loue to moueather and Brouthers and Sisters.

and So you must Excuse theas pouer Lines for I hant time to Rit as I would be glead to Rit to you this Coumes by wea of

Cape ann.

All along through the history of the fishing enterprise we have frequent records of men who were lost at sea; in several instances whole crews disappeared at once, the vessels going down with all on board. It is a pathetic and harrowing tale. In the very first years of the settlement four men were drowned while fishing from a boat at Kettle Cove, and thus the record goes on. A few instances will here suffice.[5] *Ex uno disce omnes.* In 1758, there went down in one vessel John Day, John Driver, Richard Leach, John Lee and Samuel Morgan. In 1756, Ambrose Allen,

---

[1] Barbadoes.   [2] Whether.   [3] St. Martins.

[4] Here is a cabalistic sign which cannot be represented in type.

[5] A full list of those lost at sea, so far as it is possible now to recover the names, is given in Appendix L.

Moses Trask, Jacob Lee, Daniel Davidson, William
Ireland, John Ayres, were lost coming from Lisbon.
In 1764, Benjamin Andrews, Charles Leach and
Daniel Foster were lost on the return voyage from
the West Indies. In 1772, Capt. Daniel Edwards,
Samuel Edwards, Benjamin Hill, Samuel Perry and
Frank Silva were lost coming from the West Indies.
In 1766, no less than ten were lost at sea. In September, 1843, the schooner "Vesper," of about sixty
tons, owned by Jacob Cheever and his two sons, was
lost with the whole crew, Capt. John Cheever, Rufus
Cheever, Hilliard Morse, David Hall, Nathaniel
Morgan and Merritt Lennon, all but the captain
married men and fathers.[1] Nothing was ever known
of their fate. When last spoken they had a full
fare and were bound for home. "The waves closed
over them, and no one could tell the story of their
end." No complete record exists of the losses of the
fishing fleet. But some idea may be had of the
extent to which the town suffered in the loss of its
bread-winners, from the fact that from 1745 to 1774,
the sea had engulfed no less than *ninety* men of the
inhabitants of this little town.[2]

Among the strange experiences of Manchester
men was that on board the "Troubadour," Sept. 17,
1846, on the Banks, in a heavy sea, which washed
overboard Samuel Carter and Thomas Dow, the next
wave sweeping Mr. Dow back again on deck ; the
old fisherman still living to ply his vocation as hale

[1] Of those who were thus left widows, two, Mrs. Morse and Mrs. Lennon
survive.

[2] Entry by Rev. Benjamin Tappan in Church Records. This number
includes those lost in coasting and foreign voyages.

and hearty apparently as many a man who has not seen half his years or endured half his hardships.

The loss of two vessels, the "Blooming Youth" and "Senator," in May, 1840, on the reefs of Sable Island, is an event still remembered and talked of by the older inhabitants. The site of the disaster is a well known grave of vessels off the Nova Scotia coast. "The whole region for miles around is a trap and a snare. . . . Between the years 1806 and 1827, forty vessels, and it is supposed many men, were lost."[1] The men of the "Blooming Youth" succeeded in getting ashore in the surf, and saved most of their stores, but the vessel was a total loss. The last survivor, Mr. Allen Lee, is living in town at the age of eighty-two years. Mr. Lee was born May 1, 1813, and at the age of seventeen began his seafaring life in a voyage to South America. He followed the sea for seven years until his marriage in 1837, and often went on fishing voyages afterward. His life brought him into contact with Spaniards, slaves and pirates of whom he has many interesting and thrilling incidents to narrate.

The "Blooming Youth" was built in Essex and was a vessel of about seventy tons. She was owned by Capt. Israel D. Goodridge, Dean Babcock and Benjamin Morse. She had also as crew, Mr. Lee, and a boy, Benjamin Bennett. After they escaped to land, they were kindly cared for by the "chief man of the island," called "Governor" Derby, an old English naval officer. They remained on the island twenty-four days, when they obtained passage

[1] *Harper's Magazine*, December, 1866.

(See p. 164.)   CHEBACCO BOAT.   FOSTER'S WHARF.   GRAND BANKER.   JIGGER.

to Halifax, and were sent by the British consul to Boston. The crew of the " Senator," Capt. James Pert, were taken off by Cape Cod fishermen, and the vessel bought by them for a song. She was new and staunch, and may be afloat still.

Nor were the hidden rocks and angry waves the only enemies encountered. In addition to "perils of waters," were "perils of the heathen." In August, 1747, as tradition runs, a schooner's crew from Manchester landed on the coast of Maine near Sheepscot, to procure wood and water, when they were captured by Indians, and as afterward proved all but one massacred.[1] The survivor, a lad of twelve, named Aaron Lee, was held in captivity three years, until finding an opportunity to escape, he made his way home after incredible hardships, and appeared to his grief-stricken parents who had long mourned his cruel death, as one raised from the dead.[2] Mr. Lee lived to old age, and was for many years Town Clerk. The records show him to have been an excellent penman.

In 1758, Capt. Samuel Leach, Josiah Allen, Sen., Benjamin Crowell,[3] Robert Bear, Nath. Marsters and James Allen were surprised and slain by Indians at

[1] " We hear that a few days ago, the Indians surpriz'd and kill'd at a Place call'd Wiscasset near Sheepscot in the Eastern Parts, one Mr. Hilton, his Son, and another Man, and carried another Captive." *Boston Gazette*, Aug. 11, 1747. This could not have been Capt. Amos Hilton, as Dr. Leach and others have supposed, as he had been dead almost three years when this event occurred. Capt. Amos Hilton was, however, killed by Indians, but not at the time supposed.

[2] Some particulars of his remarkable escape, as told by his granddaughter to Dea. A. E. Low, may be found in Mr. Tappan's narrative. *History of Essex County.*

[3] Dr. Leach gives the name *Jacob* Crowell.

Casco Bay. Capt. Leach was a man noted for his bravery and great muscular strength. It is said that he could jump from one hogshead into another as they stood in line on the Town Landing. He had several hand-to-hand conflicts with Indians, and had declared that he would never be taken alive.

Another peril and terror of the seas was piracy; the black flag and cross-bones had not disappeared from the Caribbean seas, in the early part of this century.[1] A brief and tragic record reads, " Capt. William Babcock was murdered at sea by pirates in 1823." These dreaded outlaws infested the Spanish main, and in their long, low, rakish schooners shot out from the keys and reefs, swooped upon merchant vessels, plundered and murdered, and slipped back to their coverts. Such incidents of adventure and peril formed a large part of the staple of " fo' cas'le yarns " a generation ago.

The fishing business was at its best in the early part of this century. It never fully recovered from the effects of the war of 1812, which drove our shipping from the ocean and left it to rot dismantled in coves and creeks, a melancholy monument to a paralyzed industry. The Assessors' Books for 1808 and 1811 show that Capt. Ezekiel Leach owned the " Jane," fifty-four tons, and the " Active," ninety-nine tons. Tyler Parsons owned one-third of the " Enterprise," ninety-nine tons. Benjamin and Samuel Forster owned a schooner of sixty tons. Maj. Henry Story owned the " Three Brothers,"

[1] *Vide* the *Official Statement* of the attack upon the brig " Mexican " of Salem by pirates, and their barbarous treatment of the crew, four of whom are still living (1894) ; *Salem Gazette*, Oct. 16, 1832.

seventy-four tons. Ebenezer Tappan owned the sloop "Primrose," twenty-nine tons, and the schooner "Nancy," sixty-eight tons. (This was the vessel run ashore at Mingo's Beach, and fired, by the British, in 1813.) Capt. Abiel Burgess owned and commanded the brig "Alonzo," 130 tons. This vessel once came to the Town Landing, and as the first square-rigged and the largest vessel that had ever been there, excited a good deal of interest. Captain Burgess was also taxed in 1811, for one-half of the ship "Hannibal"; like the "Alonzo," she was employed in the foreign trade.

After 1825, the fishing business greatly declined, and few vessels were built for the trade. In 1835, the fishing and coasting business of the town employed about 1,200 tons. In 1836, there were 150 men engaged in the fisheries, seven fish yards, and ten houses for storage.[1] In 1845, there were thirteen vessels in the cod and mackerel fisheries,[2] and the value of the catch was $21,435.

In an address on "The Gloucester Fishermen of Fifty Years Ago," Hon. Wm. H. Wonson, 3d, of Gloucester, said :

"They fitted away generally in March. The first trip was just off Point Ledge, where a fare of haddock would be secured and run to Boston. This would be secured with a

[1] *Essex Memorial*, 1836, p. 162.

[2] The mackerel have of late years almost deserted our shores. Mr. Frank Bolles, *Land of the Lingering Snow*, p. 85, suggests an explanation : "Forests of poles rising from the blue water, marking the fish-traps of the deluded fishermen, whose mackerel fleet has been swept from the sea by this sunken fleet of seine poles." Some old fishermen agree in opinion with the scholarly Secretary of Harvard University.

clam bait. Then an alewife baiting would be taken and a
trip made farther off shore. . . . The vessel generally carried six men and a cook, almost without exception a boy
ten or twelve years old. The cooking utensils were a
Dutch oven, iron pot and iron teakettle. The expenses,
including salt and stores, lines, etc., would be about $260.
At that time those engaged in fishing were nearly all
natives." [1]

About this time the increasing cabinet business
withdrew most of the inhabitants from a seafaring
life, and became for many years the leading industry.
Fish houses were left to decay, or were converted
into storehouses or barns ; flakes rotted to the
ground ; ship-building and boat-building ceased ;
and the sea-gulls and fish-hawks wheeling over Town
Hill heard the buzz of the saw and the whir
of the lathe in place of the creaking of the windlass
and the rattle of blocks on the " outward bound."
One or two small vessels,[2] a few dories and fish-traps,
alone remain to represent the earliest industry of
the town, and its leading industry for more than a
hundred years.

The hazards, exploits and hardships of the fisheries
have never been fully written. Poets have woven
them into their verse,[3] sermons have been preached
upon them, the columns of newspapers have been
full of them ; but they will never be known in all

[1] *The Fisherman*, Gloucester, March, 1895.

[2] Owned by the Jones Brothers.

[3]   " Ah ! many a lonely home is found
                Along the Essex shore,
            That cheered the goodman outward bound,
                And sees his face no more."
                                        O. W. Holmes.

their extent of loss and suffering until the sea shall give up its dead.

With all its dangers and sorrows, however, the sea which has always been the grave of so many lives and so many hopes, has been a nurse of courage and hardihood from the first voyage of the Phœnicians along the shores of the Mediterranean to the latest voyage of exploration to the Arctic seas. It has trained a class of men to deeds of heroic valor and brave endurance, surpassing any that the annals of war can furnish. The inhabitants of Manchester, no doubt, in a former age, have owed much of their pluck, their persistence, their success in life, to the ocean with whose waves they sported from childhood, and which presented at their very doors a field for their skill and an arena for their prowess.

If the history of its fishery were written, it would unfold many a tale of heroism, of self-sacrifice, of dangerous exploits, of terrible disaster, as well as of determined perseverance in the face of hardships, of successful grappling with difficulties, of patient endurance of suffering;

> " Tales of that awful, pitiless sea,
> With all its terror and mystery."

Our bleak New England shore lacks the soft beauty of Southern climes which has so often inspired the artist and poet ; but its rough winds and storm-beaten waves have helped to rear a hardy race that has made its mark in every clime.

APPENDIX.

Capt. Benjamin Hilton's Log Books.

The life of the men of Manchester on the seas, a hundred and more years ago, is made to pass before us in vivid reality, as we turn the pages of two old, timeworn volumes, now in the possession of Mr. Benjamin Hilton Russell of Haverhill, Mass., containing the nautical record of voyages made from this port to *Virginneay*, *mariland*, *Fyall*, the *West Enjees*, etc. The paper is stained and yellow with age, some pages are missing and others torn, and blank leaves contain some boyish scribblings; but the books are still in most parts a legible account of each day's happenings, including nautical reckonings, calculations in trigonometry, diagrams, sailing directions, remarks, vessels spoken, accounts with owners and crew, and such other matters as make up a logbook and journal at sea. The books were evidently carefully kept, and bear marks of a thoughtful and painstaking habit. They represent the intelligence and capacity of the men bred to the ocean in this little town by the sea.

The names of the vessels mentioned are, " Breattany," " Lucy," " Salley," " Louisay," " Patty," [1] " Corr " and " Darbey." The voyages seem to have been in general remarkably uneventful, "smoothe winds " and " smal brezes " predominating. The log

---

[1] A schooner " Patty " is mentioned with other vessels as " carried into the Bermudas and there condemned, in consequences of the British Orders-in-Council," about December, 1794. This was during the war between England and France, when American vessels were frequently searched and seized by British cruisers on pretence of having on board deserters or carrying contraband-of-war.

is methodically kept, noting each hour the knots run, the course, the wind, latitude and longitude, departure and meridian, with remarks, etc. The pages have usually a running head-line, as " A Log of our Intended Passage, by god's asistance on the good shooner Patty," etc., or, " A Journell of vige Continnered att Sea," etc. One of the books contains on a fly-leaf the inscriptions:

" Benjamin Hilton His Book Bought In Salam In the Year of our Lord 1762 the Price 13 Shilens old tenner." Benjamin Hilton His Book the Lord give him grace therein to Look and wen the Bells Do for him towl the [Lord] have marcey one his Soul

Beniamin Hilton
his hand and pean and if the peen had Been Better I Wood mended everey Latter "

The following will give an idea of the daily " Remarks " : —

Sunday the 2d of June 1765 this 24 hours we have head fresh brese of wind to the west word and South word att 3 P M Hour main touping lift gav way and att 6 A M Saw 3 toup Sail vessels bound to the East word and att 10 a m Saw 2 more Bound to the East word and we have Cloudey weather & Rain

freyday the 1st Day of august 1766 this 24 hours Begines with a smoule Brese of wind to the South word and East word and fein plesent weather and att 6 P M Caim to anchour in St. meareas and histed out hour Boot and I and Cleaves and Rouberds went on Shouer and att 5 A M went on Shouer after Soum mialk and then after that wentup to the Coustem house after a stiucket for the Last Vige and to meack Repourt and to heir Newes and So forth "

The following appears to be a letter to the owner: —

January the 8 Day 1769.

Worthy Sir

Imbrss this optunity to Writ to you to Lit you know of my Seaf arjefuell into Noncok I Entered the 27 Day of December and finding mearkets Veareay Low in these peartes molasses gowes by the hhd $^2/$ and Rum by the hh $^2/_6$ and Rum by the Barrell $^2/_9$ and Corn by the Boushell $^2/_6$ and wheet by the Boushell $^2/_6$ and Beanes thier is Non to be head I Could not hear auy Newes. . . . Corn is hurt with the froust in all the . . . and it is So Soft that I Shant Ship aney till the Last of Janueray and I Dount think that we Cant be atoum Not befor the Last of march.

Besides the name of Benjamin Hilton, those of Isaac Lee, John Driver, Robert Perray, William Tarring and John Allen are also found in these books as captains.

An autograph letter from Jeremiah Lee of Marblehead to Skipper John Allen, putting him in command of " the Sch. Derby," [1] dated Decem. 4, 1767, is a good specimen of the instructions given by owners at that time to captains in their employ, and shows how much responsibility in the matter of sale and exchange of cargoes was often placed in their hands. The only restriction made in this letter is, " Break no Acts of Trade, suffer no man to bring above six pounds of Tobacco."

[1] No doubt identical with the " Darbey " above-named.

THE BOOK-KEEPING OF THE PERIOD.

[From Leger of Tim⁰ Orne Junʳ of Salem, Anno 1750.]

1750. Capt. John Lee of Manchester, Dr.

Lawfull Money.

			£ s. d.
April 13.	To 111 Gallˢ Rum c 3/8½ p	. .	£20. 11. 7½ £ s. d.
May 22.	To 116½ Gallˢ Do c3₄	.	19. 8. 4
	Salem Dec. 27, 1750 This Day Reconed with Tim⁰ Orne Junᵉ & settled our account and there Remains Ballance Due to me Two Pounds 12/10½ Lawfull Money		
	(Signed) John Lee Junʳ		2. 12. 10½
			———— 42 12 10

1750/1			
Jan⁷ 3.	To 539 foot Boards c 56/ p m	. .	£1. 10. 2
19.	To 1, 1, 7 Turpentine	. .	17. 6
Febry 4.	To 200 Seasoned Boards	. .	13. 4
1753	To pd Samˡ Orne	. . .	4. 8
Jan⁷ 19.	To Nine pounds 6/ 6½ L. Money in full as pr Rect	. . .	9. 6. 6½
			12 12 2½

1750 CONTRA Cr. Lawfull Money

May 24.	By 5½ Quttˢ Haddock c 10/8	.	£2. 18. 8
Augᵗ 29.	By 66 Quttˢ Mid fish c 6/8 .	. .	22.
	By 35 Quttˢ Refuse Cod fish c 5/4	.	9. 6. 8
October	By 15 Quttˢ Mid fish c 6/8	. .	5.
	By 15 Qutts pollock c 4/6	. .	3. 7. 6
			———— 42 12 10
Decbᵣ 27	By the Above ballance	. . .	2 12 10½
1753			
Jan⁷ 15	By 23 Quttˢ Hack & Haddock c 8/8 pr. Quttˢ p Go Peele	.	9. 19.
			12 12 2½

Among the interesting relics of Manchester's palmy days as a seaport, is a well kept copy of Bowditch's "Practical Navigator," First Edition with Copperplates, Printed at Newburyport, 1802; the property of Isaac Preston, 1808, afterward of his nephew, Ariel Parish Lee, 1819, "on board Brig fedrick, Capt. Wm. Tuck, Commander, Latt. 40, 24, Long. 49, 54 West. Aged 23 years or there-

abouts higth of 5 feet Nothing all but one inch."
The book is now the prized possession of Mr. Lee's
daughter, Mrs. Joseph Russell. This book was
always at Mr. Lee's elbow, no doubt, in the years
of his life at sea, as the Bible, the spiritual "Navigator," was in his later life on shore. With these
two books in hand, many an old salt in days gone
by shaped his course for both earth and heaven.

CHAPTER VII.

THE WAR OF 1812.

" Is this the land our fathers loved,
    The freedom which they toiled to win ?
Is this the soil whereon they moved ?
    Are these the graves they slumber in ?
Are *we* the sons by whom are borne
The mantles which the dead have worn ? "

                                              Whittier.

CHAPTER VII.

THE WAR OF 1812.

CAUSES OF THE WAR — IMPRESSMENTS — THE EMBARGO — DI-
VIDED COUNSELS — THE WAR CLOUD — " A GLORIOUS
VICTORY " — BLOCKADE RUNNING — THE GREAT
SEA FIGHTS — RESULTS OF THE WAR —
PEACE — HOME INDUSTRIES —
" FORGING AHEAD."

THE causes of the War with Great Britain in
1812–15, were chiefly the impressment of
American seamen into the British naval service,[1] and the claim made by Great Britain to the
right of search of neutral vessels for the purpose of
arresting deserters. These claims were pushed to
such an extent, and in so arrogant a manner, and
were accompanied by so many flagrant acts of injustice in the shape of detention of ships on the high
seas, false arrests and harsh treatment of seamen
accused of being deserters, that the United States
finally threw down the gauntlet of war and became
involved in a conflict with the greatest naval power
in the world, a power which had captured or shut up
in port all the other navies of Europe.

The embargo of 1807 [2] had occasioned a great

---

[1] " The practice of impressing seamen from our merchantmen, which
had been a ground of complaint from the earliest days of the French Revolution, had been resumed on the termination of the peace established by
Treaty of Amiens." Wheaton's *Elements of International Law*, 1855, p. xix.
From 1803 to 1810 such impressments had amounted to over 4,000.

[2] One of the measures of Jefferson's administration, prohibiting all
foreign commerce, with a design of forcing Great Britain into a change of
policy.

125

deal of inconvenience and even suffering along the
coast ; commerce was paralyzed and business brought
almost to a standstill.   On September 1 of that year,
a meeting was held, and a memorial prepared and
sent to Congress, setting forth the loyalty of the
town and its distressed condition by reason of the
embargo, and the gloomy outlook for the future.
As this memorial failed of procuring relief, on
Feb. 8, 1809, a petition was adopted to be presented
to the Legislature, asking that some action be taken
to induce the General Government to afford redress.
A series of spirited Resolutions was also adopted
at this meeting, and " ordered to be signed by the
moderator and Town Clerk and a copy forwarded
to the Editor of the Centinel for publication." [1]
The following extracts show the difficulties the town
had to contend with and the spirit in which they
were met :

6ly Resolved That we dispise and will ever hold in contempt those Interlopers & Night walkers who have of late
broken open our fish houses stores and vessels to gratify
their base designs.

7ly That we will ever hold in disdain those pimps &
spies so often seen in our streets and that we will take all
Lawful and Constitutional measures to bring them to the
light and make their works of darkness manifest.

9ly Resolved That we view with equal detestation the
Idea that the Nation is to be plunged into a war with great
Britain, for the purpose of being intangled in an alliance
with France.

[1] The original paper is on file in the Selectmen's office, signed by Abial
Burgess, Moderator, and Delucena L. Bingham, Town Clerk.

PETITION TO THE LEGISLATURE.

" *To the honorable, the Senate and House of Representatives of the Commonwealth of Massachusetts, in general court assembled.*

" The inhabitants of the town of Manchester in legal town meeting assembled, humbly represent that such is their local situation, the soil of the town being in general rocky, broken and barren, they are obliged to repair to the Ocean for the means of subsistance for themselves and families. This invaluable privilege which the God of Nature has afforded them, they have hoped to enjoy unmolested. But the restrictions laid on them in the several Embargo Laws enacted by the Government of the United States, has excited sensations truly painful and distressing to your memorialists as well as many others. We have indulged a hope that the government of the United States would not continue to interdict that commerce on which we have depended for our support. Your memorialists do consider that the abandonment of the Ocean, to them is as oppressive, distressing and unjust as a prohibition on the produce of the land would be to the farmer. While our brethren in the country enjoy the privilege of cultivating their land and reaping the fruit of their labors, we are under the restraints which forbid our industry and deprives us of our only means of support. Your memorialists have petitioned Congress for relief, but in vain, now turn their eyes to this honorable body, the more immediate guardians of their constitutional rights, praying them to take such measures as in their wisdom they shall conceive best calculated to afford us relief and save us from beggary and starvation.

" Your memorialists pledge themselves as ready at the risk of their property and lives, to support you in any constitutional measures you shall adopt for the redress of our grievances, and likewise to prevent an unjust war with Great Britain.

" Your memorialists, as in duty bound, will ever pray. Done in town meeting this 8th of Feb., 1809."

The wars of Napoleon continued to produce disastrous results in this country, in the interference with trade and especially with maritime pursuits, and the time was one of much depression and anxiety. The country, too, was divided in its counsels, party feeling ran high and political animosities were violent. On July 19, 1812, a county convention was called to meet at Ipswich, to consider " the awful and alarming situation of the country." William Tuck, Esq., was delegate from this town. Resolutions were adopted by the convention strongly opposed to the impending war, which was greatly deprecated on the seaboard as likely to destroy the commercial and shipping interests. At the same time, a feeling that the insolence and injustice often displayed by Great Britain could not long be borne by a free and growing people prompted many to patriotic resistance, whatever might be the result. Before the Declaration of War, there was great division of feeling, but when the War was actually begun, when the settlement of the questions at issue was transferred from the council-chamber to the field, all hearts beat in unison, every other sentiment and interest yielded to the overmastering determination to uphold the honor of the nation and to defend the flag.

The first warlike measure adopted in Manchester was the appointment of a Committee of Safety. These were Maj. Henry Story, John Allen, Andrew Marsters, William Tuck and Samuel Forster. They were instructed to place a watch along the coast, erect flag-staffs and provide flags for signals and alarms. A breastwork was thrown up on Norton's Point,[1] and the present Powder House built on Powder House Hill. The seaboard was in particular danger from the enemy's cruisers, and was almost wholly unprotected from Salem Harbor to Eastern Point. Petition was made to Government for powder and two six-pound cannon, and the people drilled and armed themselves in almost constant expectation of an attack.

The Inspection Roll of "Capt. Joseph Hooper's Company of Foot," May, 1812, is preserved in the Town Archives. The officers' names are given as Joseph Hooper and Daniel Friend; the sergeants, Ebenezer Tappan, Jr., and Amos Knight. The names of men, rank and file, number eighty. The worn and faded sheet, with its carefully filled returns of equipments, is evidence that the inspection of the militia was no mere farce. We can almost see these sturdy men, some of whom survived until a quite recent period, mustered on a bright spring morning, at sound of fife and drum, on the Common, answering to their names, exhibiting their arms and ammunition, going through their simple evolutions in the presence of an admiring crowd of youngsters, and then adjourning when dismissed to the tavern and regaling themselves after the arduous service with cider and flip, captain and men now on a perfect equality — a part of that citizen soldiery which our country has never found wanting in time of need.

But although the English men-of-war were known

---

[1] Its remains were visible until a few years ago.

to be hovering like birds of prey along the coast, and were occasionally seen in our waters,[1] no assault was made or landing effected upon our shore. The nearest approach to anything like an invasion by the enemy's forces, and one that had a somewhat ludicrous ending, occurred at Kettle Cove. An alarm had been given, " The enemy is landing! " The militia was hastily summoned by beat of drum, the six-pounder mounted in front of the church was loaded with powder and ball, and the martial column bore away for the scene of conflict with the old field-piece in tow. The cannon was planted in a strategic position on Crow Island, and the men and boys, concealed among the rocks and bushes, awaited the approach of the enemy. After some time the boats from the frigate appeared, but seeing the cannon and hearing the strains of fife and drum, supposed that a large force was concealed, and judging " discretion " to be the " better part of valor," prudently rowed away.

The gallant defenders emerged from their hiding-place as soon as the enemy was fairly out of sight, and ere long were on their homeward way in high glee, with the old cannon and a crowd of noisy boys bringing up the rear. In coming down the " great hill," what was their amazement to find their trusty and only cannon ball quietly reposing by the wayside, where it had rolled from the cannon as it was

[1] Rufus Choate " had seen, as a boy, from the Essex hills the Shannon frigate in Ipswich bay." In a conversation with R. H. Dana, Jr., March 27, 1854, " he described beautifully the great frigate, lounging about the bay of a summer afternoon, and standing off to sea at night, proudly scorning the fleet of fishing boats about her."

being dragged up the hill. The discovery, however it might have caused a momentary chagrin, was not allowed to diminish the enthusiasm of the victors as they marched proudly back to town, and reported the success of the expedition. No doubt the *ruse de guerre* accomplished its object, and Manchester was spared an invasion. Many a victory is none the less real because it is bloodless.[1]

Another still more daring act on the part of some of the men of Manchester is related by Mr. Tappan; it is an instance of very bold blockade-running :

Mr. Ebenezer Tappan, who kept a store on Central Street, believed it possible to evade the enemy's ships, and get some supplies from Boston. His topsail schooner "Nancy" was noted for her sailing qualities, and Captain Jerry Danforth, Nathan Carter, and his son, Benjamin Tappan, were placed in charge. They kept along the shore, entered Boston harbor by Shirley Gut at night ; having secured their cargo, which consisted of flour, sugar, molasses, rum and lumber, they started homeward. All went well until they had passed Baker's Island, and they were congratulating themselves upon the success of their trip, for they were almost home. Suddenly the fog, lifting, disclosed the much dreaded cruiser quite near. A shot from her was a hint to stop, but, as there was a breeze, they kept on their course for Manchester. They could see

---

[1] The last surviver, probably of this expedition, passed away the last summer (1894) as appears from the following notice in the local prints:

Uncle George Babcock rounded out his 89th birthday on Saturday, June 30. Mr. Babcock is still quite strong and active, working about the neighborhood doing odd chores, sawing wood, etc. Although only about eight or nine years old at the time, he took part in the repulse of a British force from the shores of Manchester, his native town, during the war of 1812, when he helped drag a cannon to the beach. — Beverly *Times*.

Mr. Babcock was a resident of North Beverly and intended to attend the gathering of the elderlies this year, therefore the news of his death this week was received with great surprise. He was ill but a few hours. — Manchester *Cricket*.

two barges being made ready for a chase. When they
reflected upon the damage they might inflict on the unprotected village, they resolved to run inside of Misery Island,
and endeavor to reach the protection of the forts below
Salem. But the wind became lighter and the barges were
gaining so fast it was decided to run her on shore, which
they did at Mingo's Beach in Beverly. The men landed
under cover of the vessel, but as they reached the high land
near the road they were fired upon by their pursuers.[1] The
English used every effort to get their prize afloat, but,
failing in that, they took some of the goods, stripped the
sails and set her on fire. The militia from Beverly and
Manchester soon arrived, extinguished the fire and hastened
the departure of the barges by some musket shots. The
vessel was afterwards taken to Manchester and repaired.

This narrative is confirmed by recollections of
several old inhabitants of Salem and Beverly, published in the Beverly *Times* a few years ago. The
late Capt. Thomas Leach witnessed the affair with
his father and grandfather, with whom he rode to
the scene of action in the " square-topped chaise."
All witnesses agree as to the main facts of the case.
The presence of the Manchester company is established beyond doubt, although one witness did not
see it; a case in which positive evidence outweighs
negative.

Although the town did not suffer from any descent
of the enemy upon the coast, the presence of the
cruisers in the Bay caused a good deal of alarm at
times, especially among the women who were often
alone, and who hurried with their children and val-

[1] An interesting relic of this affair, a swivel shot, about two inches in
diameter, picked up just after it was fired from the barge, is in possession
of Mr. Oliver T. Roberts. It was long used as a pestle to break corn in a
mortar.

uables to the woods on the first alarm from the coast-
guards.   There is a somewhat apocryphal tradition
that one good woman on reaching a place of safety,
found the spoons all secure, but in the haste and
trepidation of flight the baby had been left behind.
The story may have originated in the disordered
brain of some unfortunate bachelor.

Added to this constant and wearing source of
anxiety, provisions were scarce, and no money was
to be had.   Labor commanded very small wages —
it was in fact almost a drug in the market ; and the
wages, such as they were, when there was any employment at all, were paid in " orders " on the stores.
A peck of meal was considered an equivalent for a
day's work ; and there was no ten hours' law in
force, a day was from sunrise to sunset.   But we sel-
dom or never hear a word of complaint.   Our fathers,
amidst all their privations and hardships, " bated not
a jot of heart or hope, but still bore up and steered
right onward."   It was left for a simpering and
luxurious age to ask, " Is life worth living ? "

The War did not close without its thunders reaching this little hamlet.   The famous fight between
the " Chesapeake " and " Shannon " was seen by
many from our heights, as the smoke of the guns
rolled down Boston Bay.   It was witnessed at closer
quarters than was altogether pleasant by the late
Stephen Danforth, who, as he told the writer, had a
near view of the beginning of the engagement, when
a boy in his father's fishing-boat near the scene of
action.   Manchester, too, furnished her recruits for
the naval service.   Serving on the " Chesapeake "

was Lambert Flowers, a man of herculean build and
great strength and courage ; he was wounded in the
battle, but lived to serve many years as a boatswain
in the Navy. During the fight he boarded the
enemy, but finding himself unsupported he made his
way back to his own ship undetected. Many stories
are told of his prodigious strength. It is said that
he once reefed a sail that defied the strength of four
able seamen ; and on another occasion picked up a
cannon that required four men to lift and carried it
across the deck. He is said to have been on the
" Constitution " when she captured the " Guerriere."
He was a quiet, inoffensive man, never provoking a
quarrel. He was never married, and died suddenly
and alone in his lodgings in Boston. Stories of
similar feats of muscular power are told of Paul
Leach, a ship-carpenter, and others. Some of them
are probably mythical, but not without a foundation
in fact.

There were others of the sons of Manchester in
the National war vessels and in the privateers which
wrought such destruction upon British commerce.
It is impossible now to ascertain who or how many
of the inhabitants of the town served the country on
the seas. Mention has recently been discovered [1] of
three Manchester men in an engagement between
the schooner " Sword Fish " of Gloucester, 156 tons,
twelve guns, 100 men, and two unknown British
ships, Aug. 24, 1812.

" We lay closely engaged with the two for twenty min-

[1] Communicated through the kindness of Major David W. Low of
Gloucester.

utes, and finding the ships too heavy for us, and not being able to board on account of the sea being too high, were obliged to haul off. In the action, Joseph Widger of Manchester, seaman, was killed with a round shot ; Mr. Nathan Lee, Jr., of ditto, prize-master, was dangerously wounded by a splinter which entered just above the left eye ; Archer Holt, slightly." [1]

With Perry on Lake Erie, and McDonough on Champlain, were Ephraim Clemons, John Babcock, Joseph Camp and William Camp. The last two were reported " missing," and are supposed to have been killed. Major Henry Story, Capt. Isaac Lee, Benjamin Leach and Ezekiel Leach were at one time in the famous Dartmoor prison. Mr. Thomas Dow, Senior, was taken prisoner by a British eighty-gun ship while on a coasting voyage. [2]

The War resulted in the country taking a high place abroad and winning great respect as a naval power. It achieved a second time the Independence of the United States. For generations the eastern seaboard had been famous for its ship-building ; better vessels and faster sailers had been turned out from the Yankee shipyards than even England could place upon the seas. The shipwrights of Manchester had been at work for a century, and fishing craft of from ten to one hundred tons, and if tradition is to be trusted much larger vessels, includ-

[1] *A Transcript of Journals of Vessels having letters of Marque and Reprisal, etc.*, reported to John Kittredge, Collector of District of Gloucester.

[2] Mr. Dow overheard some of the petty officers talking in a rather supercilious way about the Yankee frigates, when the old Captain said to them, "Young gentlemen, you do not know what you are saying. I know Commodore Bainbridge, and I tell you he knows how to handle a frigate." The wise heads in the British navy had great respect for American seamanship.

ing one or two ships, had borne witness in the ports of Europe to their skill and energy. George Norton had been a well known builder; others, whose works praised them in the gates of the Mediterranean and the West Indies, had laid down the keels of schooners and brigs that traded from Portsmouth to San Domingo, and run to Bilboa and Cadiz.[1] Whole fleets of American sea craft, mostly schooners, swarmed along the coasts of America, sailing to the West Indies and the Spanish Main. Every bight and bay and estuary was a lurking place of buccaneers, and the merchant vessels fought their way often to their destination and back again. Sea navigation became an instinct, and sea fighting a profession and science to these brave men.

All this experience stood us in good stead in the War of 1812, a war which was largely fought on the Ocean and the Great Lakes. The land conflicts were insignificant, and mostly disastrous to the American cause. But on the water the skill and prowess of our seamen made the young Republic the wonder and admiration of the world. With a naval force hastily improvised and equipped, and often greatly inferior in weight of metal to the enemy's ships, we were victorious in many a sharp encounter.[2] In the first six months of the War, three

[1] Besides the frequent voyages to Southern ports and the West Indies, Manchester had some direct trade with Spain. In September, 1807, the schooner "Three Sisters," Hooper, from Alicant to Manchester, was spoken at sea. Voyages to Lisbon were common, and many Manchester men were lost on these transatlantic passages.

[2] On Feb. 20, 1815, the *Constitution*, 51 guns, captured the *Cyane* and *Levant*, fifty-five guns, after a four hours' contest by moonlight, in which the American loss was fourteen to the British of seventy-seven, proving the superior gunnery of the Yankees.

British frigates and three sloops-of-war were captured or destroyed by American vessels of the same class. The great sea-fights made the names of commanders like Hull, Decatur, Stewart, Bainbridge, Porter, Dale, Perry and McDonough, and of ships like the *Constitution, United States, Essex, Wasp* and *Peacock*, familiar in song and story to coming generations.[1] "The effect of these victories was out of all proportion to their real importance; for they were the first heavy blows which had been dealt at England's supremacy over the seas."[2]

The War of 1812 has never received the attention which it deserves from modern story-writers, having been eclipsed by the greater apparent romance of the events of the struggle for Independence and of the Civil War. Yet it has been pertinently said that "If the war of the Revolution was a war for independence, that of 1812 was one for nationality, and its results, while perhaps less apparent, were none the less real."[3]

The year 1815 dawned upon a land that had looked across the seas for months in hopes of a cessation of hostilities to follow the negotiations of the

[1] Few pieces were more popular for "speaking" a generation ago than "Old Ironsides," by O. W. Holmes —

"Ay! tear her tattered ensign down!"

a lyric which saved the gallant old ship from destruction, and made it the pride and glory of the nation for years.

[2] *History of the English People*, Green, B. IV, ch. v.

[3] The younger generation of readers will get an insight into the conditions of the times of 1812, a history of the second war with England, with the results upon national life that followed it, in *The Search for Andrew Field*, by E. S. Tomlinson (Lee & Shepard, Boston), a story of American boys, full to the brim of love of country, manly in tone, and written by one thoroughly familiar with the ground.

Peace Commissioners at Ghent. It is true, the result of the embargo had been to turn the attention of the country more to manufactures, and there had been much progress made in this direction since the opening of the century. But there had been a general stagnation of industry, and upon the seaboard especially there was much poverty and distress. When news arrived in New York in February that the terms of peace had been concluded upon, there was universal rejoicing, and a general sense of relief. As the tidings spread through the land, there were bonfires on the hill-tops, firing of cannon and great jubilation. In Manchester, the event was celebrated by a great dinner at the tavern, where " the emotions of the people found vent in speeches, patriotic songs, and shouts of merriment until the small hours of the coming day."

Through all these chequered years, in light and shade, Manchester had been advancing on the whole in material prosperity. The steps are not easy to trace for want of contemporary records, but a long way had been traversed between the close of the Revolution and the close of the War of 1812.[1] The people had learned the benefits to a community of a variety of industries, and they no longer restricted their energies to the seine and the fish-flakes.

Women shared in the general activity and enter-

[1] In 1816, there were in town, three grist-mills, three lumber-mills, one mahogany veneering-mill, one bakery, twelve carpenters, one cooper's shop, one wheelwright three painters, one tailor, one brick-yard, six shoemakers shops, two blacksmiths, one manufacturer of ship steering wheels, ten furniture shops and one tannery, and the following farm products and stock : 2,500 bushels of corn, 450 bushels of barley, 290 tons of English hay, 160 cows, 60 oxen, 40 tons of salt hay, 28 horses, 50 swine, 35 tons of fresh meadow hay.

prise. Wool that was grown to a considerable extent [1] on pastures now overrun with brush or grown up to wood, was carded, spun and woven by the wives and daughters, carried to Warner's Mill in Ipswich to be fulled, and then made into substantial clothing, good not only for common but for Sunday wear. At a later period, straw braiding and the making of palm-leaf hats gave employment to women, and in many a frugal home "Hannah" might be found "binding shoes." Idleness was one of the cardinal sins. Boys were bred to the sea or put to a trade. Girls were taught household duties and simple arts; they knew how to bake and brew. to sew and darn, to spin [2] and weave, if they could not dance the latest cotillion, or trim their gowns in the newest Parisian style. They read the Bible, if they knew nothing of Browning; they were familiar with Pilgrim's Progress, if they were ignorant of Balzac and Kipling; they could sing counter and treble in the village choir, if they could not play Gounod and Wagner.

There has never, perhaps, been a more industrious community, since the days when "Adam delved and Eve span," than was Manchester down to the middle of this century. The people did not die of *ennui* and nervous prostration. They did not need for the building up of their constitutions, athletic clubs, classes for physical culture or polo grounds.

---

[1] On June 12, 1783, eight sheep were "empounded" by Aaron Lee, and advertised by written notice for a claimant.

[2] The spinning-wheel was an important article of household furniture in almost every family. It was quite as common as the sewing machine to-day.

They had their play-times, but they did not make play the business of life.

With meagre advantages at the outset, as compared with towns having more fertile soil or greater commercial opportunities, and with many obstacles to contend with in the smallness of its population and the great losses of property and life at sea, Manchester was slowly forging ahead. She was keeping rank with her sister towns, considering the disadvantages of her lot, with no unequal step. The close of the War with Great Britain in 1815 saw the little community entering upon a career of increasing prosperity. The pluck and courage of the people were meeting their reward. Communities, like individuals, often grow strong through hardship and suffering.

> " Ever by losses the right must gain,
> Every good have its birth of pain."

CHAPTER VIII.

THE CABINET-MAKING.

"In all labor there is profit."

Proverbs.

"The only noble man that I know anything about is the honest laborin' man. Work is the law of natur' and the secret of human happiness. . . . If there was less money in the world, an' more stiddy work, we should be better off."

Hiram Golf's Religion, G. H. Hepworth.

CHAPTER VIII.

THE CABINET-MAKING.

HEIRLOOMS — FIRST MECHANICS — MR. ALLEN'S MILL — "THE
GREAT FIRE" — A SOUTHERN SCARE — GALA DAYS —
THE LYCEUM — THE "SECOND ADVENT" —
PROSPEROUS TIMES — A FADING MEM-
ORY — NAMES OF MANU-
FACTURERS.

THE history of cabinet-making in Manchester is
a history, like most things that have come to
greatness, of small beginnings. For more
than a century, the sea furnished the chief means of
livelihood. Something was done in the cultivation
of the soil, but little more than was necessary to
meet the wants of home consumption. If Manchester was to increase in population and wealth, it
became evident that it must vary and enlarge its
industries.

For a long time after the settlement of the country, the better class of household furniture was
brought from England. Much of it was in the shape
of heirlooms; enough to freight quite a fleet of merchantmen "came over in the Mayflower." [1] For

[1] A "chist" of drawers which had been in the Allen family for generations and which may have been brought from England, is in the possession of Mr. Josiah Allen Haskell of Beverly, a descendant of Josiah Allen,
who was born in Manchester, April 28, 1703. Major Forster had some fine
furniture from England, which is in possession of a descendant, Miss
Bethiah Tappan.

the rest, for plain, everyday use, carpenters made
tables, stools, "settles" and "presses." When the
"new departure" took place it was in a very quiet
and humble way. It was born of no concerted
action, and nursed by no municipal concessions ; it
was built by no syndicate, and launched with no
newspaper notices and amidst no applauding
crowds.

The name of Moses Dodge leads the list of Manchester's cabinet-makers. He began work about
1775, in the house lately occupied by Deacon Price,
probably in one room, where he laid the foundations
of the business carried on afterward by his grandson
Cyrus Dodge, and at present by his great-grandsons,
John M. and Charles C. Dodge. The next to enter
the business was Ebenezer Tappan, born 1761, son
of Rev. Benjamin Tappan, a Revolutionary soldier,
who learned the trade in Portland,[1] of his Uncle
Wigglesworth. He was followed by Caleb Knowlton, who was here "previous to 1808." About
1816, John P. Allen opened a small shop on Union
street. Larkin Woodberry worked for Mr. Allen as
a journeyman. In 1834, Albert E. Low became
apprentice to Mr. Woodberry. Such were some of
the genealogical trees from which the workers in
birch and cherry and pine and mahogany have
sprung ; which for a time took deep root in the land
and spread their branches by the sea. The preëminence which Manchester attained in the business
was due to no one man exclusively. The town
seems to have been noted for its many skilled arti-

[1] Then called Falmouth.

sans. The same enterprise and "gumption" that had made Manchester "jiggers" famous in the fleet of fishing craft on the Banks and around the Grand Menan, when turned into manufacturing channels, produced mechanical results that soon took their place by the side of the most celebrated productions in the warehouses of Boston and New York. The cabinet-makers of Manchester are almost forgotten, but in their day they were an intelligent, wide-awake, ingenious, enterprising class of men. To single out individuals may seem almost invidious. But two at least should be specially mentioned.

One was Col. Eben Tappan, who was not only a cabinet-maker, but a house-builder and a manufacturer of fire-engines and steering-wheels. He worked at one bench for over fifty-six years; his shop was always a pattern of neatness. One piece of his work, made in his old age, may be mentioned as a specimen of his ingenuity. It is described as " a square box frame, containing a drawer, which may be pulled out on either of its four sides; this box is about a foot square, and stands about six inches high ; it is made of black walnut, with a walnut burl top, and has a narrow moulding, and one or two narrow strips of barberry wood ; it is a remarkably handsome and well made piece of work, which would do credit by its ingenuity and style of workmanship to any cabinet-maker in the country." Colonel Tappan died in 1875, at the age of eighty-three years.

John Perry Allen had worked for Caleb Knowlton before the War of 1812 ; but the " troublous times" led Mr. Knowlton to retire from this seaboard town and settle in New Hampshire. Mr. Allen set up business on his own account during the war, employing one journeyman and one apprentice. In order to enlarge his business he carried two mahogany bureaus on a vessel to Boston. Purchasers were found, orders came in, and business prospered. A few years later he shipped a consignment of furniture to New York, to be sold at auction. This venture met with such success and resulted in such an increase of business that it was difficult to find enough skilled workmen to enable him to fill his orders. This was the time when mahogany and other veneers were very generally used. They were sawed from the log by hand, a tedious and expensive process. The attempt had been made in New York and elsewhere to use machinery for the purpose, but with little success. Mr. Allen was one of those who experimented in this direction, building a mill for the purpose in 1825, on the site of the old tide-water Grist Mill which he bought of the town for the purpose. The chief difficulty was in getting veneers after the first two or three cuts, that were not uneven and wavy; the heat caused by friction warping the saws. The cause was at last discovered by accident. Some of the teeth which were bolted to the iron frame-work of the saw became broken, and it was necessary to set out the sections of the frame to make the saw of sufficient diameter; this gave the needed room for expansion, and the machine now turned out smooth and perfect veneers. It is said that if the discovery had been made a few days earlier, Mr. Allen's machine would have been the first successful one in the country. It appears that he narrowly escaped great fame.

The sawing of veneers now became a principal part of Mr. Allen's increasing business. His "plant" consisted of two upright saws, four veneering saws,[1] jig saws, turning lathes, etc. In 1835, Mr. Allen placed a steam engine in his mill, which supplied veneers for most of the furniture and piano establishments in the United States.

It was somewhere about this time, that Mr. Benjamin Lamson of East Boston, an extensive dealer in mahogany, sent a log measuring six feet and six inches in length, twenty-six inches in width, and thirteen inches thick, to Mr. Allen, with the request that he would have it planed on its four sides, split in the middle, and write him up an account of the condition in which he found it.[2] A few days after, Captain Mackie, a partner with Jonas Chickering, came to Manchester, examined the stick, and purchased it for one thousand dollars, having previously declined taking it at five hundred dollars, through fear that it might not prove sound.

It was while the business was at the height of its prosperity, and employing a hundred men, that a spark of fire, falling into some mahogany dust and smouldering for hours, broke out at night into a disastrous conflagration that swept away mill, shops,

[1] "These saws were capable of dividing a plank four inches in thickness into sixty veneers. They were kept from public view, under lock and key, and all sorts of subterfuges were used by people from many parts of the country, who desired to see their operations that they might adapt the principle to similar purposes."

[2] Mr. Allen is said to have been the best judge of mahogany in the Boston market.

great stacks of lumber from Maine and Honduras, and reduced the whole establishment to ashes. The fire occurred Aug. 27, 1836, and is still remembered and spoken of as "the great fire." Mr. Allen's dwelling house and several other houses, shops and other buildings were destroyed. The Salem *Gazette* of August 30 gave the following account :

"It is with the deepest regret we announce that the thriving village of Manchester in our neighborhood, has experienced a severe calamity in the destruction by fire of its principal business establishments, by which upwards of 100 industrious men have been thrown out of employment, and several worthy individuals have lost their all.

" About 2 o'clock on Sunday morning the Steam Veneering Mill of John P. Allen, situated near the centre of the village, was discovered to be on fire, and the flames spread with great rapidity, communicating immediately with the two cabinet-shops, and the handsome dwelling house and barn of that gentleman, and which were totally destroyed with their contents.

" Also the large cabinet manufactory of Mr. Larkin Woodbury which was destroyed. Part of the contents were saved in a damaged condition.

" Also the dwelling-house, barn and outbuildings of Dr. Asa Story which were destroyed.

" Also the dwelling-house and barn of Mr. Solomon Lee, an aged veteran of the Revolution; a total loss and no insurance.

" Also the house and shop of Mrs. Andrew Masters, and the stable and shed attached to the tavern of Nathaniel Colby, all of which were burnt.

" The loss sustained by Mr. Allen is very great, estimated from $20,000 to $30,000, but we are glad to learn he has considerable insurance. Besides his buildings, mahogany, tools, etc., all his valuable house furniture, a large number of mahogany logs, veneers, lumber and articles of new furniture were destroyed.

"A gentleman of this city, we learn, had $1,000 worth of mahogany at his mill. Mr. Woodbury's loss is estimated at $4,000; supposd to be insured. Both of these gentlemen were absent on a tour in the interior.

"Dr. Story's loss is about $2,500; no insurance.

"Mr. Colby likewise had no insurance. When the fire was at its height it raged on both sides of the small stream, near which these establishments were situated, so that it was impossible to pass the bridge which crosses it. Owing to the dense fog the fire was not seen in this neighborhood, and it was not known until about 3 o'clock when the alarm was given, and one engine and many of our citizens proceeded to the scene of the conflagration."

Mr. Allen's losses were estimated as over sixty thousand dollars. He was insured for only about nine thousand. With indomitable energy he resumed business with a new mill and shops ; but the cabinet-making business in Manchester had reached its zenith. In 1835, the amount of sales of furniture turned out by its workmen, was $50,000. In a few years, trade began to be transferred to the larger centres and the West, where abundant lumber and cheap water-power enabled manufacturers to enter into a ruinous competition with the East. Considerable work, especially of the better class, however, continued to be carried on in small shops, until the coming on of the Civil War and the closing of the Southern market still further curtailed the business, so that it declined until it became little more than a shadow of its former name.

Mr. Allen was a man of great force of character and public spirit. He was a leader of men; having, it is said, something Websterian in his pose of head, stature and general bearing. He died in 1875, in his eightieth year.

The work that continued to be sent from Manchester maintained the high reputation of former years for excellence, even when sadly diminished in amount. The *Cabinet Maker*, a weekly paper " devoted to the interests of the furniture trade," published in Boston, in its issue of June 18, 1870, has a leading article of two columns on " Furniture Manufacture at Manchester, Mass.," from which we extract the following :

" The class of work that is made in Manchester to-day, is without doubt as fine as any work turned out in the United States, and it is retailed in the warerooms of the most fashionable furniture dealers in the country. The styles are good, and the work thorough and reliable. Were it the custom to put the maker's name on furniture, as it is on watches, fire-arms, silverware, and most other goods, these modest manufacturers, doing business in the same small routine way for the past forty or fifty years, would have an enviable reputation, wherever, in this country, handsome and serviceable furniture is appreciated."

It was during the cabinet-making period that the gold excitement in California lured many of the citizens of Manchester, with others, to join the throngs that made their way to the new El Dorado. Some went by the Isthmus, some by way of the Plains, and a party of twelve by Cape Horn, in a small vessel which they purchased, fitted and loaded with provisions and lumber for the San Francisco market.[1]

[1] *Vide* p. 350.

An amusing incident that occurred during the manufacturing era illustrates the fact that great and grave results may sometimes spring from trifling causes. The cheaper grades of furniture found a ready market in the "forties," in Charleston, Mobile and especially New Orleans, from whence they were shipped up the Mississippi, and thus found their way all over what was then the "Great West." On one occasion, in packing some goods for the "Crescent City," a quantity of copies of the *Liberator*[1] were used for wrapping, and when the cases were opened on the sidewalk on a windy day, the papers were scattered, "thick as leaves in Vallombrosa shed." Judge of the consternation caused by the dissemination broadcast of such "incendiary" matter in one of the most combustible parts of the structure of the great Southern slaveholding civilization. They must have seemed like fiery cinders rained upon the Southland, from that ever-active volcano of political and moral fanaticism known as New England. Some of them doubtless contained the words of Giddings, or Hale, or George Thompson, or Gerrit Smith, or Parker Pillsbury, or the immortal utterances — *primus inter pares* — of Garrison himself. It is needless to say that the innocent perpetrators of this practical joke were at once notified by their agent in very explicit terms that such an offence must not be repeated. The Southern constitution was too sensitive and irritable to bear so powerful a blister.

[1] Probably no other town of its size could have furnished so many copies of this paper.

It was not, as might be thought, "all work and no play," with the mechanics of the first half of the century. They worked early and late in the shops,[1] they allowed themselves few luxuries, but they had their holidays and enjoyed them with a zest unknown to those who have lived to see holidays multiplied and hours of labor diminished. Most days were "labor days" in stern reality to the generation that made Manchester a hive of industry. But now and then, on some great occasion, the town kept gala-day.

One instance of this kind was on the Fiftieth Anniversary of the Declaration of Independence, July 4, 1826. On the morning of that day, the people were awakened by the joyful ringing of bells and booming of cannon, announcing the dawn of the nation's birthday. A survivor[2] of the actors on that memorable occasion has given the writer his recollections of it. A procession marched through the village in the following order:

Capt. Benjamin Knowlton's Company,[3]
consisting of 24 young men, representing
the States of the Union.
Gloucester Company.
Orator of the Day, and Reader of Declaration.
Revolutionary Soldiers.[4]
Committee of Arrangements.
Citizens.

[1] Work was usually carried on in the shops until 8 P. M.; many worked on "stints" as many as fourteen hours a day.

[2] Dea. A. E. Low.

[3] Capt. Knowlton has been spoken of as "a born military leader," although in private life of a very mild, quiet demeanor. His company, which was uniformed in blue coat and white pants, was called the best-drilled company that took part in the local musters.

[4] These were twenty-four in number, according to Mr. D. L. Bingham, whose youthful memory as a boy of twelve vividly retains the scene.

The exercises were held in the church, and consisted of singing the Ode to Science, reading the Declaration by Capt. John Girdler, and oration by Mr. Tyler Parsons. Dinner followed in the hall. Dea. D. L. Bingham was president of the day. The citizens generally joined heartily in the celebration, with the exception of a few of the "outs," who were conspicuous by their absence, enjoying the day by themselves as best they could, and no doubt berating the administration and bewailing the degeneracy of the times.

On at least three other occasions, once on " Poplar Field " and twice at " Lobster Cove," the whole town, men and women, old and young, came together on " Independence Day " for a general jollification, in which feasting, speech-making, toasts and games were indulged in to the heart's content. At these festivities, one learns with regret, rum flowed freely, as was the custom of those days; but the drinking habits of half a century and more ago were not so demoralizing as the liquor traffic of the present day. The modern " saloon," with its progeny of evils, had not been spewed out of the mouth of the pit.

Other feastings and junketings of a more select character took place occasionally. Among these, tradition preserves the memory of certain goings-on of Manchester sea-captains and Boston merchants as their guests at the "Cold Spring." It is not difficult to picture in imagination the " solid men " of Boston, whose names were a power in the China seas, jogging down through Lynn and Salem in the early

morning in their square-topped chaises and curricles,
and spending the day in the beech grove, eating cold
fowl and chowder, and discussing Federalist politics,
exchanging ponderous jokes with their hosts, and returning in the late afternoon to their substantial and
comfortable homes on Hanover street and Fort
Hill.

It was during the industrial period that the
Lyceum rose and flourished.[1] Its record is duly
and honorably preserved in a permanent form in the
address of Mr. D. L. Bingham, at the Dedication of
the Memorial Library Building, and published in
the Memorial Volume, pp. 24–28. The following
extracts are from that address:

"The Constitution was adopted Feb. 10, 1830. Any
person could become a member by paying an annual sub-
scription of fifty cents, and signing the Constitution. Article IX declares that 'The regular exercises of the Society
shall be original dissertations, lectures on scientific and
other practical subjects, and a debate to be open to all the
members.' Dr. E. W. Leach delivered the introductory
lecture, March 3; the Rev. Samuel M. Emerson followed
with a lecture on 'The Method of Conducting Debates.'
Dr. Asa Story delivered three lectures on 'Natural Philos-
ophy.' John Price lectured on 'Schools and Methods of
Government.' Tyler Parsons, Joseph Knowlton and Daniel
Kimball of Ipswich complete the list of lecturers during the
first year of the Lyceum. The meetings for discussion
were always well attended, and the people took a deep interest in the questions brought before them. Some of the
questions were very practical; such as, 'Is the present sys-

---

[1] Hon. Robert S. Rantoul, in a very interesting chapter on "The Spirit
of the Early Lyceums" (*History of Essex County*, vol. 1, ch. lxxxiv), traces
the "root-idea of the American Lyceum" to the formation of a "Society
for Mutual Improvement," in Methuen, Essex Co., in 1824, under the lead
of Timothy Claxton, who was born in Norfolk, Eng., 1770.

tem of repairing roads judicious?' and 'Ought property to constitute the right of suffrage?'

" In the list of one hundred and twenty members were found nearly all the principal men of the town, and most of them took part in the discussions. . . . The subjects of the lectures, and the questions discussed, were talked about on the streets and in the shops. . . . Soon after the formation of the Lyceum, a movement was made to form a library. . . . The nucleus of this Library was composed of books contributed by members of the Association . . . the Library increased to nearly one thousand volumes . . . until it passed into the hands of the Town (1871)."

The following quotation is from the closing record of the Secretary, Mr. George F. Allen:

"So ends the Manchester Lyceum (first formed in 1830). It was a useful Association, and, in forty years of its existence, met the wants of the people as no other association could. Having performed its mission, if not as its founders wished, certainly with great credit to its many sustainers, it gives way to a new order of things; but though dead in name, it lives in principle and influence."

The first officers of the Lyceum were:

DR. ASA STORY . . . . President.
DELUCENA L. BINGHAM . Vice-President.
JOSEPH KNOWLTON . . . Secretary.
JOHN LEE . . . . . Treasurer.

Curators.

HENRY F. LEE . . DAVID MORGAN.

Committee.

JOHN P. ALLEN . . EZEKIEL W. LEACH.
LARKIN WOODBERRY . DANIEL ANNABLE.
DAVID MORGAN.

The Lyceum of fifty years ago was a valuable educational institution; and notwithstanding the great multiplication of magazines, newspapers, public libra-

ries and other means of popular information, nothing
has yet appeared that quite takes its place. There
is needed in our community some opportunity for
the interchange of thought and opinion in regard to
the social, business, intellectual and moral interests
of the town, and for the discussion of general subjects of popular interest, such as labor combinations,
the license question, the fostering of home industries, the books we should read, schools, roads, and
the like. It would afford a valuable training-school
for our young people, practice in debate, and famil-
iarity with parliamentary rules and principles. A
regular meeting with some important and timely
subject for discussion, opened by some speaker or
speakers prepared to throw light upon it, ought to
be an attraction to many who have now no profitable
employment for their leisure evenings.

A place, too, where the people could meet together occasionally as citizens, irrespective of church
or society affiliations, and learn to know each other
better, would exert in many ways a good influence.
We are in danger with other small communities of
becoming clannish, and with a dozen organizations
more or less, of dividing up into little knots and
cliques, each with its pass-words, grips and fellowships, but in few instances aiming to promote the
public good beyond their own little circle. A
lyceum, well conducted, would tend to break down
exclusiveness, to broaden sympathies and thought,
and to produce a better public spirit.

During the later years of the Lyceum, a course
of lectures was delivered by our townsman, William

H. Tappan, embodying some of his observations and experiences during the period of his official life in the Far West, and the fruit of large historical research. The titles of these lectures were : " The Indians of the Northwest Coast "; " The Nez Perces and Flatheads " ; " Gold and Silver Mining "; " Frontier Life, or the Infancy of States." The appreciation with which these lectures were received was expressed in Resolutions framed and presented by the Lecture Committee, consisting of Daniel Leach, W. E. Wheaton, Alfred S. Jewett, George A. Priest.

That the town was not wholly absorbed in material things in this time of manufacturing activity, that its spirit was not wholly utilitarian, is shown also by the moral and religious earnestness which inspired the Anti-Slavery movement, the revivals and the Second Advent excitement. The first of these demands for its treatment a separate chapter ; the second receive attention in the history of the churches ; the third, as a movement which started and chiefly ran its course outside of ecclesiastical lines, may find its place in its chronological setting.

The movement known as Second Adventism had its origin in connection with a general interest in the subject throughout the country, especially in New England. It was promoted in town by the preaching of Elam Burnham of Essex, and others, in the winter of 1842–43, and made many converts.[1] The movement was not looked upon with favor by

[1] " There is a very great Reformation in this Town." " The work shops and grocery stores are shut up, and about all business is suspended, and all sorts of people attend meetings." " Men, women and children spoke and prayed." John Lee's Diary, Jan. 24, 25, 1843.

the church generally or by the minister of the town;
hoodlumism was invoked to break up the meetings;[1]
but the movement was not thus to be arrested. It
received something of a check by the appearance
upon the scene of a somewhat skilled debater, a
Rev. Mr. Smith of Gloucester, who made up in tact
and good nature what he lacked in logic, and in a
public debate was thought rather to have the advantage of Mr. Burnham. The combatants were not on
the whole, perhaps, very unequally matched; if one
carried heavier metal, the other was better practised
in training his guns. Probably the friends of both
claimed the victory.

With a good deal of fanaticism and extravagance,
there was much sincerity and pious feeling; and
although the movement may be said to have col-
lapsed with the passing of the fateful day, many had
been moved by deep religious convictions and led
into serious and devout living. The Second Advent
movement resulted in the formation of a church,
which took the form, however, of a "Christian"
church, so-called, and which afterwards became a
regular Baptist church.[2] Second Adventism left
results behind it somewhat like those of a spring
freshet, of a very mixed character, results which
continue to be felt among us; but it failed to survive in any organic form.

In 1829 a Temperance Society was formed on
" the principle of total abstinence from ardent spirits
of persons in health." Larkin Woodberry was pres-

---

[1] Paper read by W. E. Wheaton before the Historical Society.
[2] Vide ch. xiii.

ident. In 1836 the Society had "nearly 400 members." It may be doubted whether the many organizations, with ambitious and high-sounding names, which have supplanted the early open temperance societies, have done more effective work.

The manufacturing era in Manchester was on the whole a period of thrift and general prosperity and contentment. The shops, some of which still remain converted to other uses, or dismantled and going to decay, melancholy ghosts of departed days, gave employment at times to three hundred men. Manchester had then home resources which gave support to an industrious community. Other industries of the time were the making of shoes in small wayside shops, sufficient to meet home wants, with a few pairs for export, reed-organs, made by John Godsoe and others in Isaac Allen's mill, and fire-engines built by Ebeneezer Tappan, Jr., which gained more than a local reputation. The wages were not high, but were fairly remunerative,[1] and the people lived in frugal comfort.

Beautiful, however, as were many of the products of the skilled mechanics of those days, a strange lack of taste for the most part continued to mark the buildings and grounds of the inhabitants, with the exception which should be noted of the planting of the noble elms which now adorn our streets. There was little of the æsthetic spirit, and small appreciation of the natural advantages of the town. The infusion of a less prosaic spirit came later.

But from 1820 to 1860, the village hummed with

[1] $1.25 per day was good average pay; board was $2.25 per week.

the sounds of busy industry and of active life.   The
coasting-trade was represented by three " packets "
plying between this port and Boston, and all departments of life felt the stir.   The population was
largely native-born and homogeneous.   The restless-
ness, the jealousy of capital on the part of labor too
often provoked by the heartless oppressions and
exactions of monopolies, the tyranny of labor organizations, strikes, boycotts and reprisals, were as yet
happily unknown, shut up in the Pandora's box of
the Nineteenth Century, that no one had had the
temerity to open.   It was a time when, practically,
" every rood of ground maintained its man," when
no great distinctions divided society into many
different strata.   The city had not, to much extent,
exerted its fascinating power upon country lads and
lasses ; contentment, simplicity and honesty were
common virtues.   Men had not yet learned how to
live without working.   There was little show, but a
good deal of substance.   If there was some veneer,
there was solid grain beneath.   The cabinet industry
was not a school of æsthetics, though it came near
being for some a school of art ; but it trained a
thoughtful, reading, intelligent class of men, who
gave weight and character to the community.   The
period was by no means one of stagnation and drow-
siness.   Other posies besides the poppy flourished in
the old-fashioned gardens.

The following official statement [1] gives at a glance
the industrial products of Manchester in 1837 :

---

[1] *Statistical Tables, etc.*, prepared by John P. Bigelow, Secretary of the
Commonwealth, 1838.

Boots manufactured, 425 pairs; shoes, 2,750 pairs; value of boots and shoes, $4,473; males employed, 11; females, 4.

Tannery, 1; hides tanned, 2,000; value of leather tanned and curried, $5,500; hands employed, 3; capital invested, $7,000.

Manufactories of chairs and cabinet ware, 12; value of chairs and cabinet ware, $84,500; hands employed, 120.

Palm-leaf hats manufactured, 3,000; value, $300.

Vessels built in the five preceding years, 4; tonnage of same, 190; value, $4,500; hands employed in ship building, 4.

Vessels employed in the cod and mackerel fishery, 14; tonnage of same, 500; codfish caught, 4,500 quintals; value, $11,200; mackerel caught, 200 barrels; value, $1,600; salt used in the cod and mackerel fishery, 4,500 bushels; hands employed, 65; capital invested, $12,300.

Ships' wheels manufactured, 25; value, $800; hands employed, 1.

In 1865, the cabinet business gave employment to 160 men, and a capital of over $60,000. The amount of manufactured goods was $92,625. There were also four sawing and planing mills, turning out $13,000 worth of work. The number of barrels and casks made was 32,600, valued at $10,600. The number of hides tanned was 5,000, of the value of $20,000. Boots and shoes were made to the amount of $12,000. Strawberries were raised to the value of $3,300. There were 40 horses in town and 34 oxen.

When business drifted to larger centres, when the small shops could no longer compete with the great factories, when those who had built up the town's industries passed away, a blight fell upon the town from which it has never recovered. The names of the men whose energy, business capacity and public spirit made Manchester so well known a few decades ago, are still remembered among us; a few articles of fine workmanship are still turned out, reminders of the town's former mechanical pride; but the thrift and enterprise of half a century ago are almost a myth to the present inhabitants, as well as to those who for health or fashion or pleasure, now seek these romantic shores. The cabinet-making industry is fast becoming but a memory, but it is a memory worth embalming.

NOTE. — The following List of the Cabinet Manufacturers of Manchester, it is hoped, will be found reasonably complete. Those marked (ˣ) had mills connected with their factories; other mill proprietors, not in the manufacturing business, were Lord and Lee, Bailey and Bingham, and Enos G. Allen.

Moses Dodge, Ebenezer Tappan, Larkin Woodberry, Eben Tappan, Long and Danforth (afterward J. Danforth, and Leach, Anable & Co.),ˣ Kelham and Fitz,ˣ Henry F. Lee, Isaac Allen, Jerry Danforth,ˣ S. O. Boardman, John Perry Allen,ˣ Smith and Low, Cyrus Dodge,ˣ Luther and Henry T. Bingham, John C. Long & Co., H. P. & S. P. Allen, Samuel Parsons, Allen and Ames, Albert E. Low, Isaac S. Day, William Hoyt, John C. Webb, Severance and Jewett (afterward A. W. Jewett, and A. S. & G. W. Jewett), William Johnson, C. B. Hoyt, Warren C. Dane, Felker and Cheever, Hanson, Morgan & Co., E. S. Vennard, William E. Wheaton, Charles Lee, John C. Peabody, Isaac Ayers, Crombie & Morgan,

Rufus Stanley,[x] William Decker, Watson, Taylor & Co., Rust and Marshall,[x] John M. and Charles C. Dodge,[x] Samuel L. Wheaton.

" The nobility of labor — the long pedigree of toil."

CHAPTER IX.

ANTI-SLAVERY DAYS.

"God fills the gaps of human need,
Each crisis brings its word and deed."

Whittier.

"*Then* to share with truth is noble, when we share her
    wretched crust,
Ere her cause bring fame or profit, and 'tis prosperous to be
    just."

Lowell.

"No one who serves the truth, even if he sacrifice his life for
it, can do as much for the truth, no, not by an hundred fold,
as the service of the truth will do for him."

W. H. Furness, D. D.

CHAPTER IX.

ANTI-SLAVERY DAYS.

THE seeds of freedom and slavery were planted in this country in the same twelvemonth. In 1620, the Mayflower brought the Pilgrims to Plymouth: in 1620, a Dutch man-of-war entered James River in Virginia, " and sold twenty negars." Thus two opposite types of civilization grew side by side. Down to the time of the Revolution, the whole power of England supported and encouraged the African slave-trade. Under that encouragement more than 300,000 slaves were imported into the thirteen colonies. The evil gradually extended itself, and became " rooted in the habits of the people, especially in the Southern States." The invention of the cotton-gin made slavery a source of great wealth, and it speedily grew to be an enormous power.

When slaves were first held in Manchester, there are no means of determining. They are mentioned under the designation of " servants " and " servants for life," in the Assessors' books, as early as 1760, but they were doubtless here before. It is not supposed that there were ever more than seven or eight slaves at one time in town. They are known to have been owned by only two or three families. Their condition, no doubt, was rather that of indented servants than slaves.

As early as 1775, a lecture on " The Beauties of Civil Liberty, and the Horrors of Slavery " was given in town by some one whose name has not come down to us. It is a tradition that the right of liberty was claimed for all men irrespective of color or race. It would seem that this address must have been an effective one, for we find no mention of slaves, or " servants," as taxable property in town after this date. An anti-slavery sentiment may thus early in its history have found place in the town.

In all the momentous events of the first half of the century, including the Missouri Compromise, the passage of the Fugitive Slave Law and the Kansas-Nebraska Bill, Manchester people took a lively interest, and watched the veering political weathercock with eagle eye. The seeds of anti-slavery sentiment, which for years had been liberally sowed, brought forth their fruit. It is now matter of history, though then known to but few, that there were men in town belonging to a secret organization, pledged to the shielding and defending of fugitive slaves, in any and every extremity. In 1853, the following resolutions were adopted in town meeting:

" WHEREAS, The action of the United States Senate, in

the introduction and passage of the Nebraska bill, which contains a provision for the repeal of the Missouri Compromise (by the terms of which slavery or involuntary servitude was forever excluded from all the vast territory acquired by purchase of France), thereby prostituting the patrimony of Freedom to the detestable purposes of slavery: therefore

" *Resolved*, That we view with alarm and indignation, this attempt of the slave power to enlarge the area of slavery, by the violation of compacts and trampling on the rights of man.

" 2d, *Resolved*, That we hold the Representatives of the North, who may vote for the violation of the Missouri Compromise, as false to the glorious cause of Freedom and recreant to the dictates of Humanity.

" 3d, *Resolved*, That the Town Clerk be instructed to forward a copy of these Resolutions to our Representative in Congress, Charles W. Upham."

The strong Free Soil sentiment of the town showed itself also in another direction. In 1853, Manchester did itself the honor to elect Richard H. Dana, Jr., delegate to the Constitutional Convention. That Mr. Dana was highly gratified is shown by the entry in his Diary, March 8:

" I had the compliment of being elected from Manchester by a clear majority over all others on the first ballot. I have also the satisfaction to know that I was elected without a coalition, and am therefore under obligations to no party to which I do not belong. The Free Soil party nominated me, and I accepted the nomination in a letter. The Democrats refused to unite in this nomination, and ran a separate candidate. The Whigs also had a separate candidate. But there were enough of the old parties to vote for me voluntarily to secure my election." [1]

[1] *Richard Henry Dana, A Biography*, by C. F. Adams, vol. I, pp. 229, 230.

Mr. Dana was one of the acknowledged leaders and hardest workers in the Convention.

On Sept. 11, 1856, the Free Soilers of Essex County held a mass convention in Manchester, in the interest of Fremont, as candidate for the presidency. The gathering was held at Gale's Point, and not less than eight thousand were present. Mammoth tents were erected, in which distinguished speakers addressed the crowds. Henry Kitfield was chairman of the committee of arrangements. Hon. Charles W. Upham of Salem was president of the day. Among the speakers were Edwin P. Whipple, Richard H. Dana, Jr., Senator Wilson, Ex-Governor Kent of Maine, and Hon. John Z. Goodrich.

The town was early astir with the arrivals from various directions and by various modes of conveyance. Large delegations were present from many of the towns of the County, with bands, banners and various mottoes, watchwords and devices. Many of the inhabitants showed their interest and zeal by handsomely decorating their residences and erecting arches at several localities.

The Anti-Slavery people held frequent meetings in town, employed the best speakers, and exerted a deep and widespread influence. The *National Era* and the *Liberator* had many readers, and contributed much to the education of the community in the principles of Abolitionism. The movement met with much opposition, especially from the Whigs, who feared the loss of votes more than the Democrats. " Leading abolitionists were subjected to a sort of social and religious ostracism, by some who prided themselves on their wealth and high social position. They were talked about as enemies of religion, dangerous to the peace and good order of society, likened to the worst of the French Revolutionists." But the friends of freedom were not to be daunted, and while some of the earlier adherents fell away, others took their place, and the society had enrolled on its list of membership over one hundred names.

At the time of the Fugitive Slave Law excitement, a meeting was held at which strong resolutions were presented, denouncing the Law as "most unrighteous and oppressive," and as a "monstrous stride backward from the progressive and Christian civilization of the age." The adoption of the resolutions was opposed by Mr. John P. Allen, "then wielding considerable influence and power in town." Mr. Allen was replied to by some of the leading abolitionists; Elder P. R. Russell, Baptist minister, "made a powerful speech against the Law." The resolutions were passed almost unanimously. The resolutions were drawn up by Rev. O. A. Taylor, but Mr. Taylor soon after "weakened in his opposition to the Fugitive Slave Law." It was a time when many flinched and failed. The Whig-party leaders cracked the whip, and multitudes cowed before it.

One of the most remarkable developments of the Anti-Slavery movement in town, and one which was almost without a parallel, was the organization and maintaining of an "Anti-Slavery Prayer-meeting." "In some respects," says one of the survivors,

"it was one of the most singular prayer-meetings
formed in Manchester or anywhere else." "The
services of the meetings were prayer, sacred songs,
readings from Anti-Slavery publications and brief
discussions." "It could not be urged that this was
an anti-church meeting. It was organized and controlled by church-members, and the services were
always of a serious and religious character."

After the formation of the Republican party, the
work of the Abolition Society, so far as politics was
concerned, was in a great measure transferred to the
Republican Town Committee, and the Manchester
Abolition Society ceased to be. But during its
existence it exerted a great influence, and it left
behind it a worthy history. It did much to mould
public sentiment; it ploughed deep furrows and
sowed much good seed in the moral soil of the community. The great leaders of the movement were
frequently heard ;[1] the meetings were large and en-
thusiastic. The principles which were set forth in
pungent and powerful sentences on the platform were
discussed through the week in the shops and stores ;
and so general a response did the arguments and
appeals for Freedom against Slavery meet with, that
Manchester was classed among "the banner towns
of Essex County." A few of the "old guard" still
remain to rehearse the story of those stirring times.
But for the most part, the scenes are fast becoming
dim, and the heroic struggles and sacrifices of the

[1] Among them were W. L. Garrison, J. M. Buffum, S. S. Foster, Parker
Pillsbury, Fred. Douglas, C. C. Burleigh, Lucy Stone, C. L. Remond,
Theodore D. Weld.

pioneers of the cause of Emancipation will soon remain but a tradition among us.

One romantic incident, at least, belongs to this period. The time is not precisely known — it was "*sometime in the fifties*"; these men who were making history were careless about writing it. The *dramatis personæ* were a hunted fugitive from Southern slavery, and two or three friends of freedom, who were willing to risk something to befriend a fellow-being in distress and danger, even though his skin was a few shades darker than their own. The fugitive appeared in the village on a dark, rainy, chilly evening in the spring, having missed the main track of the Underground Railroad at Salem. There was one home to receive him, there was one friend to help him: wet and cold and trembling, he took him to his own house, fed, warmed and clothed him. The next day, which was Sunday, the poor man's habiliments were repaired and put in order by the good wife of another leader in the Anti-Slavery ranks, a little money was collected, and early on Monday morning, the grateful but still fearful stranger was guided on his way toward the next "underground" station. He was afterwards heard from in Canada, safe beneath the protection of the British flag. The names of the men who sheltered and befriended the fleeing bondman, at such personal risk, are worthy of being enrolled among the benefactors of the human race. They are Daniel W. Friend, Delucena L. Bingham, Thomas W. Gentlee. Others sympathized and helped, but these stand easily as "the first three."

The time was one not only of earnest thought and discussion, and of unselfish devotion, but of manful and heroic action. It was an education in itself of no mean value. It was an experience which prepared the people for the stern scenes which were to follow. It lifted the moral sense of the community to a distinctly higher plane ; it purified and energized the public conscience ; it magnified and made honorable the "higher law." It was one of the great historic periods in the life of Manchester, worthy to be classed with the strenuous times of the Revolution and the Civil War.

It is difficult for us to conceive the odium which attached to the early Anti-Slavery movement. We have at last reached the time when, so far as the negro is concerned, " 'tis prosperous to be just." But fifty years ago, to be suspected of sympathy for the slave was to be ostracized socially, politically, and, in some cases, religiously. Mr. Eminent Respectability regarded the whole thing as low and vulgar. The friends of Liberty were anathematized as pestilent fanatics and disturbers of the peace. To oppose the slave power was to confront mobs, persecution, and, sometimes, death. To attend Anti-Slavery meetings placed one outside the pale of polite society. According to every just estimate, the men and women of fifty and sixty years ago, who braved public opinion to espouse the cause of the slave, are to be ranked among the heroes of the race. Their names

"On Fame's eternal bead-roll are worthy to be filed."

CHAPTER X.

THE WAR FOR THE UNION.

"The hero's deeds and hard-won fame shall live."

Ovid.

"A war to preserve national independence, life and honor, is a war just, necessary, manly and pious, and we are bound to persevere in it, by every principle, human and divine, as long as the system which menaces them has an existence."

Edmund Burke.

"Mine eyes have seen the glory of the coming of the Lord;
He is trampling out the vintage where the grapes of wrath are
    stored;
He hath loosed the fateful lightning of His terrible swift
    sword;
       His truth is marching on."

Battle Hymn of the Republic, Mrs. Julia Ward Howe.

CHAPTER X.

THE WAR FOR THE UNION.

THE AWAKENING — THE MUSTERING OF THE NORTH — MAN-
CHESTER'S WAR RECORD — HEROISM AND SUFFERING
— THE CLOSE OF THE WAR — JOY AND SOR-
ROW — WAR MEMORIALS — WOMEN IN
THE WAR — COMPENSATIONS.

THE causes of the War for the Union must be
sought in the "irrepressible conflict" between
Freedom and Slavery, that had long been
going on, both North and South. We were in "a
place where two seas met." Following the election
of Lincoln in 1860, came the secession of State after
State from the Union, the removal of troops, ships,
and military and naval stores to Southern cities,
arsenals, forts and dock-yards; while the North
looked helplessly on, drifting into the vortex of civil
strife. The winter of 1860–61 was one of great
anxiety and suspense. There was the gravest doubt
in the minds of many, in this country as well as in
Europe, whether the Great Republic would "disap-
pear from the roll of nations, or whether it would
survive the storm that had gathered over its
head."

But when the first gun was fired on Fort Sumter,
there was at once a wonderful uprising throughout

the North.   Men of all shades of political complexion became as one; old-school Abolitionists,
Free Soilers, Democrats and " Conscience Whigs,"
forgot their differences and ceased their contentions.
There was for a time but one party at the North,
and that was the party of the Union.   A flame of
patriotic fire ran through the loyal States, and men
of all parties and creeds rallied to the defence of the
old Flag.

Who that lived at that time can ever forget those
memorable days — the intense excitement, the expectations often followed by disappointment, the
ardor often succeeded by hope deferred, the sorrows,
tragedies, triumphs and joys, the sad tidings of
defeat, the glad pæans of victory, the long-drawn
contest, evoking every generous and patriotic impulse, overshadowing all private and mercenary
interests, ending at last in the overthrow of treason,
the abolition of slavery, the preservation of the
Union ?

Manchester was not wanting in those great days.
The town met every call, kept its quota full, and was
represented on almost every battle-field of the War.

The whole number of men furnished by the town for the
Army and Navy was one hundred and fifty-nine; of whom
twenty-four reënlisted and were counted a second time to
the credit of the town, making a total of one hundred and
eighty-three men, furnished under different calls, besides
the town's proportion of the State naval credits at large.[1]

Five enlisted on the first call for 75,000 men for three
months.

---

[1] A classified list of names of all in the service will be found in Appendix F.

Sixty-eight enlisted to serve for three years or during the War, and for no bounty.

Twenty-one enlisted for three years, receiving a bounty from the town and State.

Seven were drafted, July 10, 1863, for three years, and served until discharged at the end of the War, excepting one who died in the service.

Twenty-three enlisted and served for nine months, and received from the town a bounty of one hundred dollars each.

Twenty-three enlisted for one year, who received a bounty from the town of one hundred and twenty-five dollars each.

Fourteen enlisted for one hundred days, and received no bounty.

Three paid commutation money, and one furnished a substitute.

Eleven enlisted and served in the naval service.

Sixteen died in the military and two in the naval service.

Four were killed in battle.

Two died from wounds received in action.

Seven were taken prisoners, of whom three were exchanged, and four died in prison.

Twenty-six were discharged by reason of disease contracted in the service, and wounds received in action.

Forty-eight were discharged by reason of expiration of term of service.

Sixty were in service at the close of the War, and were discharged under General Order of the War Department.

Eighteen served through the War, first enlisting in the summer and fall of 1861, reënlisting at the end of two years, and of these, two were among those who responded to the first call of the President, April, 1861.

The number of commissioned officers was four.

Eighty-four of these men were natives of the town, one hundred and thirty-nine were natives of the United States, twenty were foreigners, and three negroes.

Twenty, at least, and probably more, natives of the town residing elsewhere, were actively engaged in the War, eight of whom died in the service, three of them in Rebel prisons. Two of them were commissioned officers, one a Captain and one a Lieutenant Colonel.

The whole amount of money paid by the town for bounties and expenses of recruiting was seven thousand eight hundred and eighty-five dollars ($7,885). The whole amount of aid furnished soldiers' families to March 1, 1866, was seventeen thousand four hundred and ninety-eight dollars ($17,498).[1] Besides this sum, two hundred and forty-seven dollars ($247) was paid by the town, not to be reimbursed by the State. The estimated increase of the town debt by reason of the war was ten thousand dollars ($10,000).

Manchester can look back upon her war record with gratitude and honest pride.

" Few towns of a like population can show a better record as regards the number of *her own* citizens sent into the conflict, there being one hundred and fifty-three who were citizens of the town out of one hundred and fifty-nine — the whole number sent. The town may well congratulate herself on the record she has made in the great work of preserving the unity, integrity and freedom of the nation, inasmuch as so many of her own sons went forth to *do* and to *die* for the common weal." [2]

Their deeds are their monument, more lasting than marble or brass, in the hearts of their grateful countrymen. The Records of our Soldiers and Seamen [3] in the Rebellion, as preserved in a sumptuous

---

[1] Reimbursed by the State.

[2] Special report of the Selectmen, March 19, 1866.

[3] While we oftenest speak of the Army and the Soldiers, we should never forget the part borne by the Navy in the Great Conflict. If it had not been for the efficiency of the blockade service, the operations on the Carolina coast, at Mobile and New Orleans, and the opening and holding of the Mississippi, a fatal blow to the Confederacy, the history of the War would have been very differently written.

volume [1] in the archives of Post 67, G. A. R., furnish a mine of information and a noble memorial of Manchester in the War.

These men went forth from the fireside and the workshop, from the plough and the tiller, from the mill and the counting-room, not to carry on a war of aggression, but to defend the honor and liberty of the Country, and maintain the Constitution and the Laws. They were citizen-soldiers, bearing with them to the camp, the bivouac and the field, the best influences of a Puritanic ancestry, and of training in the town meeting, the church, the home and the common school. They were surrounded and followed by the anxieties and hopes, the prayers and blessings of parents, brothers, sisters, sweethearts, wives and children. They were overshadowed and environed by all the loving and patriotic wishes and aspirations of friends and kindred, and by the memories and traditions of a hundred years. When they fell, they were borne tenderly to their resting-place with prayer and dirge. When they returned, worn, sick and dying, they were received with flowing tears and open arms. When at last the survivors marched home from Appomattox and the honors of the Grand Review, the welkin rang with plaudits, and every heart gave welcome to the returning heroes of the Union and the Flag.

On the conclusion of the War, the town took suitable action in view of the quickly recurring events, which is still fresh in the memory of many still living. For those whose lives have been lived since

1 The gift of Russell Sturgis, Esq.

those momentous times, a brief record is here in place.   In the Town Records is found the following :

" MANCHESTER, 1865.

" Monday, April 3d, of this year, was a day of great rejoicing.   In the morning we heard our army had achieved a great victory over the enemy, but none of us dared to believe Richmond would fall so soon, if at all.   So in the afternoon when the dispatch announcing the occupation of Richmond by our forces was received, the people manifested their joy by triumphant shouts, excited congratulations and the ringing of bells.   So long had we hoped for this event and so long had our hopes been deferred, our faith had grown weak, but now great joy fell upon us and we celebrated.

" April 10th, 1865."

One week later the news was received of Lee's surrender.   The enthusiasm of the people was immediate and intense.   Arrangements were at once made for a day of public rejoicing.   The date was April 11, 1865.   The following account is from the Salem *Register :*

" Yesterday was a day long to be remembered.   At an early hour we were aroused by the ringing of bells and the glad shout, ' Lee and his whole army have surrendered.'

" Col. T. R. Tannatt and Lewis N. Tappan had made haste to ride from your city with the joyful tidings.   The people of the town were soon astir, flags were unfolded and flung to the breeze, drums and fifes brought out, a procession formed and marched to the depot, where short speeches for the occasion were made by Rev. E. P. Tenney and Rev. Mr. Thayer, author of the ' Bobbin Boy.'   These speakers leaving in the early train, the procession returned to the common, where a stage was erected at the foot of the flag-staff, from which Rev. F. V. Tenney read the despatch announcing the surrender of Lee.

"Several citizens addressed the people, setting forth in befitting terms the glories of the day. Col. Tannatt and Mr. Tappan also favored us with remarks pertinent to the glorious realities of the occasion.

"Loud and repeated cheers were given for the speakers, President Lincoln, his generals and the heroic soldiers of the army. 'America,' 'Rally round the Flag, Boys,' and 'John Brown' were sung with thrilling effect. Allusions were made by most of the speakers to that 'monster sin' which had well-nigh been our ruin. One of them was pleased to read an extract from 'Helper's Impending Crisis,' the same being a warning found in Jeremiah 34 ch. 17 verse. To make his point stronger the speaker read the following extract from a letter written in May, 1847, by a former clergyman of this town (Rev. O. A. Taylor) while journeying in the border States:

"'Slavery must and will be destroyed. It is inconsistent with the spirit of our institutions. Freedom frowns upon it from every quarter of our land. The world is against it. God's curse rests upon it. If let alone it will sooner or later poison itself to death, as do some serpents under the very malignancy of their own venom.'

"The speaker had carried this prophecy in his pocket for eighteen years, and for the most part of the time, with but faint hopes of ever witnessing its fulfillment, but to-day he was glad, and thought the prophecy of an orthodox clergyman equal to that of Jeremiah. After other congratulatory exercises the procession re-formed and marched through different sections of the town.

"In the afternoon the fire department turned out and with the citizens escorted four wounded soldiers, three of whom had lost a leg and one an arm, through the principal streets amid the waving of flags and the ringing of bells. Notwithstanding the rain the enthusiasm was unabated, and at an early hour in the evening the Baptist Church was filled with joyous people of both sexes.

"John Lee was elected as the presiding officer and Rev. F. V. Tenney invoked the divine blessing. The exercises

were all of a very interesting character, consisting of singing
by the choirs of the several religious societies, joined in part
by the assembly, and of congratulatory addresses from the
several clergymen of the town, and from other citizens,
intermingled with cheers for the different speakers and for
the great successes we celebrated — not forgetting the brave
boys now absent and the equally deserving who have returned, nor the 20 of our *heroic dead*, 5 of whom died on
the *field of battle*, 3 in *rebel prisons*, and the rest in hospitals
or at home.   Tears were in many eyes in memory of those
departed heroes.

"A collection for the Christian Commission was taken
up.   Altogether it was a day of Jubilee, and one we may
all rejoice to have been permitted to see.   E. R. N."

Four days later, April 15, the heart of the nation
was plunged in grief and consternation, by the news
of the assassination of its Chief.   From the Town
Records the following extract is made :

"'The President is shot,' and ere we could comprehend
or believe the first despatch, another said, 'Our beloved
President, Abraham Lincoln, is Dead.'

"No words can describe the feeling of *surprise*, *grief*,
indignation and *horror* which seized upon every one.   All
business was suspended.   Funeral services were held in the
Congregational Church, opened by the reading of the scriptures by Rev. F. V. Tenney, followed by an address by
Rev. E. P. Tenney.   Chastened and subdued by the solemn
lessons of the hour, the people slowly dispersed to their
homes."

Thus ends, so far as the records are concerned, the
Great Civil War.   But so long as patriotism, unselfish devotion and daring heroism are valued by men,
will the War for the Union be remembered and its
actors embalmed in oration, story and song.

Year by year, the town recognizes its debt to the

living and the dead who rallied to the defence of the
nation in its hour of peril. Memorial services give
fitting expression to the people's gratitude and
patriotism, calling together the inhabitants without
distinction of rank, creed or nationality ; a pathetic
service as time thins the ranks and reminds the survivors that a few years will sweep away every living
representative of the Union armies. Let the Veterans meet as long as they are spared, to teach the
generations that have come upon the stage of action
the value of republican institutions and the indestruc-
tible virtues of valor and patriotism, that the traditions of generous sacrifice and heroic endeavor may
continue to inspire the nation to high resolve. to lofty
hope, to simple faith, down to " the last syllable of
recorded time." [1]

" It is wise, in a nation, to foster patriotism by preserving the memory of noble deeds for the imitation and inspiration of the coming generations. Money expended in mon-
uments and statuary and memorial days is not wasted, but
wisely invested." [2]

All honor must be paid to the noble women, whose
cheerful courage in days of darkness and horror did
so much to sustain the heart of the nation and to
nerve the soldier to his deeds of unshrinking courage
and endurance. Both during the War, in camp and
hospital, and at home in many a ministry of helpful-
ness and affection, did woman prove herself worthy
of the honor and love of her brothers who went for

[1] It may be remembered that a year ago Commander Maccabe of the
Sons of Veterans delivered a ringing warning against the danger that in
the general merry-making, the real spirit of Memorial Day might be forgotten.
[2] *Gen. R. Brinkerhoff*, at Columbus, O.

the defence of home and country to the tented field.
Her example will live and pass down among the
traditions that will instruct and animate coming
generations. The wearying days of suspense, the
burdens left upon wives and mothers, the care of the
sick and wounded, the ministering to the poor and
bereaved, the preparation of stores for the camp and
hospital, the filling of the place of husband and
father often in the shop and field — made woman's
lot in those days a sad and sorrowful one; but it
was one that was bravely and cheerfully borne, re-
lieving the dark hours of civil strife with "something
of an angel's light."

Of one thing we may be sure, as we recall the
awful and protracted contest, and all that it achieved
for human freedom and civilization, that the stern
strife has yielded fruits of inestimable value to our
people and our land. Because of it, we live freer
and happier lives to-day. The blood shed upon a
hundred battle-fields has not been shed in vain. It
may be said that the War was worth all that it cost,
in the lifting higher the standard of political morality, in clearing the air of miasmatic vapors, in breaking the fetters of a nation of bondmen, in establish-
ing the supremacy of Federal authority, and in emphasizing our dependence upon Him who is " Governor among the nations " and to whom " the shields
of the earth belong."

If the lessons of the War are forgotten in a generation of peace and prosperity, of fast-growing luxury and license, if our very success and greatness as
a nation prove our weakness, it will be only another

illustration of the truth confessed long ago by the Hebrew poet, "Except the Lord build the house, they labor in vain that build it; except the Lord keep the city, the watchman waketh but in vain."

NOTE. — An account of the Dedication of the Memorial Hall will be found in Chapter XI, and of the Consecration of the Burial Lot for the use of the Post, in Appendix C.

CHAPTER XI.
THE SUMMER RESORT.

"But times are alter'd."

GOLDSMITH: *The Deserted Village.*

"I made me great works; I builded me houses . . . . I gathered me also silver and gold . . . . so that I was great and increased more than all they that were before me in Jerusalem . . . . and whatsoever mine eyes desired I kept not from them, I withheld not my heart from any joy . . . . and this was my portion of all my labor."

Ecclesiastes.

"Manchester has become in our day a splendid watering place, known as such throughout the United States; so she finds gold eagles stitched into her dress."

C. A. BARTOL, D. D.

CHAPTER XI.

THE SUMMER RESORT.

THERE is no evidence that the early settlers and
voyagers, with one or two exceptions, saw in
the picturesque scenery of Cape Ann any
beauty that they should desire it. The nineteenth
century, even, was well advanced before this region
of wonderful beauty appears to have attracted any
special attention.

Whose vision was first unsealed to the scenic
beauty of the North Shore, its wonderful combination of forest and ocean, receding bay and winding
inlet, smooth meadow and rocky rampart, neither
history nor tradition informs us. Nature waited
long for an interpreter, or even an intelligent observer — for a poet like Whittier or Lucy Larcom, or
a writer of prose poems like the author of *Corona-
tion*, who first made known to many of his neighbors
and parishioners the beauties and glories amidst
which they had lived unconscious, as their forefathers had lived before them.

The celebrated Harriet Martineau, as guest of
Hon. Stephen C. Phillips of Salem, in 1835, rode

down to Manchester and over the "Smith farm,"
stopping at the red gate which then closed the road
to stray cattle, and looking over the panorama of
sea and shore, said, "It is enough to make a poor
man envious." But for all that was said or done to
bring her into notice, Manchester succeeded for
generations, like a coy maiden, in concealing her
charms from an outside world.

The earliest "summer resident" was Richard H.
Dana, the poet. Others had been here as summer
boarders, but in 1845 Mr. Dana, struck with the
romantic beauty of the region about "Graves'
Beach," purchased some thirty acres between the
water-line and the county road, mostly covered with
a luxuriant forest growth, and built the first summer house, a plain, substantial mansion, overlooking
the sea. In speaking of this retreat, Charles Sumner pronounced it finer in point of location and
scenery than the famous Biarritz, the summer resort
of Napoleon III. For many years the Dana family
made this their summer home. Richard H. Dana,
Jr., spent several summers in Manchester, and found
here a greatly needed respite from a laborious professional life.

Following the footsteps of the pioneer in this
direction, many persons of taste and culture and
wealth have made the town their summer home,
until Manchester-by-the-Sea [1] has become famous as

[1] This name is believed to have originated with the poet-publisher and
man of letters, James T. Fields. It is not altogether an English affecta-
tion, as might at first seem; there being a Manchester in each of the New
England States, the name Manchester-by-the-Sea serves often as a useful
differentiation, preventing mail matter from going astray, not to speak of
freight and passengers even.

one of the most beautiful, and latterly, one of the most fashionable watering-places in the country. Rev. Dr. Bartol has done more than any other man to bring Manchester into notice. By his early, far-sighted and well-managed investments, he has proved himself more of a "seer," even from a financial and economic point of view, than many who have been bred to the art of money-making.

It has been remarked by a writer [1] on physical geography, that as the climate and soil, land and water, disposition of continents and islands, trend of mountain-slopes and coast-lines, affect human development; so man in his turn changes the surface of the earth on which he lives, alters its configurations, modifies its climate and productions. One instance of this at hand, on a small scale, is seen in our own town and neighborhood in the preservation of woodlands and the cultivation of barren wastes, in the opening up of vistas and the change in water-fronts. Acres once covered with a tangled growth of wildwood, and considered too valueless for taxation,[2] have been threaded by romantic avenues, and beautified by lawns and gardens. The hills that rim around the "Cove" have been adorned with stately residences, embowered in natural forests. On the "Essex road," the woods have been preserved by purchase, through the efforts and liberality of summer residents,[3] to form a continuous shaded

[1] G. P. Marsh: Man and Nature.

[2] As an illustration of the increase of land value, the "White Beach Pasture," sold in 1884 by the town for $40,000, was a part of a farm bought in 1836 for $2,200 for a Poor Farm, with the town's share of the surplus revenue ($28,000,000) divided among the States by the Federal government.

[3] Through the energetic influence of Mrs. Alice N. Lincoln, a strip of

drive under leafy arches and between mossy and
fern-covered depths, with shafts of sunlight woven
with waving branches of hemlock, oak and pine.
The whole shore, "beautiful for situation," by nature,
has been further beautified by art, which has been
made to wait on nature rather than to conceal or
improve (?) it.

From the first Richard H. Dana [1] — *clarum et ven-*
erabile nomen — to the latest representative of the
new aristocracy, from senator, ex-governor and minister plenipotentiary to champion golf-player and
imported flunkey, from "tally-ho" to donkey-cart,
from Russian wolf-hound to my lady's lap-dog — an
influence more or less perceptible, but often indefin-
able, has been exerted upon the town by its summer
population. It has furnished a new social problem.
The magnates of wealth and society and letters who
have built and domiciled among us, and made the
old roads of Cape Ann alive with their varied and
brilliant equipages, have introduced changes "surpassing fable, and yet true."

Year by year, a transformation has been going
on, until it is doubtful if the fathers, were they to
revisit this earthly scene, would know the ancient
town. If the first rude fish-house on "Jeffrey's
Creek" and the "Essex County Club-House" of
to-day are not of a different genus, it would be interesting to know by what process of evolution and

seven rods on each side of the road, for a greater part of the way was
secured partly by gift, but mainly by purchase, the sum of $3,500 being
contributed for the purpose by summer residents in Manchester and Beverly; the whole being deeded with the condition that the wood be preserved forever.

[1] The name is perpetuated in Manchester to the fourth generation.

natural selection the earlier species has been transformed into the later. The difference between the two presents at least a variation of type suggestive of the wonderful metamorphoses which Manchester has undergone in the two hundred and fifty years of its varied and romantic history.

But the gain has not been all on the side of the town so altered and adorned. From season to season it has received the invalid, the toiler of the counting-room and mart, the lover of nature, the artist, the poet, the professional man, the society dame, the college student, " the city's fair, pale daughter," the children of wealth and pets of fashion; and sent them again to their homes and the routine of life with new vigor, with ozone in the brain and spring in the step, with the bloom of the wild-rose in the cheek, and the freshness of the salty sea in the rejuvenated frame. The most beautiful months, September and October, with their bright skies, crisp and bracing air, and " softly pictured woods," witness the departure of the summer crowd, and Manchester is left to its own quiet loveliness, to the occasional artist, and the people of combined taste and leisure who prolong their stay after most of the birds of passage have flown.

The period under review has been chiefly noted for the erection of many beautiful and stately private residences, often of great cost, and of architectural display. Some of these buildings are a decided ornament to the town, built in the old Colonial style or in the picturesque " Queen Anne." A stimulus has also been given to the building, enlarging and improving of their dwellings on the part of the permanent residents.

The erection of the Town Hall belongs to the period under notice. It was built in 1868. The size of the building was sixty-two by forty-two feet, and its cost $14,000. For twenty years the building answered its purposes. But with the growth of the town, it was found at last inadequate in size and in needed facilities for Town purposes. After much discussion, and after many plans had been suggested, the building was remodelled and enlarged, in the summer of 1893, at an expense of about $18,-000. It is now well adapted to the uses of such a building, well lighted, ventilated and heated, with good plumbing arrangements, and sufficient accommodations for many years to come.

The finest and most costly Public Building that Manchester has ever possessed is the Memorial Library Building. It is a gift to the town by one of the summer residents and property-holders, Hon. T. Jefferson Coolidge. The Library, which is the continuation or outgrowth of the old Lyceum Library, passed into the hands of the Town in 1871. It then consisted of about one thousand volumes. It gradually increased by purchase and gift until it reached in 1887, the number of about five thousand volumes. It had been kept in quarters that checked its growth, that were inconvenient and constantly exposed to danger from fire. The desirableness of a new, commodious and practically fireproof building had often been discussed, especially at meetings of

LIBRARY BUILDING

the " Elder Brethren," but no active steps had been taken in that direction.[1] In 1886, Mr. Coolidge signified to the town his desire to present to the citizens a suitable building for the use of the Library, including also a Hall for the Post of the G. A. R. His generous offer was accepted, and a committee appointed to superintend the erection, which was completed in the autumn of the following year.

The dedication services were held Oct. 13, 1887, and attended by a concourse of citizens only limited by the capacity of the building.[2]

The building is located on Union street, near the centre of the town, and is constructed of cut Ashlar with natural seam face — that is, the stone used was selected in the quarries where it joined the occasional seams found in ledges, where the moisture and air works its way down through, giving the stone a reddish brown color. The effect is to give the building a venerable look, in keeping with the architectural design and general appointments.

In the western end of the building, leading out from Memorial Hall, is the Grand Army Hall.

The eastern end of the building is occupied by the library room. Here the antique is especially prominent. The library room may properly be divided into two sections — one as a sort of reception apartment for visitors and the other devoted to the bookcases. Dividing the two sections is a sort of open partition of old English oak, inlaid with genuine ancient carvings brought from across the water, and centuries old. A panel in the partition bears the Latin

[1] In 1880, a special committee reported to the town plans for a Library Building and a Memorial Hall, which were accepted; but the town failed to make an appropriation.

[2] A full account of the exercises, including *verbatim* reports of the addresses, with fine photographs, is contained in a sumptuous volume printed for private circulation, entitled *Dedication Services of the Memorial Library, etc.*

inscription — BONA SIT TIBI SELECTIO OVAE SICVT BREVIS EST ITA IN AETERNVM.[1] The ceiling is arched and finished in light oak; while the floor of the reception portion is laid with strips of light oak in " herring bone " design.

In the summer of 1895, two bronze tablets were placed in Memorial Hall, to the memory of the soldiers and sailors of the earlier wars and of the war of the Revolution. They were designed by the committee on tablets, appointed in connection with the two hundred and fiftieth anniversary, and cast by the Paul Revere Brass Foundry, Boston.

The tablets bear the following inscriptions :[2]

I.

ERECTED BY THE TOWN
IN MEMORY OF THE
SOLDIERS OF THE EARLY WARS
AND OF THE
SOLDIERS AND SAILORS
OF THE WAR OF 1812

—

IN SAVAGE AMBUSH
AND ON SEA AS WELL AS LAND
THEY WON
UNDYING FAME

—

1895

[1] This may be freely translated, " Choose wisely — brief is the act, but the results are eternal."
[2] Furnished by Rev. D. F. Lamson.

II.

IN MEMORY OF THE
SOLDIERS AND SAILORS
OF THE REVOLUTION
THIS TABLET IS ERECTED BY
THEIR GRATEFUL TOWNSMEN

———

THEY SUFFERED
THEY FOUGHT
THEY DIED
IN
FREEDOM'S CAUSE

———

1895

Manchester seems always to have possessed a certain individuality. It is unique in its combination of land and ocean scenery, in its history and customs, in the cosmopolitan character of its later population, in the manner in which the old and new jostle each other in its streets, in its contrast of antique and homely simplicity with the latest "fads." But one of Manchester's most unique institutions is the organization known as the "Elder Brethren." Other towns have their lodges, councils, orders, posts, fraternities, clubs, of high and low degree ; but no other town can boast of its "Elder Brethren." The idea first originated in the gathering, dating as far back as 1870, of the older men of the community for the purpose of eating chowder, renewing oldtime fellowships and exchanging reminiscences. The thing proved to have life, and in time provided for

itself an outward organism, "a local habitation and
a name." What had been known as "The Old
Men's Chowder Party" organized, Aug. 15, 1878,
by the choice of George F. Allen as President, and
William H. Tappan as Secretary and Treasurer.
These officers have been reëlected each year. The
name "Elderlies" was at first given to the members,
who by tacit understanding were not to be under
fifty years of age. In 1885, the name "Elder
Brethren," suggested by Capt. Thomas Leach, appears in the Records. The same year the town built
a neat and comfortable pavilion at Tuck's Point, where
the meetings had been held, and a flag-staff, the gift
of Mr. Greely Curtis, was erected, from which the
"Stars and Stripes," with the banner inscribed
"Elder Brethren," presented by Capt. Thomas
Leach, annually floats.

The charm of the gatherings is largely in their
informal character. They bring together in the
month of August, from year to year, a large number,
usually over one hundred, of past and present citizens of Manchester, who spend the day in friendly
greetings, in talking of "days of auld lang syne,"
in discussing the weather, the tariff, the changes
along the shore, and the inevitable chowder. Dinner disposed of, and an adjournment being made to
the open air and the shade of the trees, there begins,
under the lead of the president, as a kind of informal
toast-master and prompter, the "feast of reason and
flow of soul." Many are the wise and weighty
sayings of these occasions, spiced with wit and
humor, and occasionally with somewhat pungent

hits ; but there breathes over all such an air of simplicity and frankness and good nature, that all is
taken in good part, and each annual gathering is
pronounced at parting the best.

Many projects promotive of public welfare have
been originated or discussed at these gatherings ;
among them may be mentioned especially the Library
Building, for the gift of which to the town the first
inspiration is said by the donor to have come to
him while listening to these informal, after-dinner
speeches.[1] The opening of the " old Wenham road,"
also, resulted from a speech made by Hon. J. Warren Merrill at one of the dinners aforesaid ; a boon
to lovers of wildwood and of shaded, winding paths
leading to Nature's heart. In fact, it has been said,
half seriously, that whatever measure was received
favorably by the " Elder Brethren", could be carried
in Town Meeting.

Now that this annual custom has attained the age
of a quarter of a century, it may not be amiss to
express the hope that it may continue as long as the
years come and go over this beautiful town, and that
its shadow may never be less.

The time, however, is not yet, to write the history of Manchester during the period which will be
considered by some the period of the town's prosperity and glory, and by some the period of its decline
and decay. It must be left for some future historian
fully to tell the story, and to strike the balance between the advantages and disadvantages of a modern
summer resort.

[1] *Vide* Mr. Coolidge's address at the Dedication of Memorial Library
Building, *Memorial Volume*, p. 10.

CHAPTER XII.

SCHOOLS.

"Custom is most perfect when it beginneth in young years; this we call education, which is, in effect, but an early custom."

BACON's *Essays.*

"Education, a debt from present to future generations."

GEORGE PEABODY, 1853.

"A Commonwealth can only rest on the foundation of the free public schools."

GOV. GREENHALGE: *Speech at Dedham,* Jan. 11, 1895.

CHAPTER XII.

EARLY CARE FOR EDUCATION — EARLY SCHOOLS — SCHOOL
HOUSES — DISTRICTS — NAVIGATION — HIGH SCHOOL —
SOME TEACHERS — DR. ASA STORY — LATER
HISTORY — "THE NEW EDUCATION" —
MASTER JOHN PRICE.

NEXT to freedom in civil and religious "concernments," our fathers valued a common-school education. At a session of the General Court of the colony of Massachusetts Bay, June 14, 1642, it was ordered:

That in every towne ye chosen men appointed for managing the prudentiall affajrs of the same shall henceforth . . . have power to take account from time to time of all parents and masters, and of their children . . . especially of their ability to read and understand the principles of religion and the capitall laws of this country, and to impose fines upon such as shall refuse to render such account to them when required.[1]

A more stringent ordinance was passed Nov. 11, 1647. It was to the end, as stated in the preamble,

" y^t learning may not be buried in ye grave of o^r fath^{rs} in ye church & commonwealth." It is therefore ord^{red} y^t ev^{ry} towneship in this iurisdiction af^{tr} ye Lord hath increased y^m to ye number of 50 household^{rs}, shall then forthwth ap-

[1] Massachusetts Colonial Records, vol. II, 6.

point one w^th^in their towne to teach all such children as shall resort to him to write & reade . . . & y^t^ where any towne shall increase to ye numb^r^ of 100 families or household^rs^, they shall set up a grammar schoole, ye m^r^ thereof being able to instruct youth so farr as they may be fited for ye university.[1]

As this was the first law of the kind ever passed by any community of persons or any State, Massachusetts may claim the honor of having originated the free public school.

The following extracts are gleaned from the Town Records, as illustrations of the early way of doing things. The dates are given in New Style.

Mar. 27, 1696. Leift. John Siblee Robart Leach & Thomas West wear chosen A comittee for & in ye behalfe of ye towne to treat & Agree with a Scoolmaster to teach our children to read & to wright & to make an Agreement if thay can with sd scoole master.

Dec. 13, 1717. voted that John beshup & Roberd Leech iunor shall Join with the selectmen As a Commettey to Loock for a scool mestres. voted the selectmen shall a gree with a scool Marster & that every Child sent to the scool master shall pay 5^d^ per week.

Mar. 27, 1721. Jabez Doodg was Chos scool master. it is voted to leuef ye a greing with ye scool master to ye selectmen and y^t^ the selectmen shall not Give him no more than 20 pounds per yere.

Feb. 10, 1724. voted that ye town should be taxed ten pounds yerely fower yers next insuing for the support of a free scool in sd town and no more then ten pounds a yere yerely ye sd fower yere to ye sd scool which is for all sexes for Reading & Writing Englesh and for sifering that belong to the town of manchester.

[1] Massachusetts Colonial Records, vol. II, 203.

Mar. 25, 1724. nathanel Lee was Chosen Scool master for sd town for to teach yᵉ Cheldren to Read English and to writ Englesh.

May 8, 1727. Chose a Commety to treet with our Revⁿᵉ Mʳ Chever & to know of him where he will provide us a Choole or not & if he refuses to provide for us any Longer allso to Racken with him for all his disbursments for the sport of a schoole & to bring the A count to the town at the a jornment.

Dec. 22, 1729. Voted to Give Mʳ Jonathan Parepint forty five pounds for him to keep a free schole in manchʳ for one year insuing. Voted that the presant select men shall be a Commity to a gree with Mʳ parepoynt, &c.

Mar. 9, 1731. Chosen for a Comety to Reglate a schoul in Manchʳ Mʳ Aaron Bennet & Mʳ Benjᵃ Allen & Mʳ Nathaˡˡ Marsturs.

Mar. 9, 1736, voted that the £50 voted for the support of a free schoole in Manchester the one half of sd £50 to be Expended to support 4 schoole Dams to keep a free schoole one at that part of our town caled Nuport & one in that part of our Town near the Meeting house & one in that part of our town Caled the plans & one in that part of our town Caled Cittal Cove the other half of sd £50 to be Expended to support a schoole master to keep a free schoole in the schoole house in manchester the fall & winter seson.

Mar. 13, 1738. voted to Tax the Town £60 for the support of a Schoole master to keep a free schoole in Manchester & the said Schoole to be Removed to the four quarters of the Town, they in Each part to provoide a Sieutable house for the schoole Master to keepe a Schoole in on there Charge to Acceptants & the Time and Place at the Discrestion of the Selectmen.

Mar. 16, 1742. Voted that yᵉ assessers shall assess yᵉ town for to Keep a Grammer School Eighty pounds.

June 24, 1755. voted that the assess shall assess the

Town Thirty Pounds money to Defray the Charge of a gramer School maste the year in suing.

Mar. 12, 1759. Voted that yᵉ assessors this Day Chosen shall assess yᵉ Town Twenty pounds Lawfull money to Defray yᵉ Charges of a Grammer School Six months next winter; and also to assess yᵉ Ton Twelve pound Lawfull money which sum is to be distributed to Three School Mistresses in Three different parts of yᵉ Town viz. The middle part of yᵉ Town Kettle Cove & Newport, and that yᵉ People Residing in yᵉ aforementioned part of yᵉ Town pay their Part of yᵉ aforesaid Twelve pounds in Proportion to their Tax.

Mar. 4, 1765. Voted fifty Pounds for a Gramer School, the People at Cittle Cove to Draw their Proportion of said Fifty Pounds for a schoole at sd Cove, and to have no Benefit of the Schoole in the Middle of the Town.

In the War of the Revolution, the schools shared in the general distress. On Nov. 4, 1775, the town voted " to Dismis the Town School from this Day." On Mar. 14, 1785, it was

Voted to Build a school house In the Town such as the Town shall agree upon — Voted that the school hous shall be bult 21 feet wide and 26 feet Longe with a upright Chamber — Voted that the Selectmen shall be a Commett to se that yᵉ school house is Bult on the same place ware the old school hous Now Stands.

As soon as the war cloud dispersed the light of learning again appeared. The new schoolhouse was a noble monument to the public spirit and enlightened liberality of the town. It is fortunate that it has escaped the " tooth of time." The building stood near the meeting house, and was sold in 1811, and removed to School street, near Saw Mill brook, where it was converted into a dwelling-house. It is now occupied by Miss Mary D. Giles.

1785. John Foster was chosen school-master for four years, at ten pounds per annum. " The town agrees to assess £100 for four years for the support of a free school, for bothe sexes to learn reading, writing, English and cyphering."

1818. The town voted to join the " middle district " [1] in building a school-house, " the town to build one half of the house, and become proprietors of the lower part, exclusive of furnishing the inside of the district room."

The building of this temple of learning appears from time-worn papers, in a small and careful handwriting, to have been an undertaking that taxed the ability and wisdom of the district quite largely; votes passed and reconsidered, exact terms of contracts for the work, precise statements of location, dimensions, etc., show the economical and thrifty habits of the time. Nothing but the simplest and most imperative needs were provided for. This was the building on School street, on the site of the present engine-house, formerly used for the Public Library and engine-house, now removed to the rear of Samuel Knight's residence, Central street.

A book containing the warrants and records of meetings of the Middle District in the handwriting of Fran⁵ Burnham and D. L. Bingham as District Clerks, shows the business of the District to have been conducted with all the formality and careful

---

[1] In 1789, the towns were divided into districts, for the purpose of facilitating the attendance of the children upon the schools; the schools were still to be under the direct control of the town. In 1817, school districts were made corporations, and were empowered to hold property for the use of the schools.

The district system came to an end in 1851. On April 17, the district chose a Committee to " convey the property of the district to the town," and so passed away this peculiar autonomy.

adherence to forms and precedents of a Town
Meeting.

Schools were taught at different times in private
houses. The exact location of the first school-houses
is now only conjectural, except that it seems reasonably certain that according to custom, a school-house
stood very early near the meeting-house, our forefathers thus signifying that religion and education
were fast friends and allies.

After the close of the war of 1812, a great impulse was given to all seafaring industries, and there
was an increased demand for nautical education.
This want was met in town by a school taught by
Stilson Hilton, who was " noted for his mathemati-
cal and nautical knowledge." Under his tuition,
young men were instructed in the mysteries of navigation for a moderate fee; and so successful was
this school of navigation that " there were soon more
than forty sea-captains from this town in command
of merchant vessels from different ports of the Commonwealth."

The records are very meagre and scanty, and it is
difficult to trace the evolution of our present school
system through its various stages.[1]

In 1848, the town voted " that there be a High
School established for the benefit of the whole town."
This was the introduction of the " High School Sys-
tem," as it is called in the Report of the Committee,

[1] According to the *Essex Memorial*, p. 160, there were in 1836, " three
public and private schools, besides a high school, instituted in 1835, now
under the direction of William Long, having forty scholars in the higher
English branches, and the ancient languages." The whole number of
scholars was about 400, and the amount paid for the support of schools,
$1,200.

as distinguished from "the former district system." The Committee was instructed "to put the Town Hall (so called) in suitable condition to accommodate the High School." The report for 1848–49 deals largely with this matter, and covers in all twenty-five closely-written foolscap pages; it is signed by Oliver A. Taylor, John C. Long and Larkin Woodberry, as Committee.

In 1855, Latin appears as an "extra" study in the High School course. Jonathan French, Jr., was the teacher.

The Report of 1859 discloses a very unhappy contention between the Committee and the teacher of the High School. It is of course an *ex-parte* statement, but unless it greatly misrepresents the matter, the committee appear to have been abundantly justified in dismissing the teacher and closing the school.

Mr. J. A. Gould and Mr. D. M. Easton are still remembered as teachers during this middle period of our educational history. Mr. Easton is spoken of as "a well qualified and faithful teacher," whose "methods of teaching are thorough and well calculated to interest and improve the scholars." He considered himself, as another Report states, "a school teacher and nothing but a school teacher," which was perhaps one secret of his success. Mr. French is remembered by his pupils as a teacher who was qualified to fit scholars for college, and who could teach any boy or girl who cared to learn. Virgil was his favorite Latin author, and he carried one class through the Æneid. Mr. French employed assistants, among them a French teacher, at his own charges, the school at times numbering eighty pupils and over. This was about high-water mark in the history of the High School. Under Mr. French music received more attention and became a feature of the school.

Mr. Gage and Mr. Joseph A. Torrey followed, and some others who remained but a short time. There are teachers *and* teachers. Mr. Torrey approved himself as a gentleman and a competent and efficient teacher, and won the respect and confidence of his pupils and of the town.

Among the teachers of the High School none has made for himself a larger place in town than Mr. Nathan B. Sargent. For length of service he has a remarkable record. He took charge of the school in 1866 and remained until 1888. Mr. Sargent was a teacher of rare qualifications, and his influence for over a score of years made a deep and lasting impress upon the characters of those who were so fortunate as to be numbered among his pupils.

The town seems always to have taken an interest in the education of its youth. The interest has sometimes flagged, however, and the schools have not always been kept up to the same standard of efficiency. The school-buildings, too, have not in former years always been adequate or creditable to the town. At present, however, the facilities for school education compare favorably with those provided by towns of similar size. There have been many improvements within the past few years in the *materiel* of education, in houses and apparatus espe-

STORY HIGH SCHOOL.

G. A. PRIEST SCHOOL.

cially. In 1889, a new house of small dimensions, but of the best modern plan and construction, was built at the "Cove." In 1890, the large and well-appointed building known as the "G. A. Priest Schoolhouse," was erected. It is a structure worthy of the town, an ornament to the village, and admirably fitted for the wants of graded school instruction.[1] The High School House, though not a new building, has been made by alterations and improvements, very serviceable and convenient, and occupies a beautiful and commanding position, from which the prospect of sea and land must exert insensibly a broadening influence upon the scholars' minds.

Among those to whose supervision the town has been greatly indebted for the efficiency of its schools, mention should be specially made of Dr. Asa Story, whose services rendered gratuitously for more than twenty years, are considered by intelligent judges to have been of great value.[2] The name of Dr. G. A. Priest first appears as one of the School Committee in the Report of 1868. He was elected to the office as often as his term of service expired until his death in 1888. He gave much time and attention to the schools, had a high standard of excellence, and was a master of details.

Information respecting the Schools, Teachers,

[1] The town voted March 19, 1895, to add a wing to this building at an estimated cost of $3,500, to accommodate the increasing number of scholars, and to enable the committee to extend the course of instruction in the higher grades.

[2] Tardy justice has been done to the memory of Dr. Story in this respect, by a vote in town meeting, March 19, 1895, that the High School be named the "Story High School"; a well deserved tribute to a worthy man and public-spirited citizen, that is all the more an honor because paid by a generation that never knew him personally.

School-buildings, etc., since 1859, is easily accessible in the Printed Reports, which are bound and placed in the Town Library.

The Trustees of the Library afford every facility to teachers, and scholars of the higher grades, in the use of books for reference and reading, thus increasing the value of the school work by enlarging and enriching it. In the Report for 1890, the Superintendent says, " The Trustees of the Public Library have kindly arranged to allow teachers to take out at one time a number of books that may be helpful in the school work, and keep them for a reasonable time." In the Report for 1893, a valuable classified List of " Books for Collateral Reading" prepared by the Superintendent, was printed, covering five pages.

Special instruction in Music was introduced into the schools in 1890, and in Drawing in 1891, since which time these studies have been a regular part of the curriculum. An evening school was opened in the winter of 1890–91, but the small attendance did not, in the judgment of the Committee, warrant its continuance.

In the Report for 1889, the committee called attention to the matter of employing a Superintendent of Schools, agreeable to the Acts of the Legislature of 1888, chap. 431. The next year the town acted upon the recommendation, and Mr. John B. Gifford was elected Superintendent. After serving to great acceptance one year, Mr. Gifford resigned, having accepted another position. Mr. J. F. Rich served during the years 1890 and 1891; and Mr. Gifford returned to the same office in 1893 and 1894.

The present Superintendent is Mr. Henry M. Walradt.

For some reason, Manchester has not furnished so many candidates for the honors of the college and the higher schools of learning, as some of the neighboring towns. But there has been of late years, something of an advance in this direction. In November, 1893, there were twenty-six young men and women pursuing study in Business Colleges, Academies, High Schools, Normal Schools, Technical Schools and Colleges. Perhaps the general education of the many is always to be placed above the special education of the few. But it is desirable that any community, however small, should always have some of its number seeking the most liberal culture that they can command. A few well-educated persons in a town raise the standard of intelligence for the whole people. It is from the heights that the springs flow to water and fertilize the plains and valleys.

The grading of the schools and the erection of the new, costly and finely equipped building for their accommodation have been held by many not only to mark an era in the educational history of the town, but to make sure its future progress indefinitely in the right direction. This might well be so, if buildings and systems insured education. But since more personal influences must be taken into account, such a foregone conclusion is not to be relied upon. Whatever may be said of the advantages of modern school methods and appliances, it is certain that the old, with all their crudeness, turned out some well-

educated and well-disciplined minds, minds that were
not all shaped after one pattern and run in one
mould.   It is possible in these days to decry the
old-fashioned district school in the "old red schoolhouse" too much.   It may have lacked most of the
modern improvements ; its course of study, if indeed
it had one, was probably meagre and defective ; its
maps, globes, blackboards, textbooks, were very
likely somewhat antiquated, if in fact it was not
destitute of some of these entirely ; it had not the
best and most intelligent supervision ; its teachers
were often selected in a somewhat haphazard manner, and they had no idea in general of devoting
themselves to the profession of teaching.   All these
things were drawbacks.   On the other hand, the
lack of a graded system gave the younger pupils the
stimulus of the acquirements and the example of the
best and brightest of the older ones ; the personality
of the teacher counted for more ; and there was generally a more intimate acquaintance with the school
on the part of parents and committees.

Whether the bringing of most of the scholars in
town into one building is an improvement in all
respects upon the old method,[1] is still a question in
the minds of some who are not infatuated with the
"New Education."   There are evils, it must be admitted, as well as benefits; the advantages of a better
classification may be partly counterbalanced by the
disadvantages of a more promiscuous association.
"But time tests all."   Wisdom has not been buried

[1] The small number in attendance in the out districts was the best
reason for discontinuing those schools.

with the fathers, nor have their children any monopoly of it.

"MASTER" JOHN PRICE.

The name of this patriarch of the school-room will call up with many the erect and stalwart form of one who was long known far and near as a successful teacher, and who was identified for more than sixty years with the best interests of the town.

Master Price was born in Tamworth, N. H., Jan. 18, 1808. He came to Manchester in 1828, and taught first the " Newport " and then the " Middle " school. In the latter, he had in one term 159 names on his roll, and in one day 105 pupils. He taught this school five years, and it has been said, " From this time a very marked improvement in the educational system of the town may be dated." The discipline of the schools was better, and the methods of instruction improved. In 1836, Mr. Price opened a private school, which he taught until 1872, when he retired from active life. A remarkable feature of this school was that pupils came to it from almost all over the world, owing to the reputation that it had gained among merchants and shipmasters of Salem and Boston. In all, Master Price numbered as his pupils about seventeen hundred, of whom he had the names of all upon his rolls except those of the first school.

On Sept. 7, 1891, a Reunion of the old pupils was held, an occasion which proved to be of unique interest, and which was alike honorable to teacher and scholars.

It is proper to add that Mr. Price was for many years Deacon of the Congregational Church, member of the Board of Selectmen and of the School Committee, Town Treasurer, member of the Essex County Teachers' Association from 1830, and associated with educational and temperance work in many different ways while he lived among us. He was a gentleman of the old school, courteous, dignified and self-respecting. He died April 19, 1895, in the eighty-eighth year of his age. Had he lived until the town's historic anniversary in the present year, his would have been one of the most noticeable figures on that memorable occasion.

CHAPTER XIII.

CHURCHES AND CHURCH BUILDINGS.

"The church of the living God, which is the pillar and ground of the truth."

PAUL.

" Great is the Lord our God,
    And let His praise be great;
He makes His churches His abode,
    His most delightful seat.

These temples of His grace,
    How beautiful they stand !
The honors of our native place,
    The bulwarks of our land."

WATTS.

CHAPTER XIII.

CHURCHES AND CHURCH BUILDINGS.

THE TENT AND ALTAR — THE FIRST MINISTERS — THE CHURCH
AND LATER MINISTRY — THE SUNDAY SCHOOL — THE
MEETING-HOUSES — THE PARSONAGES — THE
BAPTIST CHURCH — OTHER CHURCHES
— PAST AND PRESENT.

IT was found impossible to present the subject of this
Chapter with anything like completeness, without extending the History beyond desirable limits. Much
matter prepared with considerable labor was necessarily
omitted in the final revision. Ample materials exist for a
history of the old church and parish, which it is to be hoped
will be undertaken sometime by some competent hand.[1]
If the earlier history seems to occupy a disproportionate
space, it is to be remembered that in Massachusetts for a
long time the parish and town were practically one.

One of the first things with our fathers was a care
for the maintenance of a gospel ministry. Life
without the institutions of religious worship would
have been a meagre thing. The church was the
centre around which all the interests of the community revolved.

The first meeting in town for public worship, according to tradition, was held under a tree on

---

[1] Besides the Town, Church and Parish Records, there are Dr. Leach's
"Collections," a MS. History of the First Church by O. A. Taylor, and a
volume of notes on the Ministers and their Families by the late Dea. John
Price, presented by his direction, after his death, to the Historical Society.

"Gale's Point," but the name of the preacher around whom gathered the little band of settlers with bowed heads and reverent hearts, is lost in oblivion.

Dr. E. W. Leach has preserved, pasted on one of the leaves of his "Collections," a little scrap of yellow paper, giving in the handwriting of Rev. Ames Cheever the names of the early ministers of Manchester; the record bears date, Nov. 20, 1726. The names are as follows: — Ginners, Smith, Stow, Dunnum, Millett, Hathorn, Jones, Winborn, Hubbard, Emerson, Goodhue, Eveleth, Webster.

Of most of these early ministers we have but very slight information. Some of them may have only supplied the pulpit for a time. We know as much, perhaps, of Ralph Smith as of any; and of him it may be said that we know too much. He is spoken of as "a man of low gifts and parts." Cradock warned the colonists against him, adjuring them not to suffer him to remain "unless he be comfortable to our government." He was probably a man with too many defects of character to be useful in the ministry, and he soon laid down the office. John Winborn, who came in 1667, found his residence here far from pleasant. In 1686, the town voted "that he forthwith provide for himself and family some other place"; after considerable altercation, the money questions involved were settled by compromise. In 1689, Rev. John Everleth was invited to preach as a candidate. In September, he engaged to preach for £23 per year. In 1690, it was voted that a contribution be taken up each

Sabbath for the minister in addition to the salary ; the gifts to be " wrapped in a paper, with the name of the contributor upon it " ; practically, the modern " weekly envelope" system. In 1693, Mr. Everleth seems to have been formally called to be the minister of the town. The following action shows the reverence which the fathers paid to Scripture precedent and precept :

Att a town meeting legaly warned & mett together on ye 7th of July 1693 to consider of some efectuall way for ye incorigment & setling a minister in our town namely Mr. John Evelyth hom we have already had experience of his preaching ye gosple to us & knowing it is our Duty to Doe our utmost endeavour for ye obtaining & maintaigng ye ministry of ye gosple Amongst us considering also ye ill consequences may follow if we should neglect our Duty herein & soe be Destitute of such means whom god hath ordained for ye everlasting salvation of immortall souls for which we have remarkable instances in ye Scriptures which is written for mans instruction as in ye 2d book of cronicles ye 15 ch: 3 & 5 ver: now for a long seson Israell had been without A teaching profit & what folowes in ye 5th ver: it is said their was noe peace to him yt went out nere to him yt came in but great vexation wear upon all ye inhabitants of yt people & in prob: ye 29th chap. 18 ver: wheir their is noe vision ye people perish & against ye prists lips should preserve knowlige & thou shalt enquire at his mouth & contrarywise when Duty is atended in this great & momentary work as we may in ye 2d of chronicls 31 ch: 10: ver: when ye people brought in freely great store of provitions for ye prests of ye Lord yt ye Lord blessed ye people greatly & in ye epistle of corinth 13 ch: 14: Doe you not know yt they which minister about holy things live of ye things of ye temple, & they yt wait at ye Alter as pertakers with ye Alter soe hath ye Lord ordained yt they which preach ye gosple should live of ye gosple. Under this & ye like considerations it is voted & fully

Agreed by yᵉ town upon yᵉ Day Above written firstly to
pay to Mr. John evely yᵉ sum of 35 pounds per annum in
mony for his yearly salary yᵉ sᵈ salary of 35 pounds to be
paid on every quarter or quarterley by equall proportion yᵉ
1ˢᵗ year begining upon yᵉ 1ˢᵗ Day of August next ensuing
yᵉ Date heir of so long as he doth continue with us, etc.[1]

After all this, Mr. Everleth, it seems, would not
consent to settle in town as its minister, but he continued to preach until August, 1695. Mr. Everleth
is spoken of as a man of good attainments, and was
highly respected. In 1690, after the arrival of Sir
William Phipps with the new Charter, which was
not altogether to the liking of the people, Mr. Everleth was sent to Boston as deputy to present the
town's objections to it, an evidence that he enjoyed
the public confidence.

The next minister who was settled was Rev. John
Emerson. He remained but a few years. He is
spoken of as "an eminent and faithful preacher."
The Rev. Nicholas Webster was settled in 1698, and
remained until 1715. But little is known of him.
There is a tradition, however, that he filled the office
well.

At a town meeting on Dec. 5, 1715, it was

Voted to have a minester to pretch the gospell to us as
soone as we can conveniently in order to a furder setlement
and a commete is chosen to look out for a minester and
seack the advice of our neighboring minesters in the towns
next to us which are as followeth Mr. Robbert Leach sener
Samuell lee sener Samuell allin sener Aron bennet william
hilton John bishop Beniemen Allen thomas pitman Samuell
leach Robert warin John foster John lee junʳ & nathaniell

_____
[1] *Town Records*, i, 53.

marsters which commete are hereby fully impowered to
mete & agree with a minester to preach the gospell to us &
to give such incorragement to him as they can agree for and
the above s^d commete are impowered to intreat our neighboring ministers to help us in keeping afast Day to seke of
god a right way for ourselves and our children & so pray
unto god that he would be pleased to send forth a faithful
laborer into this little parte of his vineyard, etc.[1]

As the result of this action, Rev. Ames Cheever,
a grandson of the celebrated Ezekiel Cheever, was
ordained Oct. 4, 1716. The church was organized
on Nov. 7 of the same year. The church members
had been connected with the church in Salem up to
1677, when they were gathered in Beverly, until
they were dismissed " in order to their coming into
a church state by themselves." The names of those
thus dismissed were, John Sibley and wife, John Lee,
Robert Leach, Samuel Stone, Samuel Lee, John
Knowlton and children (John, Joseph and Abigail),
Benjamin Allen, Joseph Allen and wife, Jabez Baker
and wife, Josiah Littlefield, Jonathan Allen.

With Mr. Cheever's ministry we emerge from a
haze of antiquity, in which the forms of the earlier
ministry are seen in shadowy outline. With Mr.
Cheever commenced the history of the church. He
was a man of good parts and highly useful in the
formative period of the church's history. He took a
warm interest in education, and appears from the
records to have supplied in part by his private tuition a frequent lack in the public provision for schools.
Mr. Cheever was pastor of the church for twenty-
seven years, and died Jan. 15, 1756. His grave has

[1] *Town Records*, i, 131.

recently been located with reasonable certainty, and marked with a simple tablet erected by his descendants. Among Mr. Cheever's memoranda, brought to light a few years ago, mention is made of Elizabeth Bennett, "an aged widow," who was the "first born in Manchester in 1644." She was "baptized" by Mr. Cheever in 1717, at the age of seventy-three years. Her maiden name was unknown.

Mr. Cheever's pastorate closed Feb. 27, 1743. The church was for nearly two years without a pastor. But they were not content long to remain so. The times might be hard, but our fathers in all their poverty and straitness did not feel that they could afford to be without the ministrations of the church. In 1744, the town voted "not to Chouse A Represantivie having ye Leberty of the Law so to Do," and a "Committy" was chosen to "apply themsevels to a Seuttebell Person to Prepare a Pretion to ye Generall Court for sum relese under our Decaing Surcomstances." At an adjourned meeting, to hear the report of a committee appointed to "Tack Advice in our Reselment of a Pastar," it was "voted to apply our savels to Mr Moses Hall In order to here him Prach sum time among us."

After hearing several candidates, in 1744 the town invited Mr. Benjamin Tappan to be their minister. A committee was chosen to arrange the terms of settlement. The original document, a somewhat lengthy paper, and in some respects curiously illustrative of the times, is in the possession of the Historical Society. The town agreed to give Mr. Tappan Four Hundred and Fifty Pounds, old tenor, towards

his " settlement," and to pay yearly One Hundred
and Forty-eight ounces of silver, or Bills of Credit
equal to 148 ounces. They also promised " a suffi-
ciency of fire wood for his own family," and declared
it to be their " Intent and Design to cut and Hale"
the same, though " not absolutely engaging to cut &
Hale it, lest the same should come to be a Town
charge." Mr. Tappan continued in the ministry
until his death, May 6, 1790. An idea of his exact
and methodical habits may be had from a communication from him to the Town Treasurer, a fac-simile
of which is given.

A letter written by Mr. Tappan to his son Benjamin,
dated Manchester, February 7, 1770, with the address, " *For
Mr. Benjamin Tappan, of Northampton, Goldsmith,*" is
printed in the Memoir of Mrs. Sarah Tappan, p. 136. It
shows Mr. Tappan to have been a most affectionate father,
and deeply solicitous for his children's welfare. Its closing
appeal reminds one of David's lament for Absalom, in its
tenderness and pathos. It would seem that Mr. Tappan's
character was one that has not always been fairly estimated.
The more that is known of him, the more he appears to
have been a most excellent and estimable man. He was
probably somewhat reserved, and only children and near
friends knew what depths lay beneath the calm exterior.

[A picture of ecclesiastical affairs and Sabbath customs
in Mr. Tappan's time will be found in Appendix A. See
also Appendix B for a more detailed biographical notice of
Mr. Tappan.]

After the decease of Mr. Tappan the vacancy was filled
by Rev. Mr. Blake and Mr. Worcester until September,
1791, when a committee was chosen in behalf of the church
and parish to give an invitation to Rev. Ariel Parish to
settle with them. He accepted, and a committee of eleven
were chosen to determine the conditions of settlement, and

March 12. 1784.

Dear Sir!

When I gave you a receipt, upon the receipt
instant, for seventy pounds for the year 1783,
my meaning was to acknowledge a receipt, togra
and the Tax, the receipt of all which was so-
from for that year— & the so saying, & a my act
and to help no to friend.— and the same was and is
the meaning that and every of the receipts I gave
heretofore given to you and for my Treasurer.—and
if it will give any satisfaction, I am ready to pro-
vise get the Town of Manchester that several have a
farthing demanded of it by me or any of mine, upo
either of they accounts, for any on of the Years for which
they settled with the Treasurer and gave receipts;—and
this I do hereby promise perminic & engage.—

Your Sincere friend, &c—

Benja Tappan

B: The money is intended
to find me and mine for
every year antecedent to
seventeen hundred eighty
four—excepting 1778.—

Mr. Parish was ordained April 4, 1792, and labored dili-
gently until May, 1794, when the church and the people
were called to mourn his early death. He died in the
thirtieth year of his age, and in the third year of his
ministry.

A writer of an obituary notice thus remarks :

" While he was decidedly one of the strictest of the
Calvinistic school, no man ever manifested a more candid
or placid temper towards those who had adopted a different
creed. The uniform decision, with which he embraced his
own opinions, led him as decidedly to yield the same privilege to others. His sermons were uniformly plain and practical, without harshness of controversy or the show of
ornament. His elocution in the pulpit was manly, distinct
and pathetic, and doubtless had his days been prolonged, he
would have risen to eminence. Whilst he lived, he was
distinguished for his easy and social suavity of manners by
which he won the affections and reigned in the hearts of his
people; for he shared their joys and sympathized in their
sorrows. A letter from a member of his church thus closes:
' He was cut off in the morning of life and the tears of
many watered his grave.' "

Mr. Parish was the son of Elijah Parish, of Andover ;
was born in 1764 ; he graduated at Dartmouth College,
1788 ; he married Hannah Chute, of Byfield, and had one
daughter, who died in Manchester in 1793 ; another was
born after his death.

Mr. Parish occupied the house now owned by
Mrs. William Hooper, on Washington street. His
grave is in the " Old Burial Ground," next to that of
his predecessor, Rev. Benjamin Tappan. Mr. Parish's
death was the second in the dreadful fever that
almost decimated the little town.[1] The early death of
the young and beloved pastor must have caused a

[1] *Vide* Appendix L.

heavier gloom of sadness to fall upon the stricken village.

A vote passed by the town Jan. 12, 1792, gives a glimpse of a historic controversy in the New England churches. The vote reads as follows : " That Mr. Ariel Parish Baptize all Children who Shall be offered upon what is Called the Half Covenant." From this it appears that the Church at this time held to the " Half-way Covenant." It was the resistance of Edwards and others to this measure that finally led to the formation of the Unitarian and Orthodox parties in the Congregational churches of New England in the early part of this century. It is a long-since extinct controversy, which we can now survey as calmly as tourists survey the burned-out crater whose active fires once carried devastation to many a smiling hamlet and fruitful vineyard.

From the death of Mr. Parish in 1794, to 1801, a period of seven years, the church was supplied by different ministers. The names of seventeen of these ministers have been preserved.[2] Through all this interregnum, it seems that there were watchful and jealous eyes upon the walls, lest some thief or robber should climb up some other way ; for in 1795, August 10, we are told, " The Methodists were forbidden to worship in the Town house " ; the fol-

[1] The original document is in the possession of the Historical Society ; it is written in a handsome hand, and signed

" A Trew Coppy, Attested

Aaron Lee T Clerk."

Mr. Parish, we are told, was opposed to this measure. *Brief History, Articles of Faith*, etc., 1851, p. 11.

[2] They are Hall, Neal, Wood, Kimball, Merritt, Jackson, Tompkins, Stone, Page, Crafts, Coffin, Dow, Spofford, Long, Flint, Mercy, Dana.

lowers of John Wesley then being objects of almost universal suspicion and dislike. What would the fathers have thought if they could have cast the horoscope of a century? Under the same date it was ORDERED, that "the article in the warrant respecting a Hopkentian minister be passed over," a reminder of the Hopkinsian controversy between the disciples of Samuel Hopkins and Jonathan Edwards that was then at its height.

May 23, 1801, Abraham Randall, of Stow, "the fortieth candidate," accepted an invitation to settle as pastor. He was ordained Sept. 2, 1801. He had a "settlement" of five hundred dollars, and a salary of three hundred and thirty-four dollars, with the "improvement of the ministerial land." Mr. Randall was born in Stow, 1771; graduated at Harvard, 1798, and studied divinity under Prof. David Tappan of Cambridge and Rev. Dr. Dana of Ipswich. He was dismissed, Aug. 17, 1808.

The next pastor was Rev. James Thurston, who was settled on Jan. 10, 1809, with a salary of five hundred and fifty dollars, and "the use of the parsonage property." Mr. Thurston's pastorate was marked by an extensive and powerful revival of religion during its first year, illustrating the principle, "One soweth and another reapeth." In 1810, one hundred and ten were added to the church.[1]

In the same year, a Sunday school was organized, being one of the earliest formed in New England. The origin of the school was due to two young

---

[1] An account of this revival was published in the *Panoplist*, vol. III, p. 550.

ladies who afterward became famous as Harriet
Newell and Ann Haseltine Judson, two of the earliest of American missionaries to the East. It was
through their influence that Miss Eliza Tuck, Mrs.
Martha Lee, Miss Mary Bingham, and Miss Abby
Hooper undertook what was then an almost untried
experiment, which proved so successful that the
school soon gained the confidence of pastor and
church, and became in a few years large and flourish-
ing. The years from 1837 to 1843 are spoken of as
"palmy days" in the history of the school. On one
Sunday, the number present was 355. The ages of
the scholars ranged from three to eighty years. Mr.
Andrew Lee was an earnest worker in the school.
Dea. John Price was Superintendent about thirty
years. "One hundred names appear on the records
of persons who recited the Assembly Catechism, and
received a Bible as a reward." This was during the
period from Feb. 2, 1848, to May 17, 1857.

On June 24, 1885, the Sunday school celebrated
its seventy-fifth anniversary. There were present
two ladies who were present at the first session of
the school, three quarters of a century before —
Mrs. Lydia Osborne, aged eighty-three, and Mrs.
Hannah Colby, aged eighty-two.

The beginning of Mr. Thurston's pastorate seemed
bright with promise; the large additions to the
church and the interest in the new department of
the Sunday school augured well for the future.
But the day that dawned so bright, was soon
clouded, and Mr. Thurston's pastorate was on the
whole a stormy one. An unfortunate cause of mis-

understanding arose, criminations and recriminations followed, and witnessing angels sorrowfully turned their faces aside. The contention resulted in the dismissal of Mr. Thurston, July 9, 1819.

On July 27, 1821, the church and society united in calling Rev. Samuel M. Emerson, a graduate of Williams College, as pastor. They offered him a salary of four hundred and fifty dollars, fourteen cords of wood "at the house," and "the improvement of all the parsonage land." Mr. Emerson was installed, Sept. 12, 1821. The commencement of Mr. Emerson's pastorate was a somewhat troublous one owing to dissensions in the church; but his wise, energetic and peace-making administration resulted in a restoration of harmony. He labored assiduously and acceptably until his health began to fail in the spring of 1839, and in September following he asked for a dismissal, which was granted.

Mr. Emerson's ministry was marked by several important events in the history of the church. In 1825, the articles of faith and covenant of the church were printed for the first time, with the names of the members. In 1833, the church put on record the following Minute, taking advanced ground in the matter of Temperance; for it must be remembered that no such stigma attached to the use of intoxicating liquor as a beverage as at present; it was freely dispensed on all occasions, at ordinations, at weddings, at funerals ; it was used by ministers and deacons ; the "Washingtonian" movement was yet in the future. This vote has therefore special significance: —

"Whereas the use of *Ardent Spirits* has been the fruit-ful cause of numerous evils, which admit of no remedy but that of *total abstinence*, and as it is the incumbent duty of the churches to maintain a high standard of Christian morality, it will from this time be required of all persons presenting themselves as candidates for admission to this church, to abstain from the use of *Ardent Spirits* in all its forms, except as a medicine."

In the winter of 1838–39, while Mr. Emerson was in feeble health, a revival occurred under the preaching of Rev. Leonard Griffin of Gloucester, a Methodist minister. Mr. Griffin was a man of power in the pulpit, and of a truly Christian spirit. The revival was conducted with wisdom, and resulted in large additions to the church. Mr. Griffin is still affectionately remembered by the few who remain who shared his evangelistic labors. Mr. Emerson preached a few months in Heath, Mass., after leav-ing Manchester, and died in that mountain town, July 20, 1841.

With regard to the dissolution of the pastoral re-lation, his daughter, Mrs. Mary Emerson Brown, writes under date, Nov. 21, 1894:

"Though but ten years of age when broken health obliged my father to leave his much loved charge, I have not forgotten those days, so sad to my parents, of parting from the many friends who during all the years of faithful ministry had become very dear to them. I remember hear-ing my mother say how very patient the people had been through all my father's protracted illness, hoping these months of waiting might result in ultimate recovery."

This is a testimony honorable alike to pastor and people.

The successor of Mr. Emerson was Rev. Oliver A.

Taylor, who accepted the charge of the church, with a salary of seven hundred dollars. He was installed Sept. 18, 1839, and continued his labors until his death, Dec. 18, 1851. Mr. Taylor spent his boyhood days in Hawley, Franklin County; graduated at Union College, 1825; and studied theology at Andover. He was one of a remarkable family, both father and mother being distinguished for piety and character, and four of the sons becoming ministers of the gospel.

Mr. Taylor was somewhat noted among his ministerial brethren as a scholar and a writer. His life, written by a brother, Rev. Timothy A. Taylor, shows him to have been a man of strong character, of well-disciplined mind, of large attainments, and thoroughly devoted to the work to which he had been called. He suffered for most of his life the drawback of ill health.

Mr. Taylor was a good Hebraist and was acquainted with the Arabic. And what was still more remarkable in his day, he was a good German scholar.

Mr. Taylor was not a man who loved controversy. He admitted that he "could not bear the cross-cuts and sharp retorts of debates." He was ill-fitted for the stormy era of anti-slavery discussion, and sometimes seemed to his friends over-cautious and timid. But none ever doubted his sincerity and true goodness of heart. When he finished his course, the town lost a faithful minister and a true man. His funeral was attended in one of the wildest winter storms that ever swept our coast.

Rev. Rufus Taylor, a brother of the former pastor, was installed May 6, 1852. On his return from a voyage to Russia for his health, in 1856, he was " very cordially received," and presented with a purse of one hundred and twenty-five dollars by his parishioners. The next year, however, a growing dissatisfaction resulted in a sundering of the pastoral relation. Mr. Taylor continued to preach in the meeting-house until late in the fall of 1857, when with a minority of the church and society he began to hold services in another building, " they claiming to be the First Congregational Church." A council, convened Dec. 16, 1857, decided " that neither party without the other had a claim to be the Congregational Church, and dismissed Mr. Taylor from all his church and parish relations." The number of seceding members was seventy-nine, the number who remained was one hundred. Mr. Taylor wisely accepted the decision of the council and left the town. He afterward received the degree of Doctor of Divinity, and died at his home, Beverly, N. J., Aug. 18, 1894, at the age of eighty-three years and a few months.

The minority continued to maintain separate services, effected a church organization, and called Rev. Francis V. Tenney as pastor. He was installed Aug. 15, 1858, and the present Chapel was fitted for the use of the church and society. A reunion of the two churches was brought about in 1869, and the Chapel was presented by Mrs. Abby H. Trask to the original society by whom it is now used for social meetings.

The successor of Rev. Rufus Taylor was Rev.
George E. Freeman who was ordained October 5,
1858, and dismissed at his own request, November
18, 1862.   Mr. Freeman's pastorate was not
noteworthy in any particular.   He had the confidence of the people as "a good minister of Jesus
Christ."

Rev. Edward P. Tenney became pastor, Nov. 3,
1862, and continued in that relation until Sept. 30,
1867.   Mr. Tenney's pastorate included the greater
part of the period of the Civil War, and was helpful in many ways to the interests not only of the
church but of the town.   It is not invidious to say
that Mr. Tenney's preaching was of an original
order, suggestive and richly imaginative, reminding
the more thoughtful of his hearers of the odor of far-
gathered herbs and flowers.   Since leaving the pastorate, Mr. Tenney has been engaged in educational
and literary work.

Rev. George L. Gleason succeeded Mr. Tenney;
he was installed April 7, 1869, and dismissed by
council at his own request, Sept. 21, 1881.   He is at
present pastor in Haverhill, Mass.   Mr. Gleason is
pleasantly remembered by many not belonging to his
particular sheep-fold as the genial minister and
everybody's friend.

In recent years the changes have been frequent.
Rev. D. O. Clark was installed April 20, 1882, and
left Feb. 6, 1885.   Rev. Daniel Marvin followed
from March, 1886, to November, 1892.   He was succeeded by Rev. J. P. Ashley for about six months,
and by Rev. Samuel Reid for about the same length

of time. The present pastor, Rev. Francis A. Fate, was installed Nov. 1, 1894.

The later history is briefly dismissed, chiefly because it lacks perspective. Events which seem unimportant in the passing, stand out with bold relief very often when viewed through the lengthened vista of years. And men who are seen too close at hand do not always show their real stature and dimensions to us. We know men better, often, after they are dead than when they are living.

Names of the Deacons of the Church.

Benjamin Allen, Samuel Lee, Benjamin Lee, Jonathan Herrick, John Tewksbury, John Allen, Jacob Tewksbury, D. L. Bingham, Nathan Allen, Andrew Brown, Enoch Allen, Albert E. Low, Henry Knight, John Price, John Fowler, Oliver Roberts, Andrew Brown, Daniel Leach, F. A. P. Killam.

MEETING HOUSES.

The meetings of the first settlers for religious worship were probably held in private houses. In 1656, appears the following record:

" Ye 2ᵈ of ye 12 mo. It was at a general town meeting agreed upon that a meeting-house should be built, 18 feet long, with two Gable ends, to be set near the Landing-place, and the planters are to come and cut the timber this day fortnight. William Bennett, John Pickworth and Samuel Friend are to oversee the getting of the timber and if any man neglects to work he is to give a sufficient reason for his absence or pay 5 shillings for his neglect." [1]

In 1691, the meeting-house was found too small and much in need of repair. The following record is dated " eighteenth day of January 169½ " ;

" Whereas our old meeting house being the most part Considerable part of it Rottun and the sd house also being too small to Acomodate our people When Conveined to gether for the Worship and service of god It is therefore voted and fully agreed to have a new meeting hous built of these Dimentions [thirty by twenty-five feet, sixteen feet in height], with a — belvery on the top of sd house suteable for a good Bell of about a hundred Waight or more and three galeries to be built that is to say one on won side of the whole Length of sd house and the other tow at each end the whole breadth of sd house . . . the sd house be every ways Completely finished with seats and all other decent and suteable Apartainances theirto Convieniant.[2]

This house was not fully paid for until 1695, when an assessment was made on forty-nine persons

[1] This action on the part of the town anticipated by almost twenty years any compulsory legislation. It was in 1675 that it was enacted that a meeting-house should be erected in every town in the colony.

[2] *Town Records*, i, 44.

to defray the cost, amounting to £111 16s.   It was sold in 1720 for £12.   In 1695, a Bell was presented by George Norton; it was not hung, however, until the following year.

In 1696 a Committee was appointed

" to seate each and every parson from time to time as thare is ocation in the sd meting hous Acording to each and every persons proportion that he paid towards the building of the sd hous and allso According to what such Doe now pay to the ministry as nere as they can unless in case of any antient grave sober persons and of good conversation."

AN ANCIENT LANDMARK.

THIRD MEETING-HOUSE, 1720-1809.

Oct. 28, 1696, " it was voted and agreed to give to Ephraim Jons one pound and fower shillings per year for to ring the bell and swepe the metting hous and to perform the office of a sacston acording to the orders of the sealect men."

This house seems not to have met the wants of the people, as in less than thirty years it was re-

placed by another and larger house; the action of
the town betokens earnestness and liberality, joined
with a thrifty economy. A vote was passed, Dec.
22, 1719, "to bueld a new Meting house as fast as
it can be Dun." This house was to

"be buelt 49 feet Long and 35 feet wied and 20 feet stud,"
and was to be "planket and not studed." At the same
meeting, the Committee were instructed to "agree with a
artefeshal workmen to oversee yᵉ workers & to work themselves as Cheep as they can."

The front door of this house, with its home-made
latch and strap hinges, has done
duty for many years in the southern end of the Foster warehouse;
it is now much dilapidated. The
sounding-board, after being built
into the ceiling of a house at
West Manchester, was secured a
few years ago by Dea. A. E. Low
and deposited in the Public Li-
brary Building. A "pew for Negroes" was built
in this house in 1737.

In 1750, the town voted "To Repear the Meeting
house." It was at this time that the remarkable
action was had:

"Voted that the Proprietors in the Meeting house in
Manchester And the Non propritors vote together in Town
Meeting in the affair under consideration viz for Repear-
ing or Inlarging the said Meeting house any Law or Reason to the Contrary notwithstanding."[1] In 1752, it was
voted "To Build a Stephel." It was in 1754, however,
that it was actually built "from the ground upward."[1]

[1] *Town Records*, ii, 58.

In the same year a weathercock was provided by the town.[1] In 1785, a bell was purchased weighing three hundred pounds, and costing £58 3s. 7d. This bell remained in the steeple until 1845, when it was replaced by the munificence of a citizen by a much larger one.

In 1809, a new Meeting-house was built at a cost of eighty-five hundred dollars. It is a fine specimen of the church architecture of New England of that period. It occupies about the same site as that occupied by the former meeting-houses. It has undergone but little change in its exterior, the proprietors wisely withstanding any tendency to modernize the historic and venerable structure. It was built of the best materials, and its solid timbers bid fair to outlive another century. The interior of the house was remodelled in 1845 ; the old square pews were removed and some other changes were made. The arched window in the rear of the pulpit has rendered a useful service since taken from its original position, in a small building belonging to Mr. Solomon D. Allen, on Bennett street. An oval tablet which was above the window and bore the inscription, " BUILT, 1809," has recently been discovered in the tower among some rubbish, and has been regilded and now marks the date of erection on the front of the edifice. Another tablet on the front of the pulpit with the ecclesiastical device " I. H. S.," has long since disappeared. It would be interesting to

[1] This is the same as still surmounts the tower of the present church. having looked the wind in the eye for one hundred and forty years. Its cost was £7 10s. 8d.

242]   CONGREGATIONAL CHURCH.

know the history of such an inscription in a church and town of so purely Puritan lineage.

It was not until 1821, that the house possessed any means of warming it in the bitterest winter weather. Our ancestors were content with "foot-stoves,"[1] and sat out the long sermons and prayers without flinching. After considerable delay and opposition, and many arguments that the proposed innovation would render the young puny and effeminate and endanger the health of the congregation, "a heavy cast-iron box stove, absurdly small for the large space it was expected to warm," was placed in front of the pulpit. Mr. Tappan relates an amusing incident in connection with this event:

"The first cold Sunday after it had been placed in position, the people all went to meeting fully prepared to watch the result of the experiment. Many felt it uncomfortably warm; and two young women were so overcome by the 'baked air' they fainted, and were taken to the vestibule where the atmosphere was of a better quality. But the next day it was learned, the wood for the stove had not been received, and no fire had been made: this proved a fatal blow to the opposition, and but little was said upon the subject afterwards."

Times change, but the old meeting-house on the village green still stands, a symbol of the ancient faith.

---

[1] Even these were used only by ladies and invalids.

March 20, 1775, it was voted "that the Saxton be and hereby is appointed & Impowered by the Town to sue for and recover, of any Person that shall Leave a stove in the Meeting House on any occasion whatever, a fine of two shillings and to have the same for his Trouble." This was, no doubt, on account of the great dread of fire.

PARSONAGES.

The first minister's house was built, it is supposed, in 1685, and stood near the present site of
Daniel W. Friend's house, on School street. The
land was given by the Proprietors, and is described
as " a small parcel of land lying on the north side
of the Brook below the Saw-mill, it being about ¾ of
an acre lying between said brook and the highway."
On the 23ᵈ of April, 1699, this house was sold to
John Tarrin, shoemaker, " for the sum of twenty
pounds curant money of new ingland. . . . the
mony to be Improved towards a ministry hous."
The house was afterwards moved, enlarged and
finally taken down in 1853, having stood nearly one
hundred and seventy years.

At a town meeting, April 23, 1699, a Committee
was appointed to build a new Parsonage, " forty-two
feet long, eighteen feet wide and fourteen feet stud,
to be located near the meeting-house." This house
stood near where Capt. John Carter's house now
stands, and was occupied by Rev. Nicholas Webster.
In 1716, it was given by the town, with an acre and a
half of land adjoining, extending to the lot on which
the Baptist Meeting-house stands, to Rev. Ames
Cheever. This land was given to the town by the
Proprietors of the Four Hundred acres, April 6, 1716.

The third Parsonage was bought by the town in
1745, for Rev. Benjamin Tappan. The estate was
on the northerly side of Saw Mill brook, and nearly
opposite the first Parsonage. It comprised a dwelling-house, barn and five acres of land. (*Vide* Appendix B.)

" Near yonder copse, where once the garden smiled,
And still where many a garden flower grows wild,
There, where a few torn shrubs the place disclose,
The village preacher's modest mansion rose."

244   OLD RED HOUSE.

The fourth Parsonage was built for Rev. Abraham Randall in 1803, the town furnishing the timber from the Parish Woodland. This house is still standing on Union street. It has been greatly altered and modernized within a few years, and is no longer recognizable.

The fifth Parsonage was built in 1811–12, for Rev. James Thurston, the town conveying the lot to Mr. Thurston for the consideration of one dollar (which was paid for him by a friendly parishioner). The house was occupied by Mr. Thurston and by his successors, Rev. Samuel M. Emerson and Rev. Oliver A. Taylor. It was afterwards purchased and occupied by the late Thomas P. Gentlee. It is of the style common in the early part of the century, with a hall running through the house and four large rooms in both stories. In front of it stands a weeping elm (a variety of the Wych Elm or Wych Hazel, *ulmus montana*), whose branches droop across the highway in a beautiful and graceful sweep.

The sixth and present Parsonage is situated on a court leading from Union street. This house has had a varied history. It first stood on the street and was used as a barn ; it was afterwards converted into a store, with a hall on the second floor which was used at one time as a chapel or vestry, and also by " Master " Price as a schoolroom. This building, after being moved to the present site, was presented with about an acre of land to the church by Mrs. Sarah Allen in 1853, " for a parsonage forever." It has been occupied by the pastors of the Congregational church, since the time of Rev. Oliver A. Taylor.

THE BAPTIST CHURCH.

[A part of this sketch was furnished by the author for the *History of Essex County*, Philadelphia, 1888, vol. II, p. 1288.]

It is not difficult to picture in imagination, a small shallop bearing down from Salem to Jeffrey's Creek on a summer day, somewhere from 1631 to 1635, having on board Mr. Roger Williams, "teacher," and afterwards "minister," of the First church in Salem, on his way to break the bread of life to the few fisherfolk who lived along the shore, and whose log-cabins began to rise here and there in the woods. There is no historical mention, or even tradition, however, of such a visit; and if the apostle of "soul-liberty" ever stepped on the shores of Manchester, he appears to have left no footprint behind him.

The history of Baptist *opinions* in this town it is impossible at this late day to rescue from oblivion; but the history of the Baptish *church* may be briefly told. There had no doubt been persons in town who held more or less clearly and fully the views of doctrine and Christian ordinances which serve to differentiate Baptists from their fellow-believers. But events waited long for the hour and the man; and the first movement was not in the direction of the formation of a regular Baptist church.

It was in the summer and fall of 1842, that Elder Elam Burnham, of Essex, began to hold meetings from time to time in the room formerly occupied by the Public Library, on School street, on the site of the present Engine-house, and afterwards in a hall

BAPTIST CHURCH.

Space here left for the new Unitarian church until the work went to press.

in the Tavern. The preaching gave special prominence to the Second Advent of Christ, and, as was
common at that time, aroused a good deal of interest,
and was met by corresponding opposition. Elder
Burnham was a man of strong nature and indomitable will, and his preaching was with power. A
number were baptized by him, and on April 10,
1843, thirteen men and women met and formed
themselves into a church. A few days later, fifty-
seven others joined the new organization, making
seventy in all. The body called itself a " Christian "
church; it adopted no creed but the New Testament,
and claimed to be independent of any religious denomination; it was organized, however, on the model
of the so-called " Christian Connection."

Measures were taken at once to build a meeting-
house, and on Feb. 28, 1844, the building was
opened for worship.

Mr. Burnham remained with the church but one
year, his gifts fitting him better for pioneer work
than for the work of a pastor. He was succeeded
by Rev. O. J. Waite, from 1844 to 1848. Rev. P.
R. Russell became pastor in 1848, and remained
three years. It was during Mr. Russell's pastorate
that the church became a regular Baptist church,
and on Feb. 28, 1850, was recognized by a Council
called for that purpose, according to the usages of
the Baptist denomination. Mr. Russell was a man
of ability and character, and his pastorate was a
means of uplifting the church in the community.
During his ministry, he preached a series of discourses on the Life of Christ, which were afterwards

published ; while not showing any originality or literary finish, they are said to have been highly valued by many who heard them. He also lectured and wrote on Universalism and Materialism. Judging from his published works, Mr. Russell's strength seems to have been in handling controverted subjects.

Rev. G. W. Davis served the church in 1851 and 1852. He was followed by Rev. G. F. Danforth from 1853 to 1856. Mr. Danforth is remembered as a man of excellent and amiable qualities, who served in the ministry in the weakness of declining health, until compelled to relinquish his loved work by the disease which soon after terminated his useful life. He was a man of the Beatitudes.

Rev. C. W. Reding was the next pastor, from 1856 to 1861. His ministry was a pleasant and prosperous one; he had a large place in the hearts of the people. Mr. Reding is living at an advanced age, in Beverly Farms, loved and revered by all who know him. He was succeeded by Rev. L. B. Hatch, 1863-68, Rev. H. F. H. Miller, 1870-71, Rev. C. D. Swett, 1873-75, Rev. C. T. Holt, 1879-81. For three years the church was without a pastor, and was in a depressed condition. On Jan. 1, 1884, Rev. D. F. Lamson, of Hartford, Conn., began his service as stated supply of the church.

There have been but few Sundays when the meeting-house has been closed for want of a preacher, although there have been several periods when the church was for a considerable time without a pastor. During these times recourse was often had for a pulpit supply to Newton Theological Institution. Mention should also be made of the helpful labors of " Father " Fitts [1] (as he was familiarly and affectionately called), at various times, also of Rev. W. C. Richards, whose faithful and tender ministrations are still remembered. Under the labors of the former of these brethren, especially, whose " praise is in all the churches," and during the pastorates of Brethren Reding and Hatch, seasons of revival interest were enjoyed, which materially strengthened the church as well as enlarged its membership. During the present pastorate, forty have united with the church by baptism.

The church has never been a strong one in numbers or in wealth. It has had much to contend with in its early history and its subsequent growth. It has suffered much by removals and deaths; the manner of its formation was peculiar, and after circumstances were not favorable to homogeneous development. At one time, in its earlier days, it was threatened with a formal division; but wiser counsels prevailed, and the church has grown in harmony within, and increased by additions from without.

The church has licensed three ministers of the gospel, Samuel Cheever, Thomas C. Russell (son of Rev. P. R. Russell) and Benjamin F. Tuck.

Mr. Cheever labored chiefly as an evangelist; he retired from the work some years before his death in 1892.

Mr. Russell was ordained at Barnstable, Mass., Nov. 17, 1858; he has had pastorates also in Billerica, Mass., New

---

[1] Rev. Hervey Fitts, Missionary of the Baptist State Convention.

Boston, N. H., Leominster, Mass., Mansfield, Mass., Palmer, Mass., Springvale, Me., Swampscott, Mass., Suncook, N. H.

Mr. Tuck was ordained June 7, 1871, at Bernardston, Mass.; his other places of settlement have been Belchertown, Mass., Hinsdale, N. H., South Acworth, N. H., South Windham, Vt., West Sutton, Mass., Amherst, N. H. He is at present on the retired list.

The church and society have been out of debt since 1884, when an indebtedness resulting from a remodelling of the house of worship a few years before was cancelled.

THE EPISCOPAL CHURCH.

A little west of the Masconomo House, on the road to Lobster Cove, stands Emanuel Church. It is on the land of Russell Sturgis, Esq., and its erection is due to that gentleman. It is a churchly little building, with lych-gate, mantling ivy and " storied window richly dight." It is for the use especially of summer residents, and is open only during the " season," when it receives within its walls more wealth and fashion and culture than are found often in churches of much larger size and greater pretensions. It is viewed, however, rather as an exotic by some of the permanent residents.

THE CATHOLIC CHURCH.

The Roman Catholics have a building on School street, built in 1873. It is a small, neat structure, sufficiently large for the wants of its winter congregations, but inconveniently crowded in summer. It belongs to the parish of St. Mary Star of the Sea, Beverly.

EMANUEL CHURCH.

CATHOLIC CHURCH.

THE UNIVERSALISTS.

Members of this denomination have held meetings at different times, in the Town Hall, but have had no permanent organization.

THE UNITARIANS.

In the summer of 1895, a building to be used for Unitarian services was erected on Masconomo street, by some of the summer residents.

The dream of ecclesiastical unity indulged in by the fathers has not been fulfilled in the later history of their descendants.   Perhaps the hope of any external and formal union in matters of conscience and religion is a delusive one.   But it is to be hoped that denominational walls are not so high but that we can at least see over them, though we may be of less stalwart stature than those who first reared them.   We shall do well if, in this age, we can live up to the spirit of the ancient maxim, " *In essentials, unity; in non-essentials, liberty; in all things, charity.*"

APPENDIXES.

APPENDIX A.

A Sunday in the Olden Time.

It is needless, perhaps, to say that in this sketch the author has allowed some play to the imagination, and represented some things as synchronous which were really separated by an interval of several years. But nothing is narrated but *might* have occurred in Manchester about a century and a half ago. The *atmosphere* is historical, as are many of the names and events. The paper was originally read before the Historical Society, July 7, 1890, and was published in the *Magazine of American History*, September, 1890. It is here reproduced by request.

THE first rude cabins of the men of the "Dorchester company," and others, who had landed at Jeffrey's Creek, or had come overland from Naumkeag, and had "set up a fishing-stage" and broken the forest here and there, had given place to somewhat more commodious and permanent dwellings. The meeting-house of the humble size of "eighteen feet in length with two gables," which the piety of the early settlers had erected near "the landing," and whose plain appearance aptly symbolized the simple faith of the Puritans, had been succeeded by one of somewhat larger proportions, but of the same unadorned style, where the people gathered on the Sabbath to listen to argumentative discourses and to feed their devotion on long prayers and the Psalms of David "done into metre."

It is a Sunday in May, 17——. The corn has been planted; the shad bush and wild plum are in flower; the waters of Saw Mill brook, swollen by the late rains, rush and foam through the woods to the sea; the expanse of ocean as seen from Image Hill sparkles in the morning sun; for, notwithstanding the "eastern glint"

in the morning, the day proves cloudless; water-fowl
wheel their flight slowly through the air; the only
sounds are the distant lowing of cattle, the songs of in-
numerable birds, the gentle sighing in the tree-tops, the
lap of waves on the shingly shore. With the going
down of the sun on the previous day, the labors of the
farm and the household ceased; the fishing-boat was
drawn up on the beach; the clatter of the mill-wheel
was hushed; and, after an early supper, each quiet Puritan household "prepared to keep the Sabbath."

It is now nine of the clock; the simple breakfast of
corn mush or potatoes and milk, with the addition, perhaps, of fish or bacon, has long since been disposed of;
the Sunday clothes taken from the press, carefully
brushed and donned, and the serious business of the
day commenced. The house-dog wears a sedate look,
and plainly thinks that a Puritan Sabbath is no time for
frisking and frolic. What is more strange, even the
youngsters have an air of gravity, the modern "small-
boy" not yet being evolved in the process of New England development. The bell presented by George Norton in 1695, sounds over the hills to call the little community to worship. Few houses can boast of any other
time-piece than a "noon-mark" on some southern win-
dow-sill, and the ringing of the bell is not only a matter
of pride but a necessity. Soon, along quiet woodland
ways, across pastures and over hills, the forefathers and
foremothers, with a goodly array of children, some in
arms, some walking demurely in their parents' footsteps,
glancing now and then at some squirrel frisking across
the path or some jay chattering in a tree overhead,
gather to the Sunday rendezvous, the village Meeting-
house.

There is no laughter or loud talk, only subdued greetings and quiet interchange of rural intelligence, as

acquaintances meet after a week's isolation. The news
that Captain Hooper or Captain Leach has got in with
a good fare from "Georges"; or that Samuel Morgan,
just returned from the eastward, has brought tidings
from Pemaquid of the murder by the Indians of the
Hiltons, father and son; or that Goodman Bennett's
heifer has been found by the "deer-reaves"; or that a
son and heir has gladdened the hearts of the worthy
household of Malachi Allen, and has been named Onesiphorus, for as the father said, "Peradventure he will
be to us in our old age a true help-bringer"; — these
and similar harmless bits of gossip have just time for
expression, but not for enlargement, when the groups
gathered on the green observe Parson Tappan slowly
marching from the parsonage-house on the hill toward
the Meeting-house. With stately and measured step
the village pastor enters the house, gravely bowing to
right and left, stopping to inquire of Mistress Lee for
the welfare of her aged mother, who has just "turned
of ninety," and perchance to pat the head of some
trembling and awe-struck urchin, delighted to win "the
good man's smile," or to cast a reproving glance at some
young men of rather light behavior, who had come down
the day before on a sloop from Boston, and to look
around inquiringly for Goodman Babcock, the "tything-
man." The people take their places as they have been
"seated" by the Select-men. A few of the more distinguished citizens, those who bear the title of colonel,
or captain, or squire, — and they are very few in this
essentially democratic community [1] — have been permitted to "set up" pews; others must fain content
themselves with benches. The congregation does not

[1] On the Assessors' books of this time is found the name of Honorable
Daniel Edwards, Esqr., and in the church records, under date of May 22,
1754, is the entry, "Died the Honorable Judge Marston Esqr." (Col. Benj.
Marston?)

present so picturesque a sight as in Ipswich or Newbury meeting-houses, in communities of greater wealth
and more aristocratic pretensions,

"where in order due and fit,
As by public vote directed, ranked and classed the people sit ;
Mistress first and goodwife after, clerkly squire before the
    clown,
From the brave coat lace-embroidered, to the gray frock shad-
    ing down."

But all ages are here, from the patriarch with snowy
hair to the little babe; quavering voices join in the
psalm, and young hearts under kerchief and doublet
beat quicker at the thought of the "banns" that are to
be "published" next Sabbath. A few Indians and
Negroes, and two or three "Frenchmen,"[1] complete
the congregation, made up for the most part of "freemen" and their families. Only the sick and infirm,
the very aged and the very young, are missing; for is
there not a fine of five shillings for absence from public
worship?[2] The congregation soon settles itself; a faint
aroma of lavender and southernwood is in the air; the
rustle of leaves and the songs of birds float in through
the open door, mingling with the breath from the pines
and from the sea, and the worship begins.

From the "singing-seats" sounds the "pitch-pipe,"[3]

[1] In the town records for 1757 is the following : "The selectmen are empowered to let the French men to John Foster for one year for one hun-
dren and ten pounds, Old Tenor." These were neutral French (Acadians)
who were compelled to leave Nova Scotia after it had been conquered by
the English, and were town charges. The forced expatriation of the inhabitants of Acadia by the British, with which we have been made familiar
in Longfellow's *Evangeline*, is frequently brought to mind by references
to "Frenchmen," in the Records of the Town. "Little dreamed the village
Saxons of the myriads at their back."

[2] Mass. Records, vol. II, 208.

[3] Jacob Allen, probably great-grandson of William Allen, and grandfather of John Perry Allen, "pitched the tune in the old meeting-house on
the Landing, for forty years, without pay."

and tenors and basses, trebles and contraltos, join in
Mears or St. Martin's, Dundee or Old Hundred, making
such harmony as they can in voicing one of the para-
phrases of *Tate and Brady*, or of *Watts'* " Psalms and
Hymns." [1]   Before the " long prayer " a note is read,
" put up " by the family of Captain Leach for his safe
return from Bilboa, and another by Nathaniel Marsters,
Constable, asking the prayers of this congregation that
the Lord will prosper his journey to Boston the coming
week.

Without the reading of Scripture — something which,
strangely enough, was supposed to squint at least
towards Rome — the parson turns the hour-glass, names
his text from the Book of Judges, and proceeds with
his discourse. With formal divisions and scholastic
phraseology, for Parson Tappan was one of the " painful " preachers of the time, and adjusting Hebrew history to the exigencies of New England life, the sermon
comes at last, with another turn of the glass, to " nine-
teenthly " and the close. Good, solid, Puritan theology,
with no suspicion of clap-trap or sensationalism from
beginning to end. The pulpit had not found the need
of resorting to such " popular " subjects as the latest arrival of the *Speedwell* or the *Hind and Panther*, with
news of the battle of the Boyne, or " the recent ship-
wreck at Sandy Bay," or " the truth concerning Captain
Underhill and the Cocheco scandal."

In the course of the sermon a disturbance is caused
by some " pestigeous " boys, and especially by one

---

[1] Watts' *Hymns* were published in England in 1707, and his *Songs of
David* in 1719. They were introduced into the church in Manchester in
1753. (Palfrey says that they began to be generally adopted in the Revolutionary period. Vol. V, 221 n.) They were a great advance upon the often
uncouth rhymes of *Tate and Brady*, and gradually supplanted that collection in the psalmody of the New England churches, and for wellnigh a
century held an almost undisputed place.

Pomp, a negro,[1] making strange contortions of countenance, whereupon he is called forth and reproved with great awfulness and solemnity; some children, and also a mulatto woman, are reprimanded for laughing at Pomp's scandalous demeanor.[2]

The service was simple and bare of anything that might appeal to the senses or an æsthetic taste.   Our fathers had suffered too much and too recently, to be very tolerant of anything that savored of a liturgy or reminded them of the church of Laud and Cranmer. They had as scant respect for processions, genuflections, antiphons, and such like performances, as had the Devonshire clerk for the proceedings of his ritualistic rector: " First he went up the church, and then he went down the church, side-a-ways, here-a-ways, and theer-a-ways, a scrattlin' like a crab."[3]   Puritanism was an extreme reaction from ritualism.

The noon intermission is welcomed, and parties gather here and there, some to listen to Lieut. May's story of the siege of Louisburg, others to discuss the sermon and the tides, Solomon Driver's black steers, the sailing of Skipper Bear's "Chebacco boat," the meeting of the Great and General Court, the ghost lately seen on the Gloucester road, the "greate black oke" struck by lightning in the swamp near Wolf Trap brook, and the mysterious disappearance of Goodwife Parsons' molasses, which all agreed was "bewitched."[4]   Luncheon is

[1] According to a census of the town taken in 1761, there were then twenty-three negroes and mulattoes in Manchester, seven Acadians, one Indian.

[2] Such scenes, and others even more mirth-provoking, were not of infrequent occurrence, as the old records testify. We read in an old autobiography, " diversions was frequent in meeting, and the more duller the sermon, the more likely it was that some accident or mischief would be done to help pass the time."

[3] *Charles Kingsley, His Letters, etc.,* 125.

[4] A common explanation of anything mysterious and annoying, even long after the terrible Witchcraft delusion had disappeared from these shores, like the sea-wrack before the besom of a Nor'wester.

eaten, the horizon is scanned, prognostications are sagely made on the weather, with glances at the weather-cock, bravely looking eastward, the whipping-post and stocks just made by Thomas Lee are examined and criticised, notes are compared on planting and on building a weir at Kettle Cove, the young men and maidens return from the short and discreet Sunday ramble to the brook, in which they have talked, perchance, of other things besides the morning sermon, such as the wondrous cures wrought by Molly Morgan, a "charmer of warts," who having climbed to the top of Moses Hill "was astonished to find the world so large," and some other things not strictly in the "odor of sanctity," and all gather quietly and devoutly for the afternoon service. This is similar to that of the forenoon, except that the preacher seems to aim to come a little nearer, to use Lord Bacon's phrase, to his hearers' "business and bosoms."

His text is from the words of Paul, respecting those who "having itching ears, heap to themselves teachers." He takes occasion gravely to warn his flock against certain irregularities of which he is pained to hear in the parish of Chebacco, where Rev. John Cleaveland, one of the "New Lights," is stirring up the people, and where a good deal is heard of "new measures," "experimental religion," and the like.[1]

The plain words of the parson produce a decided effect upon the congregation, and make many an ear to tingle; for is it not known in all the parish that Edward Lee and some others have been going over to Chebacco of late to meeting, declaring that their souls are not fed by Parson Tappan? There has been talk, too, of a Council; it is even whispered that letters have passed between Parson Cleaveland and Parson Tappan, and

[1] *Vide* "A Patriotic Parson," by D. F. Lamson. *Magazine of American History*, vol. XVIII, 237.

many wise ones are of the opinion that something must
be done to put a stop to the erratic goings-on of breachy
parishioners, and to preserve the order and peace of the
churches.

Such monitory discourses have multiplied of late.
The shepherd has seen the wolf coming. The times are
full of excitement and peril. The French war has left
the country demoralized. Ominous signs have appeared
of late over seas. Faint mutterings of the gathering
storm of the Revolution have been borne fitfully on the
breeze even to this out-of-the-way hamlet. But, worse
than all, rumors were abroad the previous winter, that
certain persons called "Dippers," or "Anabaptists"
had come secretly into town, and had even held some
meetings in a small house in the outskirts. It is true,
these rogues had been closely watched, and on one occasion, it was reported, were so hotly pursued by the
constables that they were glad to get out of the precinct without being set in the pillory and having their
ears cropped;[1] whereat sundry "antient, grave and
sober" persons were greatly aggrieved. All these
things had of late kept the usually sedate community
in an uncommon state of perturbation.

But at last the service ends, as services do, and the
congregation take their homeward way, circumspect
and serious, with matter enough to think about and
talk about till the next Sabbath. The supper of
baked beans, brown bread and Indian pudding, drawn
from the brick oven, with the unusual luxury of a cup

---

[1] As late as 1752, the mother of Dr. Isaac Backus, the historian of New
England Baptists, was thrown into jail, when sick of a fever, because for
conscience' sake she refused to pay the State-Church tax.

"It is a sad story. Most pure and excellent and otherwise inoffensive
persons were the sufferers, and generally patient ones. But the struggle
was a brief one. The Baptists conquered in it, and came to equal esteem
and love with their brethren." (Winsor, *Memorial History of Boston*,
vol. 1, 179.)

of tea, is eaten with honest appetites and thankful hearts. The catechism is recited by the younger members of the family, the "heads" of the sermons are given, the cows are brought to the barnyard, the milking is done, and sunset melting down the amber sky ends the sweet, peaceful, healthful, uplifting Puritan Sabbath.

No song of the drunkard has polluted the sweet air, no "meets" have flaunted along the highways, no railway trains have disturbed the quiet, no Sunday papers have flapped their huge wings like birds of evil omen athwart the sky. All day long the earth has been at peace, and has reflected back the smile of heaven.

As the stars begin to come out in the pure skies, the young people join in the free-masonry of hearts as old as the race, tales are told, songs are sung, or thoughts are breathed too deep for words, until nine o'clock finds the last suitor departed, the last "good-nights" said, the doors closed, but not barred,[1] and the full moon, which had risen high in the eastern heavens, looking down on the sleeping town.

[1] With the disturbed state of the country, incident to the Revolution, and especially the fear of a landing from the enemy's ships upon the coast, more precautions began to be taken. A stout, wooden bar, bearing evidence of long service, belonging to this period, is still in use in the Kitfield house at the "Cove," to fasten the door o' nights; another may be seen in Mrs. Abby Baker's house.

APPENDIX B.

A Typical Oldtime Minister — Rev. Benjamin Tappan, 1720–1790.

As more is known of Rev. Benjamin Tappan than of any other of the earlier ministers of Manchester, and as he served the church and town for so long a time and during so momentous a period — that of the Revolutionary epoch — and has left so many descendants; he was, in short, so representative a man and minister, that this biographical sketch is appended, it being too long and of too personal a character for a place in the body of the work. The paper was originally written by the author for the *Magazine of American History*, December, 1890.

Mr. Tappan, whose ministry of forty-five years was closed only by his death, was a good representative of the Puritan clergy. He was the son of Samuel Toppan, of Newbury, Mass., and was born in 1720. He was graduated from Harvard College in 1742, settled at Manchester, as successor to Rev. Ames Cheever, Dec. 11, 1745, and died May 6, 1790. As in all similar instances, at that time, and for many years afterwards, Mr. Tappan was called and settled by vote of the town. The time of the separation of church and state in Massachusetts was yet far in the future. The town called the minister, voted his salary, built the meeting-house, set apart ministerial lands, made arrangements for ordinations, even to the supply of rum deemed necessary on such occasions — in short, transacted all the business involved in ecclesiastical relations that was afterwards transferred to the parish. The town *was* the parish. The ministerial tax was levied on the taxable property, irrespective of creed or religious preference.

Mr. Tappan's relations to the church and town appear to have been cordial throughout his ministry. As a mark of confidence and esteem he was voted for three successive years a gift, in addition to his salary, amounting, in 1769, to £46. The records show a mingled dignity and consideration on the part of both pastor and people.

As Mr. Tappan's ministry covered the troublous period of the Revolution, with many years before and after, when the country was in an extremely depressed financial condition, it is not surprising to learn that at one time the impoverished people were unable to pay the stipulated salary. To the credit of the minister, we are told that he "maintained uninterruptedly and with faithfulness the ministrations of his pastoral duties." Such a course must have strengthened the ties that united pastor and people in those "times that tried men's souls." [1]

Mr. Tappan's theology was of the type generally prevalent in the "standing order" in New England, in the latter half of the eighteenth century. He appears to have belonged to the more conservative school. As none of his sermons are extant, all that is known must be matter of inference. About 1760, a controversy arose between Mr. Tappan and Rev. John Cleaveland of Chebacco, which has left its record in some correspondence, preserved in a rare tract written by Mr. Cleaveland, and entitled after the manner of the time, "A Plain Narrative," etc., Boston, 1767. The case in brief was this: Some persons in Manchester, among them the celebrated Edward Lee, "The Apostolic Fisherman," had for some time been attending Mr. Cleaveland's ministry, alleging that Mr. Tappan's preaching was Arminian. Some had even gone so far as to join

---

[1] To show the difficulties to which ministers were often subjected, one of them writes, "In 1777 your Pastor gave the whole of his year's Salary for one sucking Calf, the next year he gave the whole for a small store pig." The spirit of this poor parson is seen in what follows; "your pastor has not asked any consideration being willing to Scrabble along with the people while they are in low circumstances." One minister in Maine was paid £5,400 in paper money to make good his salary of £60 in gold.

the church in Chebacco, a grave offence in the eyes of
our fathers, who considered the parish a kind of ecclesiastical preserve to be jealously guarded against ministerial and other poachers. It does not appear that Mr.
Cleaveland was guilty of any breach of ministerial
courtesy in the matter ; but Mr. Tappan was one of the
New England ministers who were not in sympathy with
Whitefield and what were known as the " new measures,"
while Mr. Cleaveland was an ardent supporter of the
revival movement. Mr. Tappan complained of the interference, as he considered it, with his rights as minister of Manchester, and it seemed likely for a time that
a serious and lasting strife between the neighboring
parishes would be the result. The language of Parson
Tappan, in some of his letters, bears a tinge of acerbity,
that, considering all the circumstances, is perhaps no
occasion for wonder. Mr. Cleaveland was a man who
had "the courage of his convictions," was skilled in
debate, and a firm and decided but courteous contro-
versialist. The case was a typical one. It was a skir-
mish of outposts, but the conflict which half a century
later convulsed the churches of New England was already
impending.

   In common with most of the ministers of the period,
Mr. Tappan was an ardent patriot. He not only coun-
selled resistance to the oppressive measures of the king
in council, and gave two of his sons to the Continental
Army, but when British cruisers were menacing the
shores, he carried his musket with him to meeting,
leaving it at the foot of the pulpit stairs, ready for an
emergency.

   Of Mr. Tappan's manner and style of preaching, not
even an anecdote remains. We can imagine him in
knee-buckles, small-clothes and broad-brimmed cocked-
hat, in bands and wig ; he is said to have been stout and

well-built, and fancy pictures him as somewhat grave
and sedate. No portrait or even silhouette is known to
exist. Nor have we any means of rehabilitating the old
parsonage with its active, intelligent, busy life.[1]

Dr. Leach says of Mr. Tappan, "His character as a
scholar was very respectable, as appears from the testimony of his professional brethren, among whom, as
among the people of his charge, he was highly esteemed,
and his death deeply lamented.[2] And Dr. Leach, who
was born in 1809, must in his youth and early manhood
have known many who were the parishioners and acquaintances of Mr. Tappan. That he was a man of
strong character is shown not only by his hold for so
many years upon the town, but by the character of his
descendants. Mr. Tappan had eleven children, among
whom was Benjamin,[3] an eminent citizen of Northampton; David, who was made Hollis professor of Divinity
at Harvard College, 1792, and who died in 1803, of
whom Dr. Holmes remarks, "His death threw a gloom
over his bereaved family, over the university, the
church, the commonwealth, and the country"; Samuel
and Amos, who became successful educators, and
Ebenezer, who was in the army of 1776.[4] The family
has always been distinguished for intelligence and
public spirit. It is represented in Manchester in the
third and fourth generations.

[1] Since the first publication of this article the writer's attention has
been directed to the *Memoir of Mrs. Sarah Tappan*, wife of Benjamin
Tappan, of Northampton, by their son, Lewis Tappan (N. Y.). On page
126, referring to Parson Tappan, the author says : "He had young men
studying with him from time to time. . . . His eyes were small and
deep in his head; he had a dent in his chin, dimples in his cheeks, and
was inclined to corpulency."

[2] Rev. Eli Forbes of Gloucester, in his funeral sermon, preached at
Manchester, May 10, 1790, says of Mr. Tappan, "He was a man of fixed
probity — great candor — very cautious — of a most tender conscience, and
extensive benevolence."

[3] Father of Arthur and Lewis Tappan of New York.

[4] Grandfather of Lewis N. and Wm. H. Tappan.

The house in which Mr. Tappan lived, long known as
"the old red house," and said by tradition never to have
been painted any other color, stood on the east side of
School street, opposite Friend court. It has been described as "a fine old house in early times, the walls
being plastered with mortar made of burnt clam-shells
and sand." It was of "the long sloping-roof style,
probably built about the time of the first parsonage-
house," in 1685. It was purchased by the town in 1745,
for Mr. Tappan; connected with it were about five
acres of land on the northerly side of Saw Mill brook.
The demolition of this house a few years ago was
greatly regretted by those who have a regard for "the
ancient landmarks which the fathers have set." But
much as the removal of such a house is to be deplored
on sentimental grounds, it is better that it should not
longer have survived, to be occupied by alien and un-
sympathetic tenants.

Mr. Tappan was buried in the old burial-ground on
Summer street. The slate stone above his grave is in
good preservation, and the lettering quite legible. It
bears the inscription, supposed to have been written by
his son David : —

In Memory of
BENJAMIN TAPPAN, A. M.,
late pastor of the church in Manchester,
who expired May 6, 1790,
in the 70th year of his age,
and 45th of his ministry.
He was a sincere and exemplary Christian,
a tender Husband & Parent,
a judicious & sound Divine,
a prudent & faithful Minister.

O ever honored, ever dear, adieu;
How many tender names are lost in you;
Keep safe, O Tomb, thy precious, sacred trust,
Till life divine awake his sleeping dust.

The generations overlap each other in their influence, as well as in their physical life. Few and fragmentary as are the facts which have been preserved respecting the life of the Minister of Manchester during the last half of the eighteenth century, and shadowy as his figure may be to us, his character is still moulding the life of the community after the lapse of more than a hundred years.

APPENDIX C.

CEMETERIES.

ONE of the first cares of the early settlers, after putting up some rude shelter for the living, was to provide a resting-place for the dead. Even before the meeting-house rose on the Common, the Silent House was made ready for its tenant.

It is possible that the first graveyard, which tradition locates near the present Library building,[1] may have been a private burial-place. Nothing certainly is now known of it. The very names of those who were buried in it have long since been forgotten. The earliest burying-ground of which any trace now remains is that on the road from the "Cove" to the Magnolia R. R. Station. No mention of this is found in the records. Within the memory of persons now living, several stones remained, among them one of white marble bearing the name of Abigail Gilbert. But these have been broken down and have disappeared many years ago. There are a few small rough stones, without name or date, rising a few inches above the turf, the only memorials that mark the resting-places of the unknown dead. Nothing could be more simple, rude, primitive. But it is "God's Acre." Within this little plot, far away from the turmoil of life, were laid the mortal remains of some of the founders and first inhabitants of the town. Probably John Kettle was buried here, and the Hoopers,

[1] *Memorial Library Volume*, p. 50.

Allens, Kitfields, Stones, and others, whose descendants are now scattered from Maine to Montana. The town has within a few years taken measures to protect the spot from further desecration, but nothing can repair the ravages of the past.

The earliest record that exists of a piece of land being set apart by the town for burial purposes, is in 1668.[1]

Att a towne meeting the 16ᵗʰ of march 1668 it was confirmed by most of yᵉ inhabitents yᵗ wear their mett yᵗ in consideration of sum Ground yᵗ they make use of for a bureall place which was Samuell friend owne land possessed & planted by him in Lieu therof he has to have a neck of Land yᵗ Lyes betwen the Saw mill and his Island upon which now his house doth stand which was granted formerly but being confirmed & now recorded.

Reference seems here made to former action on the part of the town.

yᵉ 17ᵗʰ of June 1661 Att a town meeting at Manchester it was ordered & aGread upon by yᵉ inhabitents of yᵉ plantation yᵗ Samuell friend is to have yᵉ Little Island yᵗ is joyning to his marsh at yᵉ great neck of Land where they now plant this was granted to him with the Generell consent of yᵉ plantation.[2]

The meaning is not altogether clear, but it would seem that in 1661, the exchange of land was agreed upon, by which the town obtained possession of the present burial ground on the corner of Washington and Summer streets. It was in use "for a bureall place" in 1668, when, on account probably of some informality, the grant of " Little Island," was " confirmed," and with an additional grant of land " joyning," was " recorded." The location of the land thus granted to Samuell Friend

[1] Dr. Leach gives the date, on what authority is not now known, as 1653. This history simply follows the record.

[2] *Town Records*, vol. I, p. 9.

in exchange for the land which the town took for a burial ground "by right of eminent domain," cannot now be ascertained. Dr. Leach assumes that it is what was later called the "Island wharf property," on the Smith farm; but this is doubtful.

This burial ground extended across the present highway, the road to Gloucester running at that time along the line of what is now Sea street, through the Towne and Dana estates.[1] In 1701, the town ordered the burying-ground to be fenced in, and "whoever neglect to work on the same shall be fined 3 shillings," showing the scarcity of money and the low price of labor. In 1716, the burying-ground wall was built, and "six feet in its whole length given in by John Lee Jun." At a Town Meeting called on the 10th Day of March, Anno Domini 1760, it was "Voted that there be a new and Lawfull wall Erected and new set against y⁰ Burying yard and a handsome Gate Erected and Compleated at y⁰ Entrance of said Burying yard in y⁰ Room & Stead of Barrs."[2]

The article in the Warrant included also, "to see if the Town will take some method to accomplish the Destruction of Briers: which seem to have almost universally Overspread the Congregation of the Dead: By which means following our Dec⁰ˢ Relatives to their long homes is attended with no small degree of Inconveniency."[3] This part of the article seems to have failed of being acted upon; while the briers, however they were fought shy of, showed their usual persistency, and continued to thrust themselves into notice. In the Warrant for the March meeting, 1772, occurs this article:

[1] Traces of this old road may still be seen. The more direct road was laid out in 1684.

[2] *Town Records*, vol. II, 85.

[3] *Town Records*, vol. II, 84.

" To see if the Town will determine upon something
respecting the Burying Yard : on consideration that
Those : who are Called to follow their Deceased Friends
to the Grave may be delivered from those Briers which
have: and yet do Encumber such Followers." [1] This
time something was done : "34ly voted that Mr Jacob
Tewxbury have the use and Improvement of the Bury-
ing-Yard free and Clear of Rent untill he shall accomplish the Destruction of Briars growing in said Yard :
provided from this Time he makes use of his best Endeavours for so doing."   As no further record appears,
it may be supposed that Mr. Jacob Tewxbury's " best
Endeavours " were successful, and that the thorny subject ceased to perplex the ways of the fathers.

The oldest stones in this Cemetery on which the inscriptions are still legible are those of Joseph Woodbury
and Wife, 1714 ; George Norton, 1717 ; Elizabeth, wife
of Thomas Lee, gent., 1720 ; Lieut. William Hilton,
1723 ; and on a plain piece of granite are the initials,
E. H., supposed to be those of Edward Hooper.   There
are many stones which are evidently older, on which
the time-worn lines can no longer be deciphered. Many
of these, hewn and dressed by unskillful hands from the
common pasture stones, are pathetic memorials of the
simple and humble lives of the forefathers.[3]

The only inscription showing literary taste is that on
the gravestone of Rev. Benjamin Tappan, minister of
the town from 1745 to 1790.   It was no doubt furnished
by his son, Prof. David Tappan, of Harvard College.
Two inscriptions are worth preserving for their quaint-
ness. One is on the stone of Capt. John Marston, an

---

[1] *Town Records*, vol. 11, 122.

[2] *Town Records*, vol. 11, 134.

[3] The hard, dark, flinty slatestones, ornamented (?) by a death's head,
or a cherub, or a willow-tree, so common in our older grave-yards, were
imported from Wales, ready carved.

eccentric man who is said to have lived on "Smith's farm." [1]

Capt. John Marston lies here
who died May 22, 1754, being
57 years and 3 mo. old.
Art thou, curious, reader, to know
what sort of a man he was ? Wait till
the final day of Retribution, and
then thou mayest be satisfied.

An epitaph non-committal enough to suit the average politician. It is said to have been placed upon the stone by his own direction.

Sacred to the memory of
Captain John Allen
who died
August 27, 1834, aged 59 years.

Tho' Boreas' blasts and Neptune's waves
Have tossed me to and fro,
In spite of both, by God's decree,
I harbour here below.

Now here at anchor I do lie,
With many of our fleet,
I hope again for to set sail,
My Savior Christ to meet.

The grave of Rev. Ames Cheever, who was buried in this cemetery in 1756, remained unmarked until the

---

[1] Mr. Tappan preserves an anecdote of his courtship, which confirms the tradition of his eccentricity.

present year, and its site was long supposed to be unknown. It has recently been identified beyond a reasonable doubt, and a neat tablet has been placed upon it by his descendants, bearing the inscription :

Reverend

Ames Cheever

B. Oct. 24, 1686.　D. Jan. 15, 1756

Minister of Manchester

1716–1744

Erected by his

Descendants

1895.

Hoc decus exiguum sacrum memoriæ reverendi Amesii Cheever, qui cursu peracto ætatis suæ 69, 15 Januarii, anno Domini 1756, terrena pro cœlestibus reliquit.

The epitaph is from Alden's "Collection of Epitaphs," and may be translated,

"This brief honor is sacred to the memory of Reverend Ames Cheever, who his course being finished in his age 69, on January 15, 1756, left the earthly for the heavenly."

UNION CEMETERY.

This is a small burial-ground on the east side of School street, formerly owned by a stock association, which was formed July 24, 1845. It was transferred to the town, Apr. 9, 1888, by vote of the Proprietors, and accepted by the town, Apr. 23, 1888. A monument to the Rev. Oliver A. Taylor stands near the centre of the ground. It bears on two of its sides these inscriptions :

The Reverend
Oliver Alden Taylor,
Born at Yarmouth, Mass.
Aug. 18, 1801:
Installed here as Pastor,
Sept. 18, 1839:
Died Dec. 18, 1851.
Resurgemus.

———

He was a man
of clear intellect,
of deep and various learning,
of rare humility,
candor and kindness.
A laborious student,
an able preacher, a devoted pastor,
he was in every relation faithful
and lived as one
" Who must give account."
Torn, while yet in his full strength,
from the warm affection
of wife, kindred and flock,
he calmly resigned them all,
and fell asleep in Jesus.

ROSEDALE CEMETERY.

This is the prettiest and most romantic cemetery in town. It is entered from School street, opposite Pleasant street. This cemetery also belonged at first to a private corporation, dating from Sept. 14, 1854, and was transferred to the town, and accepted as a public trust, with Union Cemetery, April 23, 1888. With the enlargement subsequently made, it constitutes a burial-ground creditable to the community, and of sufficient size for the wants of a considerable time to come. Since the town has assumed the care of the different burial-places, they have been well managed and neatly kept under the efficient charge of Mr. Alhanan H. Babcock.

During the last decade it became evident that before the close of the century, more room would be demanded for death's ever-increasing harvest. After much deliberation and discussion, the town purchased a very eligible lot of land and one admirably adapted to the purpose adjoining Rosedale Cemetery on the south. This was laid out, neatly fenced, and a wide avenue opened from School street; and on Memorial Day, May 30, 1888, appropriate dedicatory exercises were held under the direction of the Selectmen, including singing, prayer, and addresses by Rev. D. F. Lamson and Rev. D. Marvin.

Two years later, May 30, 1890, a lot, set apart by the town for the purpose, was dedicated to the use of the G. A. R. Post. Rev. Mr. Lamson gave the address, as follows:

It seems to be an instinct of our nature to provide some decent sepulture for the dead. All civilized races, and some that are not civilized, have their burying places, where stately shaft, or lowly tablet, or raised mound marks the final resting spot. In accordance with this instinct, the fathers of the town in its earlier history set apart three different enclosures for burial purposes — one at Kettle Cove, one near the site of the present Library Building, and the Old Burying Ground on Summer street. To these have been added later Union and Rosedale. And this latest extension, opened two years ago, and dedicated on Memorial Day with appropriate ceremonies, it may be supposed, will afford all needed room for the ever-enlarging domain of death for years to come. In this quiet and beautiful retreat, the town, acting under a recent act of the Legislature, has wisely and patriotically appropriated this lot for the uses of the Grand Army Post, and specially for the use of the worn-out veterans whose burial may not otherwise be provided for.

After the already protracted services of the day, the fewest words will be deemed the fittest. Let us then solemnly dedicate this spot to its sacred purposes, as a resting-place of the patriot dead who gave all they had to give for their country's service ; whose bodies will here have honorable burial at the hands of their comrades and fellow-citizens. Let it be told here who those patriots were ; what sufferings they underwent in their day and generation to make this land an abode of peace, happiness and liberty to those who should live after them ; what principles they upheld in life and in death ; and what lessons should be drawn from their example by those who enjoy the fruits of their patriotism and self-denial.

Around this spot, from year to year, let the voice of prayer and the solemn dirge be heard ; upon it let the dews of tender and grateful recollection fall ; over it let the gracious heavens beam in kindly watch and ward.

And thus, with this simple but heartfelt service, we commit this hallowed spot, with all the precious dust it may hereafter hold, to the care and reverence of coming generations.

APPENDIX D.

EARLY HOUSES.

[Acknowledgments are due to George F. Allen, Esq., for most valuable information contained in this Appendix.]

THE houses of the first settlers were built near the "Landing," at the "Cove," or at "North Yarmouth." The house of William Allen was probably near the site of the present Parsonage. John Kettle's house was at the "Cove." Richard Graves had a farm near the present Dana estate. Ambrose Gale built at "Gale's Point." Several old apple trees near "Sandy Hollow" probably mark the site of John Codner's house. George Norton built about 1645 at "Norton's Point." Richard Glass came in 1660, and built at "Glass Head." John Black probably gave his name to "Black Cove Beach." Thomas Chubbs was here as early as 1636, and lived at the western part of the town. William Bennett came in 1637, and owned a house near the foot of "Bennett's Hill," and also a grist-mill on the site of the old Forster Mill.

"North Yarmouth" was first settled, it is supposed, by the grandsons of William Allen — Azariah, Jacob, Isaac, Malachi, and "Governor" Allen, so-called. This was about the middle of the last century. Azariah lived in a house near Cat Brook; only the cellar, covered by a growth of trees and bushes, now remains. One of his children, familiarly called "Bos'n John," a bluff old sea-king, built the house on Washington street now occupied by his grandson, Capt. John Allen. Jacob lived in the house nearest the woods still standing. He was a sergeant in the French war, and a man of standing in the community. One of his sons, Nathan Allen, also lived in this house; he was the father of ten children, one of whom was John Perry Allen. Isaac, an older son of Jacob, lived in the house now owned by Mr. Herbert Stanley. He was a man of great physical strength and prowess; it is said that he could catch a horse by the mane while running, and throw himself upon his back. "Governor" Allen owned and occupied the house with a sloping roof, now owned by Manuel Silva. He was a man of property and of somewhat masterful disposition. His premises had "a ponderous and ornamental gate" at the entrance. None of his descendants remained in town. This house was at one time owned by the Lee family, and was later known as the Prescott place. Mr. William Harvey Allen's house stands where one built by Malachi Allen, 2d, stood. This house was a large one with gable roof. Its white, sanded floors, huge chimney-place with crane and hooks, and mammoth oven are still remembered. It is supposed that all these houses were built by Jonathan Allen or his sons. Most of them had large families, and they were persons of mark and influence in town. The region was one attractive in its location and for the purposes of farming; but the sea and business pursuits proved too strong a counter-attraction, and their descendants have all left the neighborhood.

Near Cat Brook are several acres of cleared land where a house known as the "Molly Lendall house" once stood. Opposite the house of Jacob Allen was a house occupied by Hoopers, and afterwards by William Russell. This house was torn down some years ago, and a new one built upon the same site by B. W. Hildreth. This house was one of the oldest in town.

Here Master Moore taught "the rule of three" and navigation. The scholars were from the "Cove" and the "Row." The house standing near the old road to Gloucester is also a very old one. Isaac Lee, whose wife was an Allen, lived here. A "dame's school" was kept in this house in the early part of this century. Mrs. Rachel Lee, who lived to be 99 years and 8 months old, lived in this neighborhood. Her maiden name was Allen. She was the mother of Mrs. Mary Baker, now living at the age of 92.

APPENDIX E.

THE STORES.

THE first Store kept in town, of which any knowledge exists, was in the house of Mr. Joseph Proctor on Sea street. The storekeeper was Mrs. Samples, a woman of great energy and character. She afterwards married Col. Eleazar Crafts.[1] The "Franklin Building" has had a chequered history. First occupied by Colonel Crafts as a dwelling-house and store, it was afterwards occupied by Mrs. Elizabeth Lee, who here taught tailoring to many young women of Manchester; as a shoeshop by John W. Mann; from 1835 to 1848 it was used by John Perry Allen as a cabinet factory. In 1848 it was purchased by Capt. B. L. Allen. In 1849, Burnham and Gentlee leased it for ten years, raised it and fitted it up as a large and convenient store, regarded at the time as the best appointed country store in the county. The shelves, drawers and one counter in the northerly part of the store still remain as placed at that time. From 1859 to 1869 the store passed through various changes; at the latter date Mr. George F. Allen became the occupant, and remains to this day.

Ebenezer Tappan, son of Rev. Benjamin Tappan, began keeping store soon after the Revolution, in the building now owned by the Andrew Brown heirs, on Central street. Mr. Tappan continued in business here about forty years. He is said to have been the first store-

[1] See Appendix K.

keeper of his day who discontinued the sale of ardent spirits as a beverage.[1]

Capt. John Knight kept store in the northeasterly end of his dwelling-house, standing on the north of Saw Mill brook. An anecdote is related of a customer who came to Captain Knight's store one Saturday night to get his usual double supply of New England rum to last him over the Sabbath, as was the almost universal custom in those days. Captain Knight, not having a large stock on hand, asked the customer if he could not get along with one quart and keep the Sabbath. The reply was, " Well, I suppose I *could;* but, Captain Knight, *how* will it be kept?"

Mrs. Abby H. Trask began storekeeping in Gloucester, but soon returned to Manchester, and opened a store in her house in which she lived and died. Her business was largely in dry goods. She kept store for over forty years, and a large number of young women were employed by her from time to time.

About sixty years ago, Capt. John Hooper kept a "neighborhood" store at the "Cove." It was the resort of the Militia on training days.

Mrs. Hooper Allen was another of the old-time storekeepers, first in her house on Summer street, and later in the present Manchester House Annex on Union street. She put out a great deal of work which she paid for out of her store. She was a person of great business capacity.

Several stores were kept in early times on Washington street. A store was kept by Dea. D. L. Bingham in his house, and one by Israel F. Tappan on Bridge street. Mr. Tappan also made clocks and repaired watches and jewelry. Capt. Tyler Parsons had a store for a time in his dwelling-house. Mr. Isaac S. West commenced

---

[1] See Appendix K.

business in the store now occupied by F. B. Rust, and afterward in what was used for many years as a store by Crafts and Hooper. John Little, G. W. Marble, S. S. Colby, Samuel Adams, Larkin W. Story, A. W. Smith, John Evans, John Prince and Henry Knight are the names of others who have been in business in town. Miss Mary A. Baker kept a fancy goods store for many years in the building owned by her, on the Common, now occupied by Mrs. Hamilton.

The above list is not complete; but it includes all who have kept store in town for any length of time previous to 1880, with the exception of those now in business.

APPENDIX F.

The Military Service.

There are here given the names of Manchester men who served in the Army and Navy, (1) in the Indian Wars, (2) in the Revolution, (3) in the War of 1812, (4) in the War for the Union. That there were others in the earlier wars, there can be no doubt; but no complete record is in existence. There were also many who served on privateers, both in the Revolution and the War of 1812, of whom no full and accurate record remains.

I. THE INDIAN WARS.

No complete list is extant of the men who served in the early Indian and the French and Indian Wars.

It is known, however, that Samuel Pickworth, John Allen, Joshua Carter, and John Bennett [1] were killed at Bloody Brook (p. 55).

Jacob Morgan and John Hassam were killed at Louisburg. Jacob Foster was at the siege, and was not afterward heard from. David Allen was also among the American forces, and Lieut. Samuel May was in the engagement. Dr. Leach has also in his "Collections" the names of Thomas Jones and Samuel Foster as at Louisburg. (Pp. 62, 63.)

II. THE WAR OF THE REVOLUTION.

The following are the names of Manchester men who served in the Revolution.[2]

[1] The names of Charles Bennett and Samuel Bennett appear in some accounts.

[2] The names of the "Lexington Company" are given on p. 77. This company probably served but a short time, but many of the names subsequently appear.

Enlisted in 1775.

John Lendall,
Josiah Lee,
Wm. Kelham,
Henry Fredericks,
Jos. Kilham,
Eleaser Crafts,
Maj. Wm. Kitfield,
Lieut. Jos. Leach,
  "   Ezekiel Leach,
  "   Isaac Preston,

Samuel Bear,
John Allen,
William Dow,
Benj. Kimball,
Thomas Hooper,
John Knight,
Joseph Knight,
Dr. Joseph Whipple,
Samuel Ayres,
Joseph Haskell,
Isaac Lee.

Enlisted in 1776.

Amos Jones,
Isaac Allen,
John Kimball,
Thomas Whipple,

John West,
Abiel Burgess.
Thomas Gentlee,
Solomon Lee.

Enlisted in 1777.

Stilson Hilton,
Solomon Lee, Jr.,
Troy Lee,
John Danforth,
Jeremiah Dow,
Moses May,
James Lee,
Joseph Babcock,
Asarias Allen,
Hooper Allen,
John Dixey,

Benjamin Crafts,
John Poland,
Stephen Danforth,
Nicholas Babcock,
Israel May.
Amos Jones,
Ezekiel Knowlton,
Ebenezer Tappau,
John Babcock,
Michael Tappan,
John Lendall,
John Lendall, Jr.

In the Return of Men procured by Capt. Eli Parker, to serve in the Continental Army, Amherst, May 13, 1778, are the names of Sam. Brown and John Johnson, belonging to Manchester.

Wm. Camp was in " Billy Porter's " Company, Col. Ebenezer Francis' Regt. at Bennington.

Daniel Morgan, Ebenezer Lee, Wm. Pytman, were in Col. Jona. Titcomb's Regt.

Josiah Allen, Hooper Allen, Caleb Bartlett, Stephen Danford, Edward Hooper, Wm. Camp, Sam. Ayers, Israel May, David Morss, Matthew Sarocha, Nathan Story, Thomas Wood, John Badcock, John Bailey, Joseph Belcher, Thomas Bould, were three months' men, in 1777.

Robert Knowlton and Joseph Lee were nine months' men, enlisted April 20, 1778.

The list is incomplete. The Pay Rolls in the Adjutant General's office give other names, but it is doubtful in some instances if they were Manchester men. Probably a complete list of those who served in the Revolutionary War cannot now be secured.

The last survivor of the Revolutionary Soldiers was Ebenezer Tappan, who died May 16, 1849.

The names of Officers in the State Militia, from 1781, with date of commission, promotion and discharge, are to be found in the Adjutant General's office.

III. WAR OF 1812.

The Records of the War of 1812 are very meagre. There is, however, a list of eighty-five men who were enrolled in a Company of Foot, under Capt. Joseph Hooper. Among them will be recognized many who were the immediate ancestors of present inhabitants of Manchester.

INSPECTION ROLL

OF

CAPT. JOSEPH HOOPER'S COMPANY.

May, 1812.[1]

Joseph Hooper, Captain,
Daniel Friend, Lieut.,
Ebenezer Tappan, Jr., Sergt.,
Amos Knight, Sergt.,

[1] *Vide* p. 129.

William Lee,
Abiel Burgess, Jr.,
Levi Tuck,
Nath'l Hildreth,
James Tuck,
Jacob Cheever, 1st,
Joseph Lee, Jr.,
Nathan Allen, Jr.,
James Allen,
William Hale,
Andrew Brown, 2d,
John Driver,
Solomon Driver, Jr.,
Ezekiel Allen,
David Bennett,
Samuel Forster,
Simeon Haskell,
Andrew Roberts,
Nathan Carter,
Samuel Kinsman,
Benjamin Lee,
Wm. Norwood,
Benjamin Tappan,
James Brown,
John Miller,
John Farris,
Samuel Peart,
Eben'r Baker,
George Cross,
Nath'l M. Allen,
Aaron Lee,
Zacheus Goldsmith,
Israel Morgan, Jr.,
Thomas Ayres,
Caleb Knowlton,
Benjamin Knowlton,
Enos Merrill,
Samuel Edwards,
Abner Allen, Jr.,
John O. Morgan,

Richard Trask,
John W. Allen,
Asiah Brown,
William Goodale,
Richard Allen,
John Tuck,
Andrew Brown, 1st.,
John Cheever, Jr.,
Wm. Stone,
Joseph Allen,
Thomas H. Kitfield,
John Orsband,
Samuel Cheever,
Jacob Cheever, 2d,
Ben. Knowlton,
James Hildreth,
Ephraim Clemons,
Jacob Kitfield,
David Goldsmith,
John Goldsmith,
John Hooper,
Abraham Stone,
Abraham Stone, Jr.,
James Knight,
Benjamin Morgan,
Wm. Camp. Jr.,
Jacob Peart,
Isaac Lee, Jr.,
William Russell,
James Dow,
David Allen,
Isaac Preston,
William Mann,
Nathan Allen,
Thomas Leach,
Daniel Currier,
Wm. Peart,
Stephen Ferguson,
Nathan Lee, Jr.,
Sam'l Tuck,

Samuel Lee.

The last survivor was Jacob Cheever, who died in 1886.

IV. NAMES OF MEN WHO SERVED IN THE ARMY AND NAVY, 1861–1865.

From Report published by vote of the Town, March 19, 1866.[1]

The whole number of men furnished by the town for the Army and Navy is one hundred fifty-nine; twenty-four of whom reënlisted and counted a second time to the credit of the town, making a total of one hundred eighty-three men furnished under the different calls of the President, besides this town's proportion of the State naval credits at large.

Five enlisted on the first call for 75,000 men for three months, viz.:

Samuel W. Tuck,
Samuel Goodridge, Jr.,
Frederic W. Smith,
Albert C. Douglas,
Frank P. Haskell.

Sixty-eight enlisted to serve three years, or during the war, and for no bounty, namely:

Hugh Kinmonth,
Charles Juhnke,
Alexander Glenn,
Benjamin Allen, Jr.,
Hardy P. Murray,
Laban F. Cushing,
Edward F. Allen,
William H. Allen,
Isaac F. Allen,
Rufus S. Wadleigh,
Samuel Knowlton,
William H. Hooper,
Julius F. Rabardy,
George W. Glenn,
Henry P. Kitfield,
Thomas Poland,

David A. Lee,
Albert C. Douglass,
Samuel W. Tuck,
Ariel P. Crowell, Jr.,
Thomas D. Widger,
Dennis Donnovan,
James W. Widger,
Gilman Goldsmith,
John H. Harris,
George A. Brown, Jr.,
Frederick W. Smith,
George H. Morgan,
Stephen B. Allen,
Jacob E. Ayers,
Frank E. Tucker,
Albert H. Goldsmith,

[1] This report, evidently prepared with great care and accuracy, was presented by the Selectmen — George F. Allen, Aaron Bennett, Albion Gilman.

D. L. B. Knowlton,
William Albert,
Thomas J. Sargent,
Thomas McCormick,
Hiram C. Norcross,
William H. Bingham,
James E. Dustin,
Horace M. Osborne,
Daron W. Morse,
Frederic W. Martin,
Hiram Wagner,
Charles Cross,
Samuel Driver, Jr.,
Edwin P. Stanley,
George A. Rowe,
John C. Douglass,
William A. Stone,
Benjamin F. Tuck,

Samuel S. Hooper,
David Shepard,
Albert S. Dow,
Winthrop Sargent,
James H. Lee,
Robert T. Lucas,
John G. Lucas,
Amos K. Flowers,
Edward S. West,
William H. Haskell,
John C. Martin,
Jacob H. Dow,
Edward V. Wells,
Gilman D. Andrews,
Samuel J. Andrews,
Otis P. Gorten,
George W. Stanley,
Daniel S. Pert.

Twenty-one enlisted for three years, receiving a bounty from the town and state:

Charles E. Lee,	Town bounty.
Sewell M. Rogers,	" "
James H. Ireland,	" "
Charles W. Pert,	" "
William Miles,	" "
Charles L. Parsons,	" "
William Mitchel,	" "
Thomas G. Murphy,	" "
Samuel L. Pert,	" "
William Bourke,	" "
George H. Story,	" "
Charles E. Gilson,	" "
Larkin W. Story,	" "
Alfred S. Jewett,	" "
Charles P. Goldsmith, 2d enlistment,	" "

Andrew J. Crowell, received bounty from Hamilton, but credited to Manchester.

George H. Martin,	State bounty.
Benjamin F. Tuck, 2d enlistment,	" "
John H. Boynton,	" "
George H. Clements,	" "
Edward P. Hooper, 2d enlistment	" "

Seven were drafted July 10, 1863, for three years, and served until discharged at the end of the war, excepting one who died while in the service:

George Edward Andrews,   Charles H. Stone,
George E. Andrews,   Sam'l N. Lendall,
John H. Meader,   David C. Goodridge,
                John T. Goldsmith.

The two first named of these enlisted before the time appointed for examination, were accepted, and received the State bounty given to volunteers.

Twenty-three enlisted and served for nine months and received from the town a bounty of $100 each:

William E. Wheaton,   John H. Watson,
Jeffrey T. Stanley,   Charles P. Goldsmith,
Errol Grant,   Rufus P. Ferguson,
Luther F. Allen,   E. P. Davenport,
William J. Pert,   Joseph H. Bingham,
Francis B. Pert,   Jeremiah R. Lord,
Stephen A. Ferguson,   Milo T. Hardy,
Sam'l L. Allen,   Daniel S. Pert,
Frank P. Haskell,   Charles C. Parsons,[1]
Nathaniel M. Andrews,   George A. Foss,[1]
George Willmonton,   Edward P. Hooper,[1]
                Joseph A. Morgan,

Twenty-three enlisted for one year, who received a bounty from the town of $125 each. The first two, Higgins and Lawler, received from the citizens' fund, one $140, the other $175, additional.

Joseph H. Higgins,   George A. Lendall,
John Lawler,   Sam'l C. Martin,
Charles H. Dow,   Ezra Stanley, Jr.,
John R. Lee,   Henry C. Smith,
Edgar E. Jones,   John W. Stone,
James H. Andrews,   Benjamin Thompson,
Clarence Allen,   Edward V. Wells,
George P. Burnham,   Alex. H. C. Payson,
John A. Gilbert,   Edward Baker,
George Haskell,   Paul Stanley, 2d,
Augustus L. Juhnke,   Charles P. Crombie,
                George A. Jones.

[1] These three men received a bounty from Essex, Malden and Boston, but were credited to Manchester.

Fourteen enlisted for 100 days and received no bounty:

Clarence Allen,   William H. Elwell,
Henry C. Smith,   George N. Driver,
John W. Stone,   Thomas Morgan,
Edward V. Wells,   David F. Bennett,
Gustavus O. Stanley.   Orin W. Andrews,
Frank A. Rowe,   John G. Haskell, Jr.,
Charles G. Bingham,   Stephen G. Hildreth.

Three paid commutation money, and one furnished a substitute.

Eleven enlisted and served in the Naval Service:

John J. Giles,   Edward Baker,
George H. Story.   Jerry Kannaley,
Henry T. Bingham, Jr.,   Joseph Norcross,
Oliver F. Stone,   Wm. D. Giles, Master's Mate,
William H. Woodbury,   Oliver F. Smith, still in service,
                Isaac Baker.

Sixteen died in the military and two in the naval service:

Edward F. Allen. Taken prisoner, July 1, 1863, at battle of Gettysburg. Died Dec. 5, 1863, at Belle Isle Prison, Va.

William H. Allen. Taken prisoner at the same time, and died at the same place, November, 1863.

Rufus S. Wadleigh. Died at Culpeper, Va., Jan. 2, 1864, of chronic diarrhœa.

David A. Lee. Died at Yorktown, of fever, in May, 1862.

Horace M. Osborn. Drowned by accidentally falling from the steamer on his way to Newbern, N. C., June 18, 1863.

Samuel S. Hooper. Died of fever in Newbern, N. C., Apr. 13, 1862.

Albert S. Dow. Died at Beaufort, S. C., Sept. 14, 1863.

James H. Lee. Died in Newbern, N. C., Aug. 27, 1862, of inflammation of brain.

Charles L. Parsons. Died of chronic diarrhœa, Feb. 7, 1864.

Samuel L. Pert. Died Oct. 24, 1863, soon after arriving home.

Stephen A. Ferguson. Died July 19, 1863, of fever contracted in Newbern, at home only a few days.

Joseph A. Morgan. Died July 3, 1863, four days after arriving home, of fever and exhaustion.

George E. Andrews. Died near Washington, Sept. 26, 1864, of chronic diarrhœa.

Samuel Goodridge, Jr. Died in prison in Florence, S. C., Feb. 5, 1865.

Oliver F. Stone. Died in prison in Georgia; taken prisoner while on shore in naval service.

William H. Woodbury. Died on board of sloop-of-war Hartford, Sept. 7, 1862, off the coast of Florida, of fever.

Four were killed in battle, as follows: —

Ariel P. Crowell, Jr., at Gaines' Mills, Va., June 27, 1862.

Isaac F. Allen, at Antietam, Sept. 17, 1862.

William Bourke, at Antietam, Sept. 17, 1862.

Edward S. West, near the Weldon Railroad, Va., Aug. 16, 1864.

Two died from wounds received in action:

Hardy P. Murray, wounded July 1st, at the battle of Gettysburg; died July 8, 1863.

Benjamin Allen, Jr., wounded by a shell while under fire near the Weldon Railroad, Va., Aug. 23, 1864; was conveyed to Washington and died Aug. 29.

Discharged from service by reason of disease contracted while there, and wounds received in action:

Laban F. Cushing,
William H. Hooper,
Julius F. Rabardy,
Henry P. Kitfield,
Thomas McCormick,
James E. Dustin,
Daron W. Morse,
Frederic W. Martin,
Hiram Wagner,
Edwin P. Stanley,
John C. Douglass,
Benjamin F. Tuck,
Samuel W. Tuck,

George A. Brown, Jr.,
David Shepard,
Amos K. Flowers,
William H. Haskell,
Jacob H. Dow,
Edward V. Wells,
Gilman D. Andrews,
George W. Stanley,
William Miles,
Thomas G. Murphy,
Larkin W. Story,
Daniel S. Port,
Samuel N. Lendall.

Whole number wounded by the enemy, and now living: [1]

Charles Juhnke, in the hand.

William H. Hooper, lost an arm at Gettysburg.

Julius F. Rabardy, lost a leg at Antietam.

Daron W. Morse, shot through the body in action at Glendale, June 30, 1862.

[1] Mar. 19, 1866.

Frederic W. Martin, lost a leg in action at Glendale, June 30, 1862. [1]

Charles Cross, slightly at the battle of the Wilderness.

Samuel Driver, Jr., severely at Antietam, and the battle of the Wilderness.

Edwin P. Stanley, severely in leg at Glendale, June 30, 1862.

John C. Douglass, lost an arm at first Fredericksburg. [2]

Dennis Donnovan, wounded at the battle of Whitehall, N. C., Dec. 16, 1862, and at Cold Harbor, Va., June 3, 1864.

Stephen B. Allen, at the battle of Whitehall, N. C., Dec. 16, 1862.

Jacob E. Ayers, in action at Deep Bottom, Va., Aug. 18, 1864.

Robert T. Lucas, at the taking of Newbern.

Charles E. Lee, in action at Olustee, Fla.

George H. Story, at the battle of Cedar Creek, Va., Oct. 19, 1864. [3]

Luther F. Allen, slightly at the battle of Kingston, N. C.

John H. Meader, at Laurel Hill, Va., May 8, 1864, and at Hatcher's Run, Va., Feb. 4, 1865—serious.

Samuel N. Lendall, lost an arm at the battle of Laurel Hill, Va., May 8, 1864.

John H. Boynton, at Charlestown, Va., Aug. 29, 1864.

Jacob H. Dow, lost a leg in the attack before Petersburg, July 29, 1864, after the explosion of the mine which blew up a portion of the enemy's works.

Forty-eight were discharged by reason of the expiration of their term of service.

Seven were taken prisoners by the enemy, three of whom, Andrew J. Crowell, John T. Goldsmith and George H. Clements, were exchanged; the other four, Oliver F. Stone, Edward F. Allen, William H. Allen and Samuel Goodridge, Jr., died in rebel prison.

Whole number in the service at the close of the war and discharged by General Orders of the War Department, sixty :

Charles Juhnke,	Charles H. Stone,
Samuel Knowlton	David C. Goodridge,
Thomas Poland,	George H. Martin,
D. L. B. Knowlton,	John H. Boynton,

[1] Died Sept. 11, 1877.
[2] Died in California.
[3] Died June 16, 1877.

Hiram C. Norcross,
William H. Bingham,
Charles Cross,
Sam'l Driver, Jr.,
William A. Stone,
Albert C. Douglass,
Dennis Donnovan,
John H. Harris,
Stephen B. Allen,
Jacob E. Ayers,
Winthrop Sargent,
John C. Martin,
Sam'l J. Andrews,
Otis P. Gorten,
Charles E. Lee,
Sewell M. Rogers,
James H. Ireland,
Charles W. Pert,
William Mitchel,
George H. Story,
Charles E. Gilson,
Alfred S. Jewett,
Edward P. Hooper,
George Edward Andrews,
John H. Meader,
John T. Goldsmith.

George H. Clements,
John Lawler,
Joseph H. Higgins,
Charles P. Goldsmith,
Charles H. Dow,
John R. Lee,
Edgar E. Jones,
James H. Andrews,
Clarence Allen,
George P. Burnham,
John A. Gilbert,
George Haskell,
Augustus L. Juhnke,
George A. Jones,
Andrew J. Crowell,
George A. Lendall,
Samuel C. Martin,
Ezra Stanley, Jr.,
Henry C. Smith,
John W. Stone,
Benjamin Thompson,
Edward V. Wells,
Alex. H. C. Payson,
Edward Baker,
Paul Stanley, 2d,
Charles P. Crombie.

Three still remain in the service, one in the army,

Fred. W. Smith,[1]

and two in the navy,

William D. Giles,[1]
Oliver F. Smith.

Eighteen served through the war, first enlisted in the summer and fall of 1861, reënlisting at the end of two years; and two of them were among those who responded to the first call of President Lincoln for 75,000 men in April, 1861:

Frederic W. Smith,
Albert C. Douglass,
Charles Juhnke,
Samuel Knowlton,

William A. Stone,
Dennis Donnovan,
John H. Harris,
Stephen B. Allen,

[1] Discharged since this Report was prepared.

Thomas Poland,	Jacob E. Ayers,
Hiram C. Norcross,	Winthrop Sargent,
William H. Bingham,	John C. Martin,
Charles Cross,	Samuel J. Andrews,
Samuel Driver, Jr.,	Otis P. Gorten.

Number of Commissioned Officers, four:

Samuel W. Tuck, 1st Lieut.,
William A. Stone, 1st Lieut.,
Frederic W. Smith, 2d Lieut., Regular Army,
Charles Cross, 2d Lieut.

The above Report is of great value, and worthy of being placed in this permanent form for future reference.

Further information regarding the soldiers of Manchester, especially since the close of the War, may be found in the Records of Allen Post, No. 67, G. A. R.

The following classified list of Manchester men who died in the service will be found of convenience :

Died in Rebel Prisons.

Edmund C. Morgan, Co. G, 23d Reg't Mass. Vols., at Andersonville, Ga., Aug. 5, 1864.

Samuel Goodridge, Jr., Co. G, 23d Reg't Mass. Vols., at Florence, S. C., Feb. 5, 1865.

Oliver F. Stone, U. S. Gunboat Sumter, at Macon, Ga., Aug. 30, 1862.

William H. Allen, Co. K, 12th Reg't Mass. Vols., at Richmond, Va., November, 1863.

Edward F. Allen, Co. K, 12th Reg't Mass. Vols., at Richmond, Va., Dec. 5, 1863.

Died from Disease while in the Service.

Samuel L. Peart, Co. D, 40th Reg't Mass. Vols., at Manchester, Mass., Oct. 24, 1863.

Rufus L. Wadleigh, Co. K, 12th Reg't Mass. Vols., at Culpeper, Va., Jan. 2, 1864.

Charles L. Parsons, Co. D, 40th Reg't Mass. Vols., at Hilton Head, S. C., March 7, 1863.

George E. Andrews, Co. G, 3d Reg't H. A. Mass. Vols., at Fort Bacon, D. C., Sept. 26, 1864.

Horace M. Osborne, Co. G, 23d Reg't Mass. Vols., drowned June 18, 1863, while returning from furlough to rejoin his Reg't.

Joseph A. Morgan, Co. A, 45th Reg't Mass. Vols., at Manchester, Mass., July 3, 1863.

Stephen A. Ferguson, Co. A, 45th Reg't Mass. Vols., at Manchester, Mass., July 19, 1863.

Albert S. Dow, Co. D, 24th Reg't Mass. Vols., at Morris Island, S. C., Sept. 4, 1863.

Samuel S. Hooper, Co. F, 23d Reg't Mass. Vols., at Newbern, N. C., April 13, 1862.

David A. Lee, Co. H, 19th Reg't Mass. Vols., at Newport News, Va., June 4, 1862.

James H. Lee, Co. D, 24th Reg't Mass. Vols., at Little Washington, N. C., Sept. 7, 1862.

William H. Woodberry, U. S. Sloop of War, Hartford, at Pensacola, Fla., Sept. 7, 1862.

Died from Wounds Received in Battle.

Hardy P. Murray, Co. K, 12th Reg't Mass. Vols., at Gettysburg, Pa., July 6, 1863.

Serg't Benjamin Allen, Jr., Co. K, 11th Reg't Mass. Vols., at Washington, D. C., Aug. 24, 1864.

Killed in Battle.

Corp. Ariel P. Crowell, Jr., Co. E, 22d Reg't Mass. Vols., June 27, 1862, at Gaines' Mills, Va.

Isaac F. Allen, Co. K, 12th Reg't Mass. Vols., Sept. 17, 1862, at Antietam, Md.

William Bourke, Co. F, 28th Reg't Mass. Vols., Sept. 17, 1862, at Antietam, Md.

Edward S. West, Co. K, 24th Reg't Mass. Vols., Aug. 16, 1864, near Weldon Railroad, Va.

> " The voice of patriot blood,
> Thus poured for faith and freedom, hath a tone
> Which from the night of ages, from the gulf
> Of death, shall burst, and make its high appeal
> Sound unto earth and heaven."

FIRST POST OFFICE.

APPENDIX G.

THE POST OFFICE SERVICE.

[The facts given below were furnished by George F. Allen and J. F. Rabardy, Esqs., whose kindness has placed the writer under great obligation.]

THE first Postmaster of Manchester was Dea. Delucena L. Bingham, who was appointed in 1803, and held the office until his death in 1837. At the beginning of Mr. Bingham's term there were three mails per week from Gloucester and Manchester to Boston, carried by Jonathan Low's coach, which left Manchester at 9 A. M., and returning, arrived at 3 P. M. the following day. Previous to this, mails had been carried "when convenient," by a Sloop commanded by the father of Dea. A. E. Low. For the year 1803, the receipts of the office were $7.00. In 1820, there were but two papers taken at the "Cove," the *Palladium* and the *Columbian Centinel*.[1] Capt. John Knight took the *Palladium*, and held it in such esteem that he named one of his vessels for it.

William Dodge was appointed Postmaster Nov. 17, 1837, and served until 1845. He owned the tavern, and kept the Office in it, being assisted sometimes by his wife. At the beginning of his term there was one mail daily, arriving about 3 P. M.; at its expiration, there were two mails, carried by the four-horse coaches which ran from Boston to Gloucester. These were the palmy days of stage-coaching.

---

[1] These were both semi-weeklies. The number of dailies now taken in town averages about 250 *per diem*; this is exclusive of the summer season.

Col. Jefferd M. Decker succeeded William Dodge, Sept. 29, 1845, both as Postmaster and proprietor of the hotel. On retiring from the hotel business, he removed the Office to the house owned by the descendants of D. L. Bingham. During his term, papers published in the county were delivered free to county subscribers. Mr. Decker was a man of military bearing and tastes ; he commanded a militia company in town, and served in the early part of the War of the Rebellion.

George F. Allen was appointed April 4, 1849, by Postmaster-General Collamore, to succeed Colonel Decker. Mr. Allen says, " In those days, the Office had no special value in a pecuniary sense, and there was no surplus of applicants. I was appointed because Mr. Decker resigned and moved out of town, and there was no other candidate." The mails at this time were brought by stage from Salem, John W. Low, Contractor. To him was remitted the amount due the Government on Quarterly Returns, averaging about $70. The Postmaster's compensation, including Box rent, amounted to about $300 per year. At the first of the term, the Essex mail was made up at Manchester. Domestic postage was forty cents to the Pacific Coast, five cents under one hundred miles, and ten cents over. Postage to Great Britain was twenty-four cents; single letters to China, sixty-five cents; to Germany, twenty-four cents. Newspaper postage was one cent within one hundred miles, one and a half cents beyond, except to California, which was three cents, and to Great Britain, four cents. Postage on papers sent to subscribers was to be paid quarterly in advance. In making up the mail, every letter had to be " billed " to the place of its destination if within the State; letters out of the State to Boston as a distributing office; a

record also had to be made of these. All letters
received came "billed" in like manner, and these
"bills" were recorded and placed on file. At the close
of the quarter these records were transcribed, and with
the "bills" sent to Washington. With the introduction of cheap postage and the great increase of business
about the middle of the century, this cumbrous system
was discontinued.

Mr. Allen kept the Office, first in the "Bingham
house," and afterward in the store now occupied by D.
T. Beaton. He held the office for four years, "until
there was no more need of a Whig Postmaster."

Mr. John Prince Allen succeeded Mr. Allen in 1853,
and proved himself a good-natured, accommodating
official. He had his Office on the northwest corner of
the Common, near the site of the present Police Station,
in a building used as a cabinet shop.

Henry F. Lee was appointed April 18, 1861 ; he was
a Republican, "but not of long standing." The Office
was kept in the room in the Lee building recently occupied
as a furnishing store, opposite the present location. The
accommodations were very good for the time. Mr. Lee
held the Office during the War, and his wife is remembered by many for her sympathetic and faithful service
in those days when the mail often came laden with
messages of sorrow to the families and loved ones left
at home by the nation's defenders. The compensation
at this time was $400 per year. The Boxes were few,
and no return was made of them to the Department.

Julius F. Rabardy, a native of France, in accordance
with a law of Congress providing that government
offices be given, when advisable, to wounded or disabled Union soldiers, was appointed Postmaster, Aug. 9,
1865, and took charge of the Office, Oct. 1. The office
was first kept in the cabinet shop above spoken of;

afterward in the store now occupied by D. T. Beaton; and later in the "old Bingham house." But as more room was needed, it was removed to its second tarrying place, and kept there until the completion of Mr. Rabardy's Block in 1885. About this time, the Democratic party came into power, and against the earnest remonstrance of a large number of the citizens, in many cases irrespective of party, Mr. Rabardy was removed from the position which he had filled with fidelity and to the satisfaction of the people generally.

It was the custom when Mr. Rabardy took the Office to put up letters, papers and other mail matter, addressed to those who had not Boxes, in the window, as they were received. Subsequently, when the business of the Office made this practically impossible, they were placed on an octagonal drum behind glass, which any one could turn by a projecting rim at the bottom. This worked well, but was discontinued by order of the Department, making it unlawful to expose letters to public view, and requiring letters not intended for private Boxes to be advertised.

Until 1872, the mails for Essex were received here, and carried by coach to that town. The Magnolia mail was also received at Manchester until the Magnolia station was built.

From Oct. 1, 1865, to July 1, 1866, the revenue averaged $60 per quarter; the compensation amounted to $100 for the same time, consequently the latter was reduced to $67.50 per quarter. But in July, 1868, the yearly pay was raised to $430, the net return for the year having been $469.25. In 1874, the net revenue was $547.35, and the salary was raised to $600 per year. From July 1 to Sept. 1, 1885, Mr. Rabardy's last quarter, the net revenue was $630.94, and the compensation $250 for the same period. The business of the Office for this quarter was: One-cent Stamps, 1,000; Two-cent Stamps, 33,000 Five-cent Stamps, 700 Ten-cent Stamps, 300. Total, including wrappers and envelopes, $746. The amount collected for Boxes was $70, returnable to Government.

Among the improvements made by the P. O. Department, during Mr. Rabardy's twenty years of service, were the reduction of Domestic postage from three to two cents per one half ounce; the introduction of Postal Cards, the Money Order system, and the formation of the Postal Union, which to-day includes over eighty nationalities, of almost all grades of civilization, and secures safety and regularity in the transmission of mails and a low rate of postage over nearly the whole world.

During Mr. Rabardy's term of office, not a single Registered letter, foreign or domestic, was lost, and no native ever asked aid in recognizing his name. In 1870 Mr. Rabardy opened a telegraph office, which was a great public convenience, at his own risk and expense, and thus placed the town under great obligations; the office was relinquished by him after fifteen years, on his dismissal from public service.

Mr. William J. Johnson received appointment as Postmaster, Sept. 2, 1885, and opened the Office in October in the place which it has since occupied. In 1887, Manchester was made a Money Order office, and the year's business in that branch amounted to about $10,000. The same year, the office became a third-class office, and Mr. Johnson was confirmed as Postmaster of that grade by the Senate, Jan. 16, 1888. In the year ending Dec. 31, 1889, the receipts of the office were $2,561.47; the salary was $1,200, fuel, light and rent being paid by the Department.

Mr. Jeffrey T. Stanley succeeded Mr. Johnson, March

1, 1890. He had served in the 45th Regiment, Massachusetts Volunteers. Mr. Stanley was succeeded in 1895 by Mr. Charles H. Danforth.

The business of the Office in 1894 was as follows: Stamps, Stamped Envelopes, Postal Cards and Wrappers, $3,079.55; Money Orders, 836; Box-rents, $334.70; Registered Letters and Packages received and sent, 662.

ENGINE HOUSE.

APPENDIX H.

THE FIRE DEPARTMENT.

THE matter of fires and methods of extinguishing them very early claimed the attention of the people in the larger towns. Buildings were constructed at first almost entirely of wood, and fires were common. There were fires in the early history of Boston which, for size and destructiveness, considering the small population and limited area, were as disastrous as many of the great fires of recent times. From 1653 to 1795, no less than twenty fires had occurred "so extensive in their desolation as to be selected for the records of history."[1] Many of these fires were accompanied by a sad loss of life.

The early records show that there was a great fear of fires; precautions were taken which seem almost oppressive. The following By-Laws were adopted by the town in 1808:

It is ordered—That no person or persons shall presume to make any bonfires, or set fire to any wood, straw, shavings, or other combustible matter, by night or by day, in any street, lane or alley, or in any private or public yard, in this town, or make any bonfire in any part of the town on the evening of the fifth day of November,[2] in any year hearafter, under the penalty of forfeiting and paying Three Dollars.

If charcoal was kindled by "any tradesmen or others in a pot or pan out of doors, nigh their house or shop," it was to be "during the daylight only," and some care-

[1] *A Brief History of the Massachusetts Charitable Fire Society*; H. H. Sprague. Boston, 1893.

[2] Guy Fawkes' Day, the Anniversary of the Gunpowder Plot, 1605.

ful person was to stand by " to watch the same while it
shall continue in the open aire." It was also ordered:

That no person or persons shall presume hereafter to carry
fire from any house or place within the town to any other
house or place within the same, but in some vessel which
shall sufficiently secure the fire from being [blown] about by
the wind, or scattered by the way—under penalty of forfeiting and paying the sum of Fifty Cents for each offence.

Chimneys were to be " Regularly and Seasonably
Cleansed." The " firing " of chimneys was to be " at
or nearly a calm time, when it shall actually rain or
snow, and between the time of sun rising and twelve
o'clock at noon." It was further ordered:

That no person shall hang any beef or pork for the purpos
of smoking the same, on the top of any chimney unless upon
an iron bar or hook, on penalty of forfeiting and paying Two
Dollars.

Defective chimneys were to be " viewed " by the
Selectmen ; it was forbidden to run any funnel through
a wooden building except it was " surrounded with
brick work," and no stove was to be placed in any
store " without a double hearth." Coopers were not to
" burn Casks but in a sufficient chimney," and Boat
builders were not to " steam or burn any boards or
plank . . . but in such place as in the opinion of the
Selectmen shall be thought safe."

From these and similar precautions it seems that prevention was considered better than cure. Our fathers
believed that " fire is a good servant, but a bad master,"
and acted accordingly. And they determined that as a
servant it should be made to keep its place. To these
restrictions, burdensome as they may seem, they no
doubt owed, in a large measure, their immunity from
serious and sweeping conflagrations.

According to one of our oldest citizens, Manchester

was very early awake to the necessity of an efficient fire
department. "The fire brigade of those days was a
voluntary institution, the members serving without pay,
but was nevertheless very effective." The substantial
citizens furnished their hall-ways with leather buckets,
in which they took great pride. "They were handsomely painted, with the owner's name enclosed in an
artistic design upon their sides." In case of an alarm,
the people rallied, a line was formed to the nearest
water, and under the direction of some influential citizen the work commenced. "During the existence of
this system, covering a period of one hundred and fifty
years, but two buildings are known to have been destroyed by fire."

Manchester adopted some enterprising measures in
the direction of protecting the town against fires, when
the Fire Departments, even in the cities, were in a very
primitive stage of development. In 1828, the town
bought the first fire engine, the "Eagle," and twelve
pairs of leather buckets, and a citizens' fire company
was formed. Col. Eben Tappan was engaged in the
manufacture of fire engines at this time, and built one
in 1832, the "Torrent," a suction engine, which was
used in the great fire of 1836, and was afterward bought
by the town.[1] This engine did good service until laid
up in ordinary, in 1885, a period of fifty-three years, a
most remarkable record.

Mr. Tappan had been in the furniture business about
eleven years, when in 1826 he began the building of fire
engines, without a previous knowledge of foundry work
or special instruction in mechanics. "The plans were
entirely his own, and he worked out his own models

[1] An engine is mentioned in the Gloucester *Telegraph*, Sept. 25, 1830, as
built by Mr. Tappan, which "held about 125 gallons," and was "capable of
emptying itself in one minute, throwing a good column of water a distance
of 105 feet."

and patterns. The village blacksmith did the ironwork under Mr. Tappan's immediate supervision. The brasswork came to Mr. Tappan from a Boston foundry in the rough, and Mr. Tappan's own hands finished and fitted it. He also did all the work of the coppersmith. In short, with the aid alone of the blacksmith, to whom reference is made above, the engines from Mr. Tappan's hands were the result of his own unaided skill and industry."[1]

In April, 1836, Engine Company No. 2 was organized, with E. Smith, S. F. Parsons and J. A. Allen as "Captains." This company disbanded, April 2, 1838, "the clerk only dissenting." A new company was formed, April 4, 1838, and disbanded April 4, 1839. On April 24, 1839, a company was again formed, with John C. Wells, G. W. Marble and John Godsoe as "Masters," and J. W. Mann as Clerk. The fire department seems now to have got fairly upon its feet, and its history may be said to have commenced.

Two of the greatest fires with which the town has been visited occurred when the department was yet young and inexperienced, and appear to have been handled with bravery and skill. These were the "great fire" of Aug. 28, 1836,[2] and the fire of Feb. 1, 1838.[3] Thus early in its history weighed, and not found wanting, the department has never failed in its prompt and efficient service in times of danger.

Some of the earlier votes on record are of present-day interest; among them are these :

April 24, 1839, "Voted the use of the Hall to the Infant Sabbath School for this season on the Sabbath."

May 2, 1842, the constitution was amended as follows :

[1] Salem *Daily Telegram*, June 6, 1888.

[2] *Vide* page 148.

[3] John and Henry Knights' Bark Mill and Currier Shop.

Art. 6. " Any person wishing to become a member must sign the total abstinence Pledge."

June 6, 1842, " Voted not to admit boys under 14 years of age into the reading room ; and all boys for disorderly behaviour to be expelled immediately."

May 17, 1843, " Voted to take the following list of papers, viz., *Daily Bee*, *Mercantile Journal*, *Zion's Herald*, Philadelphia *Saturday Courier*, *Essex Co. Washingtonian*, Boston *Cultivator*, Portland *Transcript*." May 2, 1871, " Voted that this association subscribe for two daily papers, namely, the Boston *Post* and Boston *Journal*; also four weekly papers, namely, the *Commonwealth*, *Ploughman*, Gloucester *Telegraph*, and Portland *Transcript*."

Under date of Sept. 3, 1877, mention is made of the "Franklin," a " spare engine without a company, stored in a small building owned by Charles Lee." This was an engine purchased of the city of Lynn, and was too large and heavy for ordinary use; it needed a force of a hundred men to handle it.

The "Manchester," bought in 1872, at a cost of $1,635, is a good hand engine, and still serviceable.

On Nov. 15, 1880, Mr. John Knight's Tannery was burned. This was a large fire and threatened the destruction of much adjoining property. It was got under control, however, before assistance arrived from neighboring towns.

In 1885, an Amoskeag Steam Fire-Engine, the " Seaside," was bought, costing $3,000, and a new company formed, the old company disbanding May 4, tendering its records to the Selectmen, with a " request that they be placed in the Vault of the town for safe keeping." An Engine House was built on the Common, the present Police Station. In 1891, the present commodious and well equipped Engine House on School street was built, on the site of the old Engine House which was moved to the rear of Mr. Samuel Knight's residence.

A Chemical Engine costing $1,774.50 was added to the apparatus in 1889.

The following information is from the Report of the Board of Engineers for the year ending Feb. 28, 1895.

Apparatus.

One Steamer, Fourth class Amoskeag. One Chemical Engine. One Hook and Ladder Truck, containing a good supply of sails, ropes and ladders, including one 40-foot extension ladder. Four Hose Carriages. Four Ladder Boxes in the outlying sections, well supplied with ladders. One Hand Engine, not in commission.

Force of the Department.

One Chief and two Assistant Engineers. One Engineer, one Fireman and Twenty-one Members, for the Steamer "Seaside." Ten Members for the Chemical Engine. Eighteen Members for the Hook and Ladder. Total number of men in the Department, Fifty-four.

Estimated value of property, not including Reservoirs or Engine House, about $7,500.

The material equipment of the Fire Department fifty years ago would now be considered cumbrous, weak and inefficient, belonging to a crude and altogether unscientific age.[1] But, judged by the list of papers in its reading room, and its total abstinence by-law, it must be confessed that its *morale* was high. There were, in sooth, "Great-hearts" in those days to man the brakes and pass the buckets. And the Department was well organized and well disciplined, if the frequent adoption of stringent by-laws, and the significant action of April 24, 1839, "Voted, to *abide* to our By-laws," — be any criterion. Great as has been the improvement in apparatus, the early firemen certainly possessed personal

[1] Three buckets preserved as mementoes, hanging in the Engine Room, and inscribed respectively, EAGLE, 1828, TORRENT, 1835, FRANKLIN, 1865, mark the contrast between the appliances of a former time and the present. They are a simple but picturesque memorial of departed days.

courage, skill and endurance worthy of all the praise which they have received. Modern improvements have been mainly in the line of better machinery, of greater variety and power of equipment, and in the use of horse power, steam and electricity. With their simple and meagre apparatus, the firemen of forty or fifty years ago performed feats of valor and skill, which the men of to-day will do well to equal.

In the future it will be found that it is in the prevention of fires rather than the extinguishing of them that the safety of a community mainly consists; the danger of a general conflagration seeming to increase about in proportion to the means of arresting and subduing it, as witness the "Great Fires" of recent times.[1]

All honor must be given to the brave men who spring to duty at the call of the dread alarum, who flinch not amidst flying cinders and deafening roar of flame, who with true knightly devotion fling themselves into battle with the fiercest of foes, who make their own the ancient devices of their guild, — painted on buckets and inscribed on banners,—

PRO BONO PUBLICO;

SEMPER PARATUS;

NIL DESPERANDUM.

---

[1] *Great Fires and Fire Extinction*, by Gen. A. P. Rockwell, Boston, 1878.

APPENDIX I.

Some Old Books.

PROBABLY the oldest Bible in town, and one of the oldest in the country, is in the custody of the Historical Society. It was "Imprinted at London by the deputies of Christopher Barker Printer to the Queenes most Excellent Majestie, 1599." It is a good deal worn by use and by "the tooth of time"; the following portions being wanting, Gen. i–Deut. xvi, 1 Tim. iv–Rev. xxii, besides scattered leaves or parts of leaves here and there. The title page of the New Testament is mostly preserved, giving the date. It is a copy of the Bible known as the "Bishops'" Bible, translated in 1563; it contains marginal references and annotations, and each book is prefixed by an Argument; there are also some quaint maps and diagrams of Ezekiel's temple. The ink and paper must have been good, as the type is still perfectly clear and legible except where greatly worn and defaced by handling.

Upon the blank leaf separating the Old and New Testaments is the following writing, without date, "——— sire of John Lee and Sarah ———ee the Owners of this Book that it become the Property of their Grandson Thomas Lee after their Decease." Below are the autographs, Thomas Lee, Junr, and anna allen.

It is said that this Bible was sent from England by John Lee to his grandson, Thomas Lee, Jr., who was born in Manchester in the house now owned and occupied by Mrs. Abby Baker,[1] in 1694, and where he died in 1775. After his death, the book was in the Lee family until about sixty-five years ago, when the last of

[1] Henry Lee deeded this house to his widow, in 1674; see cut, p. 49.

the family, who occupied the house above referred to,
died, and it came into possession of Dea. Enoch Allen, by
purchase at auction. After Dea. Allen's death in 1845, his
daughter restored the volume to Mr. Charles Lee, a descendant in direct line from Thomas Lee, Jr.   Soon after
Mr. Lee's death in 1889, his daughter, Miss Ella F. Lee,
of the seventh generation from John Lee, of England,
the original owner, presented it to the Historical Society
for safe keeping.

The book is an interesting and valuable historical
relic.   It was printed thirty years before the Landing
at Plymouth, and was almost half a century old when
Manchester received its present name.   For obvious
reasons, copies of the " Bishops' " Bible are more sel-
dom found in New England than those of the " Geneva "
translation, and of course are much more rare than old
copies of King James' Version.   It is of special interest
as a book that has been in the possession of Manchester families for two hundred years, and was, no doubt,
in daily use in the Lee family through several generations.   It may have been in the hands of some of the
first settlers, and is a memento to their descendants of
the source from which their religious faith and their
civic virtues took their spring.

Two old books in the Town Library are the Second
and Fourth volumes of Matthew Henry's Commentary.
They evidently belonged to different sets.   One has the
autograph of Ebenezer Tappan, 1790, and very likely
was the property of his father, Rev. Benjamin Tappan,
who died in that year.   The other was owned in partnership.   An inscription, very much faded, on the inside of the cover shows how much beyond the means of
most persons were books of this size and cost, and the
estimation in which they were held.   The writing is in
a beautiful round hand.

Manchᵣ 14ᵗʰ June 1734.

Memorandᵐ

That this Book & the Rest of the First Five Volumes of the Revᵈ Mᵣ Henry's Exposition upon the Holy Bible, Together with the Revᵈ Mᵣ Burkit's Exposition upon the New Testament are held in Partnership Between Messʳˢ Nathˡ Lee Benjᵃ Allen Nathˡ Marsters Ezekiel Goodel Rich: Coye & Robᵗ Herrick for the —— Benefit of Themselves their Heirs Execˢ & Admʳˢ Upon Condition that each Proprietor shall have the Use of but one Book at a Time, and not to Keep it longer than Six Months; and at the End of every Six Months They are to Exchange them One with another upon Demand in a numerical Order

[Here the inscription becomes illegible.]

The book is mostly in a good state of preservation, and is an interesting memorial of the intelligence and devout piety of the " Proprietors."

There are other old books in town, but few as old or as interesting as these.

Another volume may serve as a sample of a " world-lie " book. For its age, it is a decidedly handsome specimen of the bookmaking art. The book is a valuable one as evidence that there was some good learning in Manchester a hundred and thirty-five years ago. Its title, abbreviated, is as follows : The Young Mathematician's Guide ; Being a Plain and Easy Introduction to the Mathematics. I. Arithmetic, Vulgar and Decimal. II. Algebra. III. The Elements of Geometry. IV. Conic Sections. V. The Arithmetic of Infinites. With an Appendix on Practical Gauging. And a Supplement on the History of Logarithms. By John Ward, London, 1758. The title page bears the name of Simeon Miller, in a very ornate style of penmanship, with the words *Ejus Liber*, and the date Jan. 1, 1760. Mr. Miller was a teacher, and lived on the " Row "; he has no direct descendants among us.

APPENDIX J.

POLICE REGULATIONS.

IN these times when Personal Liberty is placed by many above Public Morals and Public Safety, some of the early town legislation would seem burdensome and tyrannical in the extreme, and would no doubt stir up a rebellion. Our fathers, however, believed in good manners and self-restraint, and found them an excellent schooling and conducive to public comfort, respectability and safety.

In 1808, it was ordered

That no person or persons shall presume to smoke any pipe or Segar in any outhouses or barns used for hay, at any time, or in any of the streets or lanes in this town, after sunset, and that every person offending against this order shall forfeit and pay the sum of two Dollars. [1]

There was an ordinance forbidding "Ball, Stone or Sticks" to be played with a "battler or club," within "Seventy Yards of any Public building or Dwelling house."

"Guns or pistols charged with ball or shoot" were not to be fired "within one mile of the compact part of the town, in a direction whereby the lives of any of the inhabitants may be endangered, being in such part of the town."

Carts and carriages were not to be driven "through any public highways, lanes or alleys of this town, but at a foot pace or common walk, nor without a sufficient

---

[1] Many years after this, men who were accustomed to smoke regularly, never smoked on the streets; it was not considered "good form."

driver." Minute regulations were made as to the manner of driving horses, either by holding the "thill or
hindermost horse" by a halter, or if in a carriage by
"bits in the mouth . . . with reins fastened in such
manner as to give the driver full command, etc."

Stringent measures were also taken to prevent "Persons Behaving in a Rude and Disorderly Manner" in
any of the highways or near any dwelling house in the
night time. It was ordered that any who

shall insult any Person within the town, or be guilty of
rude or disorderly behaviour, or use indecent or profane language in the night time, to the annoyance or disturbance of
any of the inhabitance, or by cutting or defacing fences or
buildings; shall forfeit and pay for every such offence, 50
cents, to be recovered by complaint or information, to a justice of the peace; one moiety to the use of the poor of the
town, and the other moiety to the use of the constable or other
person who shall inform and prosecute for the same.

We may smile at such "paternal" government, but
we might be better off if we had a little more of it. It
is possible that in some particulars our fathers were
sometimes over-governed. But the children are now
making up for it by not being governed at all.
Which is the greater evil it needs no Solon to decide.
The most singular thing about these old by-laws is, that
they were made *to be enforced*, and not simply to adorn
the records.

APPENDIX K.

Some Notabilities.

MANCHESTER has been the birthplace and home of many persons, both men and women, who were possessed of marked individuality and force of character. There was WILLIAM ALLEN, ancestor of most of the Allens in Manchester and vicinity, who came over to Cape Ann in 1624 and settled in Manchester "about 1640"; one of the first selectmen, a carpenter who built the first frame house in town, and "an influential and enterprising citizen." —— There was BENJAMIN ALLEN, one of the first deacons, serving from 1716 until his death in 1747.——There was SAMUEL ALLEN, father of *thirteen* children, town clerk, selectman and merchant, born in 1701.——There was Capt. JOHN ALLEN, "Bos'n Allen," one of the old-time Yankee Vikings, who built the brick house now owned and occupied by his grandson, Capt. John Allen, a lordly house in its time.——There were Capt. "BEN" ALLEN, and the three brothers, JOHN, JAMES and SAMUEL, all "noted shipmasters."——There was MALACHI ALLEN, 2d, a gentleman of the old school who is described by one who is still living,[1] and who worked for him when a boy at the "Cove," seventy-one years ago, as "a man of much dignity of character, of an inquiring mind, and much interested in hearing about foreign countries; always asked a blessing at meals; he was a good man; was about five feet, ten inches in height, wore short clothes, had a queue, and silver buckles on his shoes." He was able to work about his

[1] Charles H. Allen, of Salem, Mass.

323

farm when over eighty years of age, and when eighty-nine "could cut up a codfish like a young man." A fine and edifying figure must have faded out of the land-scape, when he ceased to walk abroad.——There was "Skipper" PRESTON of Newport, whose self-conscious-ness would have done credit to the quarter-deck of a frigate, a kind of self-constituted tribune of the little hamlet; a man who was a law to himself, as he very plainly gave the Selectmen to understand when they thought to instruct the District as to the duties of the District School Committee. ——There was JOHN DODGE, a representative old-time "skipper," a man of prodigious strength, who performed the astonishing feat of lifting seven fifty-six-pound weights with his teeth. He knew all the intricacies of the New England coast, and could make harbor in the darkest night from the sound of the breakers on the different reefs. He was the father of Cyrus Dodge.——There was EDWARD NORTHEY, who lived at the "Cove" and was of the craft of silver-smiths, some of whose workmanship is in the possession of a descendant in the town, and is highly valued. Mr. Northey went to New Hampshire about the commence-ment of the Revolution. His trade was one that could be carried on with greater security away from the sea-board.——There was 'Squire COLBY, a kind of natural "deemster," whose decisions according to "common statute law" were as generally accepted without appeal by litigious parties as were those of higher legal authorities.——There was Major HENRY STORY, a left-handed Benjamite, of rather dubious maritime reputa-tion, whose stalwart form and Yankee spirit impressed the guards of Dartmoor prison with a wholesome

1 The incident is given on the authority of Mr. John Lee, who repre-sented the majesty of the town in the *rencontre*, and narrated it to Mr. D. L. Bingham.

respect. —— There was EDWARD LEE, the fervid ex-
horter, whose erect figure and white locks formed a
conspicuous object in the meeting-house in his later
years, as he stood during the long service, and whose
remarkable foreboding of approaching calamity, uttered
upon his death-bed with "something of prophetic strain,"
was thought by many to have found fulfilment in the
"great sickness." —— There was Major LEE, a man of
autocratic temper, and an owner of slaves when human
flesh and blood were still bought and sold in Massachusetts; his house with the slavepens in the attic, which
occupied the site of the "Rabardy Building," surviving
its imperious owner almost a century.——There was
"Goodman" BABCOCK, the tything-man, a grizzly
veteran of Valley Forge, whose duty it was to watch
over the youths of "disorderly carriage," and see that
they "behave themselves comely"; and whose austere
demeanor, stately tread and staff of office made an impressive figure in the Sunday assembly, where he
seemed to embody in his person the combined authority
of Church and State. [1]——There was ANDREW LEE, a
notable character. Originally an ardent Universalist,
he became later in life an equally earnest disciple of
evangelical religion. He was a man greatly esteemed
for his integrity and his benevolent disposition. His
love for the Sunday school and his love of children
were prominent characteristics to the very last. His
life was written by his pastor, Rev. O. A. Taylor, and
published by the Massachusetts Sunday School Society.
——There was Mrs. (SAMPLES) CRAFT, who when

---

[1] Many amusing anecdotes are told of this village beadle's pompous
ways and eccentric manners. One of our most respected aged citizens
well remembers the terror struck into his heart as a small boy when de-
tected in some childish prank, by the stern official pointing his finger at
him and calling out in stentorian voice, "I see you, serving the devil, in
the Lord's house."

Boston was invested by the British, made a journey there on foot, eluded the sentries, procured a supply of pins and needles, of which there was a distressful need, and made her way home to the great joy of the housewives who had been using thorns for pins, and whose stock of needles had become wholly exhausted.—— There was "Aunt" MARTHA LEE, a kind of spiritual authority and "mother in Israel."—— There was "Mother" DODGE, a woman who bore her testimony on all occasions, with most unconventional freedom, often supplementing the sermon with her exhortation, a kind of modern prophetess.

The sketches which follow are selected mainly because the materials were more accessible, or because the subjects were of a somewhat representative character.

The experience of NATHANIEL ALLEN, known as "Sailmaker Allen," one of Manchester's sea-rovers, illustrates the adage, that "truth is stranger than fiction." He was a soldier in the Revolution, crossed the Delaware with Washington, was in the battles of Trenton and Princeton, and in other hard-fought conflicts, was taken prisoner, and kept for a time by a band of Indians, of whom he learned the art of making birch canoes, baskets, etc. After his release, he returned to seafaring life. In October, 1780, he shipped on the schooner "America," bound to the West Indies. On the return passage, December 31, they encountered a violent gale, and lost sails, bowsprit and rudder. In this disabled condition, they had for two months a succession of heavy winds and seas, and drifted helplessly up and down the Atlantic. For *two hundred and sixty-one days*, these men were at the mercy of the stormy waves, at times reduced almost to the last mouthful and the last drop of water, when they were rescued, and carried into New York; they finally reached home, so emaciated that they were scarcely recognized by their friends who had long since given them up for lost.

BENJAMIN CRAFT, who was at the siege of Louisburg, kept a journal of the expedition, showing a keen observation and a devout spirit. He wrote many letters to his wife also which show the religious character and loving disposition of the man. The following will serve as a specimen of his correspondence:

DEAR WIFE: We came out of Boston last Sabath Day fifty odd Sail of us, & stood off to sea that night. The wind came against us & we put in again. At night we got close in to Cape Ann, but ye wind dying away we were obliged to stand off to sea & a Tuesday we arrived in Sheepscott . . . Remember me to Mr. Choate & his family & to Brother Eleazer and to all our friends & tell them I desire & beg their prayers to God for me — Stephen Low William Allen & Joseph Emerton remember their love to their wives & families . . . Dear Wife I recommend you to heavens care & keeping. Begging your prayers for me I subscribe your loving husband till death. BENJA. CRAFT.

LOUISBURG ye 13th October 1745.
DEAR & LOVING WIFE,

Having an opertunity by the providence of God to write to send you a few lines to let you know my circumstances. I have been sick for about eight weeks past but blessed be God I have not been so bad as to keep my bed, but I am pined away to nothing but skin & bones . . . If I should not come home this winter I believe that ye Captain & Lieut. Gidding will be discharged by whom I shall send, If I cannot get discharged, so that you may receive my wages, which will be between forty & fifty pounds — I am in very good business & have been for a month past having ye care of the Commisary Business for our Regiment beside what I do for others, which is a considerable income, not less than fifteen shillings a day, beside my wages . . . If I should tarry all winter I believe I shall be in good Business for I am in considerable favour with several of the great men, & which way it came I know not — but there is nothing is any temptation to me I long so much to get home to see you & my poor children & dear friends . . .
BENJA. CRAFT.

Mr. Craft was also second lieutenant in Capt. Benj. Kimball's Company, of the 19th Regiment, at the Siege of Boston, and was in camp at Winter Hill. He kept a Journal from June 15 to Nov. 16, 1775. It is published in the Essex Institute History Collection, vol. I, Nos. 2, 3, 4, 5. He received his discharge, Nov. 11, 1775, on the ground that "his wife and family being situated in a seaport town [were] consequently much exposed to danger from the enemy."

ELEAZAR CRAFT, brother of Benjamin, served throughout the war of the Revolution. He was a lieutenant at the time of the Lexington alarm, and was afterward engaged in many battles. He rose to the rank of major of the Cape Ann and Manchester Brigade in 1777, and the next year was commissioned as lieutenant-colonel, his commission bearing date of 12 Aug. 1778. He was in the army under General Gates, when Burgoyne surrendered his forces. He kept a journal throughout the entire war, but all that has been preserved of it is the portion printed in the Historical Collection of the Essex Institute of Salem, Mass., from 9 Sept., 1777, to 1 Dec., 1777, vol. VI, pp. 181–194.

EZEKIEL CHEEVER, son of Rev. Ames Cheever, was born in 1741. He was noted for his "integrity, strong religious convictions, phenomenal memory and extreme gentleness." He was wont to restore to their native element any fish that were caught on the hook otherwise than by the mouth, addressing them in this fashion, "You are the victim of an accident; I cannot claim you; go in peace." This gentle disciple of Izaak Walton never deviated from a fixed price; an advance in the market made no difference with him. One day, as he was returning from fishing, while crossing "Smith's point," a dangerous bull charged upon him "with

mighty bellowing"; whereat Mr. Cheever calmly sat
down on his barrow, and addressed the angry bovine
with such an impressive array of Scripture texts, that
after pawing the earth awhile and sniffing at the barrow, the infuriated but perplexed beast withdrew with a
crestfallen air.

SAMUEL LEE, a man of considerable note in his day,
had many grievances against the town, of which record
remains in various communications, drawn up with a
good deal of care and forcibly worded, and signed with
a flourish and in a bold hand, " Sirs, yor most Humble
& Devoted Servt Sam^{ll} Lee."

One of these papers, dated 11 March, 1771, and addressed to the "Moodrator of ye Annuel Town Meeting," is a vigorous protest against "granting any Parson
or Parsons Liberty of Erecting Hors Houses, or Shedds
any Whare adjoyning on any of my Lands."

One dated 13 March, 1779, addressed to the "Inhaby-
tence of the Town of Manchester," declares his belief
that "Turkish Laws are Much Preffarable & Juster then
the Assessors conduct in Manchester at Present is"; he
advises "those that can Watch and Ward to Look out
for themselves and others; or I think the Town is
Ruend." He signs himself, "an Abusd, and imposed
upon, Inhabitent of Manchester." This wrathful communication was "to be Exhibited to the Inhabytene of
s^d Town, before your Choyce of Town Officers."

In 1779, Mr. Lee asked for an abatement of Taxes,
representing that the assessment of his real estate was
unfair as compared with that of "Decon Herrick and
Mr. Chever"; and says "if my tilling, moing & Par-
string, must be sot so much hier then My Neighbeours,
for the —— & Butter & Cheas I have for Winter &c, I
hope those that have any by them, May be taxt Allso;

and for there Tea, Cofey, Shugers, Cyder, flower, Wines, Porters; and all other Articuls Used in a Luxures Way of Living; letts all fare alike in taxation, and then I am Content to be Pointed at," etc. He has another grievance: "Is not Brothers Ware Hous With 2 fire places Glass & Suller, & Claborded &c Worth more than £5 More than my Barn; I thinke my Barn is two high, or his too Low, or Both."

A copy of a note to the Assessors is appended: "Gent^m, I ame at the Jenerall good, of the Town and itts Inhabitence; & my one Presarvation, by all these Papers, to lett you know thatt allmost Every Man, that keepts any stock, or had any Corn, his been taxt three times over; and ought to be abated, by a Vote of the Town; or other Wayes, according to my Judgment."

Truly, the town meetings of those days were not without their occasional spice, and a town office was not always a bed of roses for its incumbent.

WILLIAM TUCK was born in Beverly, July 5, 1741, and removed to Manchester in 1760. In 1777, he commanded the "Remington," privateer, eighteen guns, and took many prizes; he was afterward captured by a British frigate, but by a successful piece of strategy the vessel was retaken from the prize-crew, and brought into Boston Harbor.[1] Mr. Tuck was second Collector of the Gloucester district, holding the office from 1796 to 1802. He passed the remainder of his life in Manchester, where he filled the position of Justice of the Peace, and also practised medicine "very successfully." 'Squire Tuck, as he was generally called, was a public-spirited man, interested in all improvements. He was a man of great energy; as one of the Commissioners at the time of the building of the first bridge between

[1] Vide p. 85.

B. Tappan

Dr Asa Story

John Dodge

D. L. Bingham

Beverly and Salem, he rode on horseback, on the coldest day in winter, from Manchester to Boston, leaving home before daylight. He had four wives, and was the father of twenty-three children, fourteen of whom lived to years of maturity. He died March, 1826, in the eighty-sixth year of his age.

EBENEZER TAPPAN, son of Rev. Benjamin Tappan, kept a store on Central street. He was the father of a remarkable family. If one came into his store and inquired for his son, Mr. Tappan would say: "Which son? Do you want Colonel Eben, Lieutenant-Colonel Israel, Major Ben, or Captain Sam?" Mr. Tappan was one of the first, if not the first, in the town who gave up the sale of liquor, and this at a time when the traffic was perfectly reputable. So profound was his conviction of the evil of the business that he destroyed even the measures that he had used in dealing out the beverage to his customers. He was very scrupulous in his dealings, and a great practical joker. Many stories are told of the old gentleman's eccentricities. We can picture him as a man straightforward and fearless, sanguine and hilarious; in bodily presence

> "a man of glee,
> With hair of glittering grey;
> As blithe a man as you could see
> On a spring holiday."

EBEN TAPPAN, son of the above, began his business career with his father in the mercantile line, and in building and employing vessels in the coasting trade. He afterward became a manufacturer of furniture and of ships' steering-wheels. He became well known, also, as a builder of fire-engines. [1] He was a member of the Legislature in 1843 and 1844. In 1818 he was

[1] *Vide* p. 311.

Colonel of a Regiment of Militia composed of Beverly and Manchester men.

Dea. DELUCENA L. BINGHAM, a native of Canterbury, Conn., came to Manchester to teach school, in 1785. He was then nineteen years of age. He afterward filled many town offices: was Town Clerk twenty-nine years, Representative to the General Court in 1824, the first Postmaster of the town, holding the office for thirty-four years, and a deacon of the church for thirty-two years. Rev. Mr. Emerson, his pastor, wrote of him shortly after his death, which occurred Oct. 25, 1837: "His religion bore the stamp of a mind of something more than ordinary intellectual endowment; to this was added a cheerfulness blended and softened with humility. No man more conscientiously avoided saying or doing anything that would engender strife among neighbors." He was a man of marked character, and left an influence in the community which showed that his life had been a blessing and that his death was a public bereavement.

Captain RICHARD TRASK commenced his seafaring life by a voyage to the Grand Banks at the age of twelve years. He subsequently entered the merchant service, and rapidly rose until he obtained command of a ship, the "Adriatic" of Boston. He had few opportunities of early education, but having an active mind and an indomitable will, he made headway against wind and tide, and became one of the most successful shipmasters of his time. In 1828, he became connected with Enoch Train & Co., in the Russia trade. He commanded some of their best vessels and had an interest in the business. In 1839, the Company built the "St. Petersburg," a ship of eight hundred and sixty tons, the largest merchant ship that had been built in Massachusetts.

John P. Allen

John Y. Price

Richard Trask

Thos Leach

Her size, carrying capacity and furnishings, including costly woods, cut glass and silver ware, attracted attention even in European ports. Capt. Trask made his last voyages in this vessel. He retired from the sea about 1844, and died at his home in Manchester, Aug. 6, 1846, in the fifty-ninth year of his age.

Captain Thomas Leach was born in Manchester in 1807. His father was a noted mariner who had sailed in the employ of William Gray. Young Leach was bred to the ocean from boyhood. His father intending to make him a first-class sailor, the discipline of shipboard was never relaxed in his favor. In 1832, he became Captain of the brig " Oregon," and made successful voyages for many years to Russia, China, and many other ports. For fifty-one years, his home was on the ocean wave. He had many adventures and some marvellous escapes. These he was fond of recounting to sympathetic hearers, and could tell a story with a good deal of humor. One of his thrilling experiences is narrated in substance as follows : On one of his East Indian voyages, Capt. Leach sighted one day a suspicious craft, which proved to be a *prou*, crowded with bloodthirsty Malays ; the pirates with their sweeps soon overhauled him, but when almost within range, seeing the warlike appearance of the ship with its mounted cannon and its crew armed with cutlasses, prudently hauled off and left the brave Yankee skipper to pursue his homeward voyage in peace.

His last active service was as Port Warden of Boston, an office which he held for twelve years, until failing health compelled his retirement. Captain Leach was a vigorous, self-reliant, self-made man, of cheerful temperament and kindly disposition. Few men better fitted for the position ever trod the quarter-deck, or in their own community received more universally the respect of their fellow-citizens. He died, in the house in which he was born, Dec. 5, 1886.

Capt. JOHN CARTER began his profession in the fishing fleet at the age of fourteen. He soon shipped on a merchantman, was mate at twenty-two, and at twenty-seven was promoted to a captaincy; he was almost constantly afloat, either on the waters of the Atlantic or the Pacific, until he was sixty-five years old, when he retired to his home and well-earned rest. Like the two above mentioned, Captain Carter's success was the result of patient industry and unremitting attention to his duties. In a serene and peaceful old age, Capt. Carter lives surrounded by children, grandchildren and neighbors, who love and respect him for his sterling worth. He is waiting in calmness his orders to sail for the Unseen Port.

JOHN PERRY ALLEN has already been noticed in the account of the Cabinet-making, of which he might almost have said "all of which I saw and a great part of which I was." Mr. Allen was a man of great force of character and executive ability, and had great influence in town affairs. While not a man of liberal education, he was a forceful speaker and his impressive bearing added power to his speech. Few men have done more for the business interests of the place, or manifested a more marked ingenuity or a more indomitable pluck in overcoming adverse circumstances. His name is a name to conjure with to the present day.

LARKIN WOODBERRY was not a native of Manchester, but the town has had few citizens of whom it has had more reason to be proud. He was at one time an extensive manufacturer, but he met with reverses in business, adding another to the long list of excellent men who are not successful in life from a material and financial point of view. Mr. Woodberry was a man of sterling character, a strong temperance man, a warm friend of education, and a leader in the Anti-Slavery ranks. He was one of the originators and strongest supporters of the Lyceum, and though never seeking office, his opinion on public matters always carried weight. Many men have brought the wealth of gold and silver to the town, of whom nothing more can be said. Mr. Woodberry brought to it the wealth of brains, character and life.

Dr. Asa Story was one of "Nature's noblemen." He was for many years not only the physician of the town [1], but also one of its most public-spirited citizens. He was a man of large calibre, and one who did with his might what his hands found to do. His character had in it a "strain of rareness." Dr. Story was born in Essex, July 20, 1796. While working in his father's saw-mill, he was in the habit of studying evenings and nights, walking three miles on every alternate evening to recite. He graduated at Dartmouth College, where he also studied medicine and received his medical degree. After spending one year in Washington, D. C., he came to Manchester, well-equipped for his life work. He was a man of great integrity, honor, and benevolence of disposition. He never refused though at the cost of great personal inconvenience to respond to calls upon his service, even from those from whom he could expect no remuneration. His son, Charles R. Story of San Francisco, remembers that when he was a boy, his father was called up one winter night and was obliged to climb

[1] Dr. David A. Grosvenor preceded Dr. Story, from 1810 to 1820. Dr. Lakeman was here from 1801, for some years; before him were Drs. Norwood and Whipple. See *Index*. There is very scanty knowledge of the earlier physicians.

in by the barn window to get a shovel to remove the drifted snow, in order to get his horse out, then riding to a distant part of the town to see a patient who already owed him a bill for attendance and was never likely to pay a cent. Dr. Story has left no family in town, but his name is held in honor among us.

OBED CARTER was a man of somewhat eccentric traits of character, who served the town as Treasurer through more than a generation. Some amusing stories are told, which illustrate equally his simplicity, his primitive method of keeping his accounts with the town, and his unimpeachable honesty. In 1846, the following Resolution, offered by Jonathan Hassam, was adopted by the town:

Resolved, That Obed Carter, Esq' is justly entitled to, and should receive a vote of thanks of the citizens of Manchester for the faithful Zealous and Honourable Discharge of the arduous duties devolved on him in the Treasury Department for Forty years and upwards.

It is worth recording as one of the humors of the time, that the Moderator would often say when the polls were open, " Gentlemen, bring in your votes for Obed Carter for Treasurer "; and, a few votes having been cast, would declare the polls closed. Those were days when office sought the man, and not the man the office.

ISRAEL FORSTER was born May 28, 1779. He studied at Phillips Academy, Andover. He was selectman for many years and had great influence in the town. He built a grist-mill on the site of the old Bennett mill property, introducing all the improvements known; adjoining the mill, he built a wharf, warehouses, and flakes for drying fish. He gained the reputation of curing fish better than most of his competitors, and thus established a large business. With his brother, he built a schooner of one hundred tons for the Grand Banks fisheries. Mr. Forster was much interested in military affairs, and was Major of the Militia in 1812. He represented the town in the Legislature in 1810 and in 1836. His residence, built in 1804, remains as an excellent specimen of the architecture of the early part of the century; it was known for many years as the summer home of his grandson, George C. Leach of Boston.

EZEKIEL W. LEACH was born in Manchester, July 1, 1809. He received his collegiate training at Amherst, and studied medicine with Dr. George S. Shattuck of Boston, taking his medical degree in 1835. Soon after commencing his medical practice in Boston he united with the Baldwin Place Baptist Church, during the ministry of the eminent Baron Stow. He was very active in church and educational matters, and held several offices. He served the city in the Legislature in 1839 and 1840; and was again elected in 1841, but from illness was obliged to resign. Dr. Leach was never a man of robust health, and a change to a milder climate being deemed advisable, he went South, and afterward took passage from Savannah to Havre, dying on the passage, at the age of thirty-three. He was a man universally respected and loved. For many years Dr. Leach interested himself in the history of the town, and left at his death a large collection of materials in manuscript, which is deposited in the Library of the Massachusetts Historical Society.

MRS. ABIGAIL HOOPER TRASK. — Widow of Capt. Richard Trask; she was the oldest resident of Manchester at the time of her death, March 3, 1885, being of the age of ninety-six years and five months. In her prime there was probably not a person in town who excelled her in business capacity. She kept herself in touch with the present in a remarkable manner, and maintained up to her last illness a regular correspondence. She was one of the "chief women" of Manchester, and one whom convention could not keep down.

LEWIS N. TAPPAN, son of Col. Eben Tappan, was born June 25, 1831. Mr. Tappan was in business some years in Boston. In 1857, he went to Kansas, and was Secretary of the Senate under the Topeka Constitution. He was one of the Fort Scott Treaty Commissioners, and one of the fifteen armed men who captured the box containing the altered election returns at Lecompton.[1] The discovery of this fraud resulted in the overthrow of the Pro-Slavery party in Kansas. Those were perilous times, and they called for brave and resolute men, who could well claim to be the advance guard of liberty; men who could say,

> "We tread the prairie as of old
> Our fathers sailed the sea,
> And make the West, as they the East,
> The homestead of the free."

In 1859, Mr. Tappan joined the Colorado pioneers, was a member of the first city government at Denver, a member of Governor Gilpin's Council, and one of Governor Cummings' staff. He organized the first Sunday school in Colorado, started the first smelting-works, and opened the first store in the territory. Returning to Manchester, Mr. Tappan was elected to the Legislature in 1877. He was a man of public spirit, conscientiousness and integrity, and was much respected by his fellow citizens. He was identified with the interests of the Baptist church while he was a resident in town. His death occurred on the 25th of February, 1880, in the forty-ninth year of his age.

[1] American Commonwealths; *Kansas*, p. 229.

SAMUEL FORSTER TAPPAN was born June 29, 1831.
He learned the chairmaker's trade, but afterward went
into business in Boston. In 1854, he went to Kansas
with the earliest company of emigrants from Massachusetts, and located on the site of the present city of Lawrence. Later in the same year, a city government was
organized, and Mr. Tappan was elected Alderman. The
" Border Ruffians " were at this time carrying elections
by fraud and force, and mobbing and murdering generally. Mr. Tappan was one of a determined band who
saved Kansas for Freedom. He canvassed Southern
and Western Kansas, was Secretary of the House of
Representatives and acting Speaker when it was dispersed by United States troops under orders from the
Pro-Slavery administration, was Clerk of the House in
1856, Secretary of the two Constitutional Conventions,
and active in the whole struggle that resulted in driving
out the myrmidons of Slavery and enrolling Kansas
among the Free States.

In 1860, Mr. Tappan removed to Colorado, and the
next year was commissioned Captain in the First Colorado Volunteers. After seeing active service in breaking up a gang of desperadoes that terrorized the settlements, and receiving severe wounds afterward at the
hands of some of the outlaws, he was promoted as Lieutenant Colonel, and instructed to increase his command
to a full regiment. In 1861 and '62, Colonel Tappan
rendered most efficient service in holding Colorado for
the Union, and with the aid of some Regulars and other
Volunteers driving the rebels from Utah and New Mexico. The plan of cutting off the Pacific coast from the
Union was thus thwarted. The regiment was subsequently mounted, and during the rest of the War held
the frontier against Indian attacks and rebel raids, Mr.
Tappan having the rank of Colonel. Mr. Tappan has

since served on the Indian Peace Commission, and also as Superintendent of an Indian Industrial School in Nebraska. His life has been largely given to securing freedom for the black man, and equal rights for the Indian. He now resides in Washington, D. C.

HENRY C. LEACH, son of Benjamin Leach, was born Oct. 9, 1832. His home was in St. Louis from 1855 to 1861, spending the summers of 1856 and '57 in Kansas and aiding in the early contest in that Territory for free soil. He was active at the outbreak of the Rebellion as a member of a military organization, the object of which was to hold Missouri in the Union. In 1863, Mr. Leach removed to Colorado, and went into business at Denver. He was elected to the Territorial Council in 1865, serving two years, and was President of the body. This was before the days of the Pacific Railroad, and Colorado was separated from the East by 600 miles of trackless plains. To the North was an unexplored wilderness, inhabited by Indian tribes with whom the pioneers were compelled to carry on a harassing border warfare. In 1865, a Constitution was adopted at an irregular election which was obnoxious to a majority of the citizens. Mr. Leach and Col. Samuel F. Tappan spent the winter in Washington, and succeeded by enlisting the interest of Charles Sumner and others in securing the rejection of the Bill for the admission of Colorado. The time was one of intense political excitement, not unmingled with personal peril at times to the actors. Mob law was often in the ascendant, and " Judge Lynch " frequently held court. Things were in a nebulous state, "slow rounding into form." Since Mr. Leach returned East, he has been in business in Boston, having his home in Salem. For a few years past, he has made his summer residence among us, at the old homestead on the " Plain."

Capt. WILLIAM A. ANDREWS, son of Asa Andrews, was born in 1843, in the house now owned and occupied by Mr. J. Radford Lord. His grandfather, Zebulon Andrews of Essex, taught navigation, and was pilot of United States ship " Ohio " on her voyage to the Mediterranean, and was said to be the only man who could navigate that vessel, a seventy-four gun ship of the old type. The grandson performed a more hazardous feat in navigating alone a small boat from Atlantic City to Palos, Spain, in the summer of 1892, arriving in the latter city in time to take part in the festivities held there in honor of the discoverer of the New World. Captain Andrews received great attentions from the Government and was presented to the Queen. The boat, which passed through town Jan. 22, 1895, and was seen by many of our people, is 14 ft. 6 in. long over all, and is a canvas-covered folding boat, decked over, excepting a cock-pit 2 ft. by 3 ft. and 6 ft. long, fitted with a sliding hatch. She carries 350 lbs. of lead on her keel.

JOHN LEE, son of Andrew Lee, was born Dec. 6, 1813. He was identified with town affairs for an unusually long period. He served on the Board of Selectmen twenty-five years, and for a considerable part of the time was also town clerk. He was Representative in the Legislature in 1847, '48 and '68. He was a man of strength of character, and an able defender of the town's rights in instances when they were imperilled. Mr. Lee was greatly interested in historical and antiquarian matters, and contributed to the *Beetle and Wedge*, during the brief term of its existence, a number of articles on the earlier history of the town. He kept a Diary for many years which is a mine of information on local events. Mr. Lee died July 9, 1879.

These are among those who were either the "Makers" of Manchester, or who went forth from its shops and shores to plant New England institutions and ideas on other soil and beneath other skies. There were others worthy of equal mention, who lived less eventful lives, or concerning whom only scanty memories or traditions remain, but whose names deserve to be "writ large" in the respect and gratitude of posterity. "The time would fail" to tell of the Bennetts, the Leaches, the Marsterses, the Wests, the Normans, the Hiltons, the Knowltons, the Edwardses, the Sibleys, the Bishops, the Herricks, the Hassams, the Hoopers, who fished the seas, subdued the forest, laid out the roads, built the wharves, served the Church and State, and ruled the Town. Many of them were men of such strong individuality that it needs but slight effort of the imagination to reinvest them with a personal interest, till "only they who live in history seem to walk the earth again."

APPENDIX L.

FLOTSAM AND JETSAM.

ANCESTRAL NAME AND HOME OF THE ALLENS.——
The name of Allen, or as it is variously spelled, Allin,
Allan, Allyn, is doubtless the same as that of the noted
non-conformist preacher and author, Joseph Alleine,
born 1634, who is supposed to have been a descendant
of Alan, Lord of Buckenhall, in the reign of the first
Edward. The Alans of England are thus traced to a
Suffolk ancestor. Is it not possible that some of the
Allens came from Yarmouth, on the borders of Norfolk
and Suffolk, and gave the name to that part of the
town which they settled, and which later became known
as "North Yarmouth" to distinguish it from Yarmouth
on Cape Cod? A confirmation of this theory may perhaps be found in the name early given to the "Row,"
from the ancient streets called "Rows" in the English
Yarmouth; also, in the quaint lines on Capt. John
Allen's gravestone (p. 275), which are found in seaside
graveyards on the eastern coast of England.

THE WILL OF WILLIAM ALLEN. — Copied from First
Book (Old Series), page 72, Essex Probate Records:

WILLIAM ALLEN'S WILL.

the last will of Wim: Allen Senr of Manchester made the 7:
June 78:

Imp's. I doe make my wife Elizabeth Allen my full & Sole
executrix of all my lands & goods during her life: & after
the death of my wife, to be disposed in manner & forme,
as followeth, that is to say, I give to my sonn samuell
the remainder of ye 25 acre lott; which he alreddy pos-
sesseth, that is to say the vplands & the share of ye fresh
meddow belonging therevnto, I giue to my two sonns
onesiphorus & William Allen, my whole 50 acre lott, with

all the deuissions & App'tenances belonging to it, with
the propriety of all comons deuided & vndiuided belonging to it, & an acre of salt marsh, at the lower end of my
oarchard, that I purchast, this I giue to my two sonns
onesiphorus & Wim: Allen, to be equally deuided betweene them, both after the death of me & my wife & it
is further to be vnderstood, that as son onesiphorus hath
halfe an acre, in p'sent possession, joynning to his house
that lyes in my oarchard, for my son Wim: Allen to haue
halfe an acre Joynning to his house in the same maner.
In witnes where of the said William Allen has put to my
hand in the p'sence of Tho: Joans **E** Joans his mark Samuell friend

the mark of
W A
WILLIAM ALLEN

Tho: Joans & samuell friend gaue oath in Court that they
signed the aboue written as witnesses & y⁰ s⁴ Allen signed
the same & declared it as his last will & testament in theire
p'sence being of a disposing mind: alowed in court at Salem
the 16: 4: 79

atest HILLIARD VEREN cler:

An Inventory of y⁰ estate of Wim: Allen deceased 3:
mo
11: 78

house & land with all y⁰ meddow belonging	£ 140:00:00
15 acres of vpland lying within the bounds	
of Beverly: Joynning to wenham Great	
pond	" 20:00:00
2 oxen: a cow: 2 heifers: 2 sheep: a horse	" 18:10:00
Bed: with beding & other household stuff	" 08:00:00
	£ 186:10:00

(£5 to be abated for the loss of a horse)

This is aboue Inventory made by Tho: West John Sibley
17: 12: 78 the estate is d⁺ to seuerall men 19: 13: 3½

Elizabeth the relict of the deceased gaue oath to the truth
of the aboue written Inventory to the best of her knowledge,
& what comes to her knowledge afterwards; to ad to it in
mo
Court at salem: 26: 4: 79

atest HILLIARD VEREN cler.

the widdows testimony & y⁰ debtors bills filed with y⁰ will &
Inventory.

DEED OF MASCONOMO'S GRANDSONS.

SAMUEL ENGLISH and JOHN UMPEE to the town of MANCHESTER:

Samuel English, Joseph English and John Umpee all living in Middlesex county, Indians, on one party, and Robert Leach ——John Knowlton, and Samuel Lee, Selectmen of the Town of Manchester in the County of Essex, on the other party, for £3 19s. current silver money of New England received. Whereas said townshipe quietly and peaceably and without molestation enjoyed the soil, &c. for more than sixty years — and that in the first place by the consent and approbation of our grandfather Sagamore John of Agawam — alias Masconomo, or Masquenomenit, and ever since by consent and approbation of his children, and by us his grandchildren, being now the surviving and proper heirs to our said grandfather Masquenomenit.

SAMUEL ENGLISH [Mark & Seal]
JOHN UMPEE   [Mark & Seal]

Witnesses
JOHN NEWMAN
JOSEPH HERRICK
THOMAS WHITREDGE

Acknowledged at Salem
Dec. 18, 1700.
JOHN HIGGINSON

Examined
    Attest Steph Sewall
        Register.

INDIAN REMAINS. — The following account of archæological discoveries in town was written by a very careful and intelligent observer, Mr. John Lee. It is well worthy of preservation:

Many years ago one of these mounds, located near and southeasterly from the Orthodox meeting-house, and on land then owned by Capt. Thomas Leach, was levelled down, and in 1835, Capt. John Knight levelled down another situated at the head of tide-water, the spot on which the steam mill of Messrs. Kelham & Fitz now stands.

This mound was about 150 feet in diameter, and about eight feet above the adjoining marsh, and on it stood some large apple trees. It was of a conical form and had a moat entirely

surrounding it, which was filled with water at very high tides.
Large quantities of bones were found here, but very much decayed, so that they were cut with a spade or shovel as easily
as the ground they were embedded in. These bones appeared
to have been interred promiscuously, and in an erect position.
No Indian implements were found there. On the plain near
the spot where it is supposed William Allen built the first
English dwelling-house in the town, the Indians had their
wigwam fires for a long period of time, for when that elevation
of land was taken down in 1845, for the purpose of levelling off
a lot for " Union Cemetery," below the soil was found in many
places, of the diameter of about six feet, where the earth had
been burnt down by fires, and the deposit of ashes, charred
wood, burnt stones, etc., were from sixteen to eighteen inches
in depth, and the earth for some feet around was of a reddish-
yellow color, different from the natural earth; and when, in
the autumn of 1864, a gravel pit was opened into a sandy,
gravelly knoll about twenty-five rods southerly from this place,
four entire skeletons were found buried there, three of adults,
and one of a youth; one of the adults was of very large size.
They were found lying nearly side by side, with their heads
toward the west, which were raised so as to face the east.
They were found about fourteen inches below the surface,
which had been much cultivated. One of these skeletons had
its head rested upon a round piece of copper of about sixteen
inches in diameter, and where the head touched the copper
the skin and hair adhered firmly to the skull. The hair was
black and bright, and about two and a half feet long. With
them were found an iron tomahawk, and an iron knife-blade
much decayed by rust, some coarse cloth made of flags or
rushes, a short-stemmed smoking pipe, a large number of bone
arrow-heads, preserved by the copper in a sound condition.
These arrow-heads were formed something like a writing pen,
sharp at the point; some were found of stone, larger and in
the form of a heart; some lobsters' claws, a fishing line in
good form but very rotten, a portion of another line of larger
size, both made from some fibrous plant, a wooden ladle or
bowl and wooden spoons. At other times round, smooth
stones about fourteen inches long, probably used for crushing
corn, and a round stone of about the size of an eight-pound
iron shot, with a groove around it in two ways, deep enough
to receive a small rope or withe, were found.

"FRENCHMEN" IN MANCHESTER. — Reference is
made on page 258 to the "Frenchmen" mentioned in
the Town Records. They were, as Bancroft says,
"a simple, harmless people torn from their homes, and
scattered in broken families from New Hampshire to
Georgia." Those that were landed at Boston were distributed among the towns, to be cared for at the public
charge. The following action of the General Court
throws light upon the matter:

IN THE HOUSE OF REPRESENTATIVES Dec. 27, 1755.

Whereas a considerable number of the inhabitants of Nova
Scotia arrived here the 26th inst. being removed by the Governor and Council of the Province for the security thereof; and
no provision being made for their support here, they are in
great danger of suffering during this rigorous season, without
the interposition of the Court. Ordered, that Mr. James Russell, Mr. Cooper and Mr. Hall, with such as the honorable
Board shall join, be a committee to provide for the support of
such inhabitants of Nova Scotia until advice may be had from
Governor Lawrence, and his orders concerning them; or until
there may be an opportunity of applying to his Excellency
General Shirley, Commander in Chief of his Majesty's forces
in North America, for his directions concerning them. And
the Committee are to dispose of them in the meantime in
such Towns within this Province as they shall judge least inconvenient to the public. And the Selectmen or Overseers of
the Poor of the several towns to which they may be sent as
aforesaid are hereby authorized and required to receive them,
and employ or support them in such manner as shall incur the
least charge. And the said inhabitants of Nova Scotia being
so received and entertained in any Town, shall not be con-
strued or understood to be an admission of them as town
inhabitants; the Court relying upon it that some other provision will be made for them without any expense to this government, signed etc.

In pursuance of the above Order, we direct that the Town
of Manchester shall at present receive Joseph Janwise his
wife 1 Son, 3 Daughters in all 6, and the Selectmen or Overseers of said town are to dispose of them in any method they

apprehend most likely to answer the ends proposed by this government

SAMUEL WATTS,
In the name of the Committee.

To the Selectmen or Overseers of Manchester.

Boston Dec. 29th, 1755.

1777.

SHIPPING PAPERS OF SCHOONER "HAWKE," PRIVATEER,
CAPT. J. HIBBERT.

Now fitted for Sea

and ready to proceed on a cruise the privateer Sch. Hawke a well built vessel of seventy five tons burthen, mounting 10 carriage guns 8 swivels — small arms &c. — She is a prime sailer and has on board evry convenience for such a cruise and is to be commanded by Capt. Jeremiah Hibbert.—The whole crew are to draw one half of all prizes out of which the Capt. will draw 8 shares — First Lieut. 5, second do 2. Master 4 — Prize Masters 3, first mate 2½ second do 2. Surgeon 5 — and the remainder a single share —

We therefore the subscribers do severally engage and enlist ourselves &c—&c—

Jeremiah Hibbert Captain
Marston Watson 1st Lieut
Caleb Ray Surgeon
Samuel Bennet Master
Ezekiel Leach Mate
Israel Morgan Gunner
Benjamin Leach Prize Master

The names of some of the crew were Thomas Steele, Theophilus Lane, Joseph Perry, Nicholas Babcock, Stilson Hilton, Abial Lee, John Knight carpenter.

NAMES OF MANCHESTER MEN, MASTERS OF VESSELS ON FOREIGN VOYAGES.

[It is perhaps too much to expect that this list is free from errors; but it has been made up with a great deal of care.]

Benjamin Allen.
James Allen.
James G. Allen.
John Allen.

John Hill.
Amos Hilton.
Jacob P. Holmes.
John Hooper.

John Allen.[1]
John W. Allen.
Joseph Allen.
Richard Allen.
Samuel Allen.
William Allen.
Peter Ayres.
William Babcock.
—— Babcock.
Delucena L. Bingham.
James Brown.
Abial Burgess.
Abial Burgess, Jr.
David Burgess.
David Burgess, Jr.
Benjamin Carter.
David Carter.
Ezekiel Carter.
James Carter.
John Carter.
John W. Carter.
Nathan Carter.
Obed Carter.
Henry Cheever.
Jacob Cheever.
David Crafts.
Ambrose Crowell.
Ariel P. Crowell.
Samuel Crowell.
Hilton Dow.
David Driver.
David Driver, Jr.
John Driver.
John Girdler.
John Girdler, Jr.
Israel D. Goodridge.
Simeon Haskell.
Jonathan Hassam.
William Hassam.
Amos Hill.
Benjamin Hill.

William Hooper. (2.)
William Hooper, Jr.
William Kelleham.
James Knight.
Benjamin Leach.
Benjamin Leach, Jr.
Charles Leach.
Daniel Leach.
Ezekiel Leach.
Thomas Leach.
Thomas Leach, Jr.
Edward Lee.
Isaac Lee.
John Lee.
Nathaniel Lee.
William Lee.
William Lee, Jr.
Benjamin Lull.
William Lull.
Andrew Marsters.
Isaac Morgan.
Isaac Morgan, Jr.
Samuel Morgan. (2.)
William Morse.
Tyler Parsons, Jr.
Jacob Pert.
William Pert.
—— Prince.
Augustus Smith.
Abram Stone.
Nathan Stone.
Abram Symonds.
—— Tarring.
Richard Trask.
John Tuck.
William Tuck.
William Tuck, Jr.
Samuel Wells.
Thomas Williams.
Jacob Woodbury.

[1] Grandson of John.

If the adventures, "hair-breadth 'scapes," ingenious
expedients, nautical skill and business enterprise of
these men could be related, the tale would equal in
interest, if not in wonder, the "Arabian Nights." They
sailed every sea, visited every clime, saw the far-famed
capitals of Europe, the old empires of the East, and
lands unknown to history or song. They encountered
savages, pirates' and enemies' fleets, typhoons in the
China seas, icebergs in the Atlantic, doldrums and tidal
waves. They made the name of the American sailor
everywhere a synonym for hardihood, intelligence, pluck
and sagacity. They built up a commerce which was
once our national pride and the envy of the world.

THE GOLD HUNTERS. — In 1849 a unique voyage was
made from Manchester to California. A party formed
a stock company, bought a schooner, the "Billow," of
about 100 tons, and freighting it with the frame of a
house and provisions, set sail for the new El Dorado.
They manned the vessel themselves, and on arriving at
San Francisco sold it and the freight, and betook themselves to the mines. After varying fortunes, most of
the number found their way back to their eastern homes.
Three died in California. It was not a very profitable
venture, but it was an illustration of pluck and enterprise worthy the men of Cape Ann. None became mil-
lionaires; all secured a portion of that which is often of
more value than riches — experience. The following is
a list of the company.

Albert E. Low, John Kemp, Isaac Allen, D. W. Friend,
William Sturgess, Henry Sawyer, Henry Stone, Albert Dow,
William E. Wheaton, Joseph Morgan, George Thompson; J. D.
Winn,[1] Sailing Master; A. W. Smith, Captain. A. E. Low and
D. W. Friend are the only survivors of these modern Argo-
nauts. The vessel also carried as passengers, Joshua Younger,
Charles Smith and ——— Hunnewell.

[1] Captain Winn accompanied the famous Wilkes Exploring Expedition.

EARTHQUAKES. — Several severe shocks of earth-quake were experienced in New England in the early days. One of these on the 29th of October, 1727, greatly alarmed the people of Manchester. The motion was so violent, that those who were standing were obliged to sit down to avoid falling. An old writer says :

The heavens were clear, the atmosphere perfectly calm, the moon shining in her glory. The shock extended several hundred miles; its greatest force was displayed at Newbury, in Essex county; the earth burst open in several places; more than a hundred cart-loads of earth were thrown out, which in a few days, emitted a loathsome smell.

On the night on which Lisbon was destroyed, Nov. 1, 1755, it is said that the Leach family was gathered around the fireplace (in the house owned and occupied by the late Mr. Charles Wilmonton), when the house was violently shaken and bricks came tumbling down the chimney, to the great alarm of the family in front of the fire. Is there any record of similar seismic disturbances in New England at that date ?

EPIDEMICS. — In 1748, the *throat distemper* prevailed and many children died. " The throat swelled with white or ash-colored specks, an efflorescence appeared on the skin; with great debility of the whole system, and a strong tendency to putridity." This disease was the scourge of New England in the last century.

Early in 1775, the greatly dreaded small-pox visited the town, and many people fell victims to its ravages. " The pest-house " was built at this time. The town voted, March 20, " to Choose a Committee of three men to Look out and purchas a place to sett a small Pox & smoak House upon and to agree with a Person or Persons to Build said Houses in the Cheepest manner." Again, in 1791, a house was built at Graves'

Beach for small-pox patients, indicating a recurrence of the malady.

The following Report of Committee (without date) is on file in the Town Clerk's office:

The Committee Appointed to Look out a Suitable Place to Sett a House for the Vse of the Small pox and also to put the poor in when Not used for the Small pox and to procure a Frame for s^d house have attended that Sarvice and Do Report — That the Common Right belonging to the Estate of Mr John Eskort Dec^d they Judg to be a most Conveniant place for that Purpose and that they have agreed with Mr Jacob Allen for a frame for said House for the Sum of Seven pound, Six Shiling Eight pence A Plan of which House is Herewith Exhibited ——

Signed By order of the Committee
Andrew Woodberry Clerk.

In 1794, occurred the "great sickness," in which according to the memoir of Edward Lee, sixty-four persons died (page 28). "It visited every family but two in town." Dr. David Norwood is said to have "labored excessively" at this time. There was great difficulty in obtaining persons to care for the sick. "Many suffered for want of attendance."

LONGEVITY. — Statistics hardly bear out the assertion sometimes made that the average of life is less than in former times. No doubt, our forefathers possessed vigorous constitutions, and were capable of enduring great hardships. But the burdens imposed upon the earlier generations in New England told upon them, and the average of life appears to have been less than at present. Bradford, in his *Memoir* of Elder Brewster, speaks of many of the people living to "very olde age," and goes on to say that many had "attained to 60 years of age, and to 65, diverse to 70 and above, and some were 80," and adds, that in view of "ye many changes and hardships these people went through, and ye many enemies they had and difficulties they mette with all, it was God's vissitation that preserved their spirits." There are no records of deaths in town prior to 1749. From that time to 1800, we find but thirty-two who reached the age of eighty; from 1800 to 1850, there were seventy-one, with a gap of twelve years in the records; from 1850 to 1887, there were no less than one hundred and thirteen. Allowance must be made, of course, for increase of population. Mrs. Lucy A. Roberts, who died in 1881, reached the age of one hundred and three years and ten months.

RATTLESNAKES.——There are no snakes, so far as is known, of the species *Crotalus horridus* at present in Manchester. But rattlesnakes formerly abounded in the ledges and rocky hillsides, much to the terror and danger of the inhabitants. These reptiles were no mere myths, but a very awesome reality; so much so that so late as 1844, the town offered a bounty of one dollar per head for their destruction. While found more or less in different parts of the town, as near the village even as Powder-house Hill, they seem to have had their headquarters in a den in the woods near the Essex line.[1] Their extermination is due to a single mighty hunter of Ophidians, Mr. John D. Hildreth. This slayer of dragons received a considerable revenue in bounties, in the oil which was considered by many a specific for rheumatism, and for living specimens secured for museums and showmen. He had an ingen-

[1] There were at least two severe cases of rattlesnake bites. In 1799, Capt. Henry Lee was bitten, but by prompt treatment his life was saved. A few years later, Ebenezer Tappan was bitten; with him, although vigorous application of remedies neutralized the effects of the bite, discoloration of the skin, inflammation and lameness recurring about the same time every year until his death, some forty years after, witnessed to the virulence of the venom. Among the remedies used in these cases, were fresh earth, baths of warm milk and application of pelts from a newly killed sheep. .

ious method of ensnaring them. With a dog to arouse the reptiles, and armed with a slender stick with a slip noose attached to it, he watched his opportunity as the head was lifted in anger to strike, and dextrously lassoed his victim which he then easily despatched. At last he laid siege to their stronghold, when they were in a state of hibernation, and by building a fire at the mouth of their den, lured them forth, when he caught them one by one, flinging them upon the snow which chilled them and made them an easy prey. This *ruse* proved so successful that apparently not one escaped, as no rattlesnake has been seen in town since. Mr. Hildreth well deserves to be called a public benefactor. He died in 1885.

TRAVEL ONE HUNDRED YEARS AGO. — An interesting letter, preserved in the *Crafts* Genealogy, gives a glimpse of the perils of the road only a few miles from Boston, near the close of the last century; and also furnishes a personal reminiscence of Prof. David Tappan, of whom so little is now known, which shows him to have been a man of nerve, and equal to an emergency. The scene is laid in Brookline, Mass.

Mr. Jackson has the rheumatism, he is not confined to the house, but is at times lame. Mr. Tappans of Cambridge preached for him yesterday. He was very unfortunate in coming over the bridge in the new lane as it is called. The violent South storm we had Saturday night carried off the snow & raised the water to such a degree that none attempted to pass but Mr. Tappin & his son; in passing the horse went off the bridge, Mr. Tappin, son & carriage were plunged into the water, it is said his son had liked to have been drowned, but they got out safely. Mr. Tappin sent his son back to Capt. Crafts to get people to assist in getting the horse & chaise out of the water, while he went on to Mr. Jackson's, dripping. This was the report yesterday, your brother has this minute come in from town meeting, says Mr. Jackson told him, after Mr. Tappin had sent his son to call assistance he staid in the water while he disengaged the horse from the carriage, then mounted bare-backed, followed his son, borrowed a saddle, & rode round by White's to Sumner's store. This accident happened at first bell-ringing, he did not get to Mr. Jackson's till after the second began. He was so fatigued he could not give much account of himself, only that he had been in the water. Mr. J. drest the poor unfortunate then in a suit of his cloaths, but as his small cloaths did not cover his knees he was obliged to wear his wet ones or go without. David H——— said he was very sorry he did not send to him for a pair, but as the legs of the lame are not equal, if one knee had been covered, the other must have been bare, but he dried & fixed himself as well as he could and went clumping into meeting with his borrowed shoes, just as Mr. J. had done his first prayer. Mr. J.'s cloak was so short for him, he could not look very Buckish; altho' there were some circumstances a little diverting it was really a serious affair. . . . Mr. Tappin put his notes & his Bond [Bands ?] in his Book & put them on the cushion on behind him when he set out from Cambridge. The current was so rapid they were all carried off. Notwithstanding he preached two excellent sermons from notes he happened to have in his pocket The chaise which he borrowed of the President was very much damaged. It seemed as if fire & water was against them Sunday; his son staid at home in the forenoon to dry himself, left his shoes in the sitting room & went out to the kitchen fire, — meanwhile a brand fell down on one of them & burnt the heel quarter almost up, but Mr. Jackson was kind enough to look up one that answered to follow his father to meeting in the afternoon.

CONVEYANCES. — There could hardly be a better illustration of the changes of the past century, than the contrast between the lumbering stage-coach that once accommodated the travel between Gloucester and Boston by its triweekly trips, and the eight or ten long, well-filled trains that now run daily each way between the "Hub" and the "City of the Sea." The picturesqueness of the old method of conveyance, when the arrival of Captain Trask from a Russia voyage would be known to the loungers at the tavern as soon as the

stage hove in sight, by its "list" to port or starboard,
as the case might be, has been more than counterbalanced by the ease and quickness of transit on the "Flying Fisherman."[1]

SAW-MILLS. — The first settlers built their houses of
logs; the earliest frame buildings were constructed of
hewn timber. But saw-mills were erected at a very
early period in different parts of the town. There was
one on Cheever's Creek, north of the High Schoolhouse;
one still farther north; one on School street, near the
brook, which was referred to as the "old Saw-mill" as
early as 1694; there were three at the "Cove," and
one on the Baker farm, the only one now remaining.
The small streams in town must have been of much
greater volume formerly than at present, "Wolftrap
Brook" having almost entirely disappeared; changes
in the surface of the country, the building of roads and
drains, and the partial clearing of forests, have no doubt
contributed to this result.

THE GRIST-MILLS. — These were John Knowlton's in
the centre; Easkott's at West Manchester; Israel Forster's (still standing); and one at the "Cove," near the
road to the Magnolia station; a wind-mill for grinding
grain was built by the town on the "Plain."

THE SHOEMAKERS. — John Cheever, Andrew Lee,
Nehemiah Goldsmith, Daniel Anable, Edward Goldsmith, James Hooper, John W. Mann, Benjamin Morgan, John Robinson, Isaac S. West, Stephen Story,
Benjamin Morse, William Stone.

These disciples of the "gentle craft" worked in small
shops, with sometimes an apprentice or two, or a journeyman. The days of immense factories, of machinery,
and of strikes, were yet in the distance.

[1] Not to speak of the "Subscribers' train," somewhat irreverently
dubbed the "Dude" by some of the natives.

THE PRESENT BUSINESS. — Of late years, the business of the town has depended largely upon its summer population. Roberts and Hoare began business, Jan. 1, 1884, as successors to the firm of Friend, Roberts and Hoare, and have built for summer residents thirty-two houses, at a cost of $225,000, and twenty-one stables at a cost of $75,000. This is in addition to work done for permanent residents, and out of town, aggregating $216,000. Employment has been given by this firm alone to forty men on an average in carpentering, and to fifty or more, in all departments of their work. Other builders have been F. W. Churchill, and Phillips and Killam. E. A. Lane and A. P. Crowell do an extensive business in painting.

Brick-making, of which there are early traces, has lately assumed considerable importance; one hundred and six thousand brick having been shipped from the yard on Summer street in the month of August, 1894.

Ice-cutting employs in the season about 30 men, and keeps quite a force of men and teams employed in the summer. The business has been built up by the energy of Mr. Amos F. Bennett, who has invested in it $9,000, in buildings, machinery, etc. The ice is cut from artificial ponds, and great care is taken to secure purity in the water supply.

With the failure or departure of its native industries — its fishery, its ship-building, its cabinet-making — the town was somewhat in the position of Dominie Sampson, who had " fallen to the leeward in the voayge of life," when it was grappled to by the smart summer resident, and brought up to the wind. Since that time, by the application of new steering apparatus, change of rig and restowing of cargo, it has gained seaway, and now presents a brave sight among its sister craft along

shore, albeit its build is somewhat old-fashioned and its
top-hamper partly ancient and partly modern. With
a good wind on the quarter, the old ship may still lift
her bows to the sea, after the strain and storms of two
hundred and fifty years. Her children can say with our
much-loved poet:

> " Sail on, nor fear to breast the sea!
> Our hearts, our hopes, are all with thee,
> Our hearts, our hopes, our prayers, our tears,
> Our faith triumphant o'er our fears,
> Are all with thee, — are all with thee!"

SHIPWRECKS. — Taking into account the rocky nature
of the coast, it is surprising that so few vessels have
been lost in this vicinity. It is probably due to the
fact that a good offing is usually kept from Eastern
Point to Baker's Island. On Nov. 28, 1878, at an early
hour in the morning, the schooner " Charlie Cobb," of
and from Rockland, Me., for Providence, R. I., loaded
with lime, came ashore on " Singing Beach." The vessel took fire and burned to the water's edge. The mate,
a Norwegian, was knocked overboard by the main
boom and was drowned before the vessel was beached,
his body afterwards washing ashore. On Jan. 6, 1892,
the U. S. Revenue Cutter, " Gallatin," was wrecked in
a thick snow-storm on " Boo-hoo Ledge," about two miles
from " Eagle Head." One seaman, a Dane, was struck
by the falling smoke-stack, knocked into the water and
drowned; the rest of the crew, with the officers, all
landed safely on the beach near the summer residence
of Mrs. Bullard, and after being cared for by the town
authorities were forwarded by the late afternoon train
to Boston.

NAMES OF PERSONS LOST AT SEA.

In order to secure as full a list as possible of those who have been lost
at sea, a request for information was published in Salem, Gloucester and
Boston papers as well as in the Manchester *Cricket*. As the result of this

inquiry the following list is appended, which is probably as complete as can now be made. Special thanks are due to John T. Hassam, Esq., of Boston, for valuable assistance, also to William H. Tappan, Esq. A number of names have been furnished by the Church Records, as kept by Rev. Benjamin Tappan, 1745-1790; others have been gathered from various sources.

1717. John Peirce, drowned in the harbor.
1719. Ezekiel Knowlton, drowned at Sable Island.
1748. Benjamin Allen, William Hassam.
1749 or '50. Benjamin Hassam, on a voyage to Lisbon.
    William Lee, Isaac Presson, on a voyage to Lisbon.
1752. Ezekiel Allen, Mallaca Allen, Azariah Allen, Joseph Allen, Jonathan Hassam.
1754. Amos Allen, John Tarring, Robert Safty, Joseph Safty, Thomas Hoole, coming from Virginia.
1756. Ambrose Allen, Moses Trask, Jacob Lee, Daniel Davidson, William Ireland, John Ayers, coming from Lisbon.
    James Allen, died at sea.
1757. Daniel Leach, Israel Morgan, died in England (?).
1758. Joseph Allen, John Day, Simeon Wilson, John Driver, Richard Lee, Jun., John Dennis, Josiah Lee, John Sears, Samuel Morgan, Jun., Joseph Lee.[1]
1759. John Hassam, drowned at Louisburg.
    Lewis Degan,   "   "   "
    John Badcock, died near Louisburg.
    Moses Bennet,   "   "   Isle of Orleans.
1760. William Bennett, Aaron Dennis, Robert Leach, died at sea in the West Indies.
1765. William Edwards, Samuel Carter, Samuel Jones, drowned in the harbor.
1767. Benjamin Allen, Thomas Ayer, Benjamin Allen, Ezra Allen, John Leach, Richard Kitchin, Timothy Donnaway, Joseph Easty, John Marshall, Josiah Hassam.
1768. Benjamin Andrews, Charles Leach, Daniel Foster, coming from West Indies.
1770. Amos Allen, Thomas Allen, Bartholomew Allen, Jacob Allen, Crispin Joynt, Jacob Lee.
1772. Daniel Edwards, Samuel Edwards, Samuel Perry, Frank Silva, Benjamin Hilton, coming from the West Indies.

[1] There is some confusion in names this year.

1773. Edward Lee and "five others." [1]
1774. Benjamin Masters Allen, Charles Hill, Moses Bennett, John Easty, John Morse, Edward Lee, Amos Morgan, Samuel Lee.
1776. Daniel Morgan, Daniel Ober, Nicholas Babcock, James Pittman, John Allen, John Carter, ———— Tucker, Amos Allen, Daniel Brown, Jacob Lendall, Simeon Webber, Azariah Allen, James Morgan, Andrew Brown, Dr. Joseph Whipple, lost with Privateer "Gloucester."

Andrew Leach, and "ten others," with Privateer "Barrington."
1777. Captain Jeremiah Hibbert, in command of Privateer "Civil Usage," lost near Portland. [2]

John Allen, Azariah Allen.
1780. Jacob Allen.
1781. Samuel Edwards.
1783. Amos Hilton.
1787. Thomas Allen, died at sea.

Malachi Allen.
1793. Arthur Allen.
1796. Amos Hilton.
1798. Luther Allen, Jacob Perry.
1801. John Lee.
1803. Isaac Allen, William Hassam.
1821. John Hooper.
1823. Capt. William Babcock. [3]
1824. Daniel Allen.
1827. (Sept.) ———— Hassam, " age 28." [4]
1829. Josiah Hassam, drowned at Boston.
1830. Joseph Killam, on a voyage to the West Indies.
1838. John W. G. Allen.
1843. John Cheever, Rufus Cheever, Hillard Morse, David Hall, Nathaniel Morgan, Merritt Lennon.
1844. Horatio Allen.
1852. George F. Allen.

[1] Perhaps this and the list for 1774 are the same.

[2] Capt. Hibbert had previously commanded the Privateer "Hawke."

[3] Murdered at sea by pirates; p. 113.

[4] This is from the Church Records: "Josiah Hassam b. Aug. 19, 1797, died Sept. 1824 at City Point, Va." They may have been the same.

1877.   Edward L. Wheaton, Charles Allen. [1]
1894.   Edward W. Leach.
        Vincent R. Burgess, lost overboard in the Indian
        Ocean.

The above list gives nearly or quite 130 between the years 1717 and 1894. How many names are lacking appears from the record made by Rev. Benjamin Tappan, November, 1774: "N. B. About 97 have been lost at sea and buried in distant ports since I came to town" (1745).

[1] On voyage to India, on ship "Iceland," one of three ships built for the India trade, the others named the "Iceberg" and the "Ice King." The "Iceland" was spoken a few days out from port, and never again heard from.

APPENDIX M.

The Water Works.

Among the great works of art of the old world, rivalling its Pyramids and Temples, are its Aqueducts, the ruins of which still challenge admiration for their solidity, costliness and engineering skill. The "water question" presents one of the great problems of our modern civilization. Happily, it seems to be solved in Manchester, at least for the present generation. And there is no reason to doubt that the supply will prove adequate to meet all reasonable demands upon it, so long as the springs run among the hills.

The town had depended for nearly two hundred and fifty years of its history upon the natural water supply by means of wells and cisterns for domestic purposes, and upon reservoirs in case of fire. It was as well provided for, perhaps, as most towns of similar size and population. It had been felt for many years, however, that a larger and purer water supply was demanded. Various plans were discussed, but nothing definite was accomplished until April 23, 1890, when Samuel Knight, T. Jefferson Coolidge, Jr., William Hoare and Roland C. Lincoln were chosen a Committee "to take into consideration the expediency of introducing water into the town for general town purposes, to ascertain the best source of supply, the quality of the same, the best method of procedure, and to make an estimate of the probable cost thereof, together with such information as will enable the citizens of the town to act thereon understandingly." This Committee employed Mr. Percy

M. Blake as Engineer, and proceeded at once to make a
series of investigations and surveys, resulting in the
recommendation to the town in an able and elaborate
Report, of the present system of Water Supply, including driven wells, a large filter-well, a pumping-station
and stand-pipe.

The thoroughness of the work of this Committee left
little to be done subsequently but the carrrying out of
the original plan with some slight necessary modifica-
tions and enlargements. The town was fortunate at the
outset, in the selection of its Committee and its Engineer. The finances of the enterprise were also successfully managed from the start, consisting in the issue of
a series of gradually maturing Bonds, so as to distribute
the cost of the work over twenty successive years.

The following account of the construction of the
Works, and the introduction of water into the town, is
little more than a compilation from the admirable Reports of the Water Commissioners, Engineer and Superintendent. These are of necessity the chief, and in some
instances the only, source of information.

In pursuance of a vote at a town meeting held Feb. 2,
1891, at which the above-mentioned Report was sub-
mitted, the Committee petitioned the Legislature for
" an Act to supply the town of Manchester with water."
The Act was passed, and was approved by the Governor, March 20, 1891. The Act was accepted by the
town April 4, 1891, by a vote of two hundred to seventy-
six. At this meeting the town also voted to take " the
waters of Sawmill Brook and its tributaries, and from
springs and underground and surface sources adjacent
thereto," and to issue bonds to the amount of $125,000,
and elected Samuel Knight, Roland C. Lincoln and
William Hoare Water Commissioners, for three years,
two years and one year respectively.

On April 15, operations were begun for the driving of test-wells along the valley of Sawmill Brook, as recommended by the State Board of Health and by Mr. Blake in his report, in order to ascertain more fully the nature of the subsoil and to determine the point of largest yield remote from habitations. No satisfactory results could be reached above the so-called Coolidge Springs, though many wells were sunk to obtain them. Finally, a well, No. 30, was developed near the junction of the Eastern and Northern Valleys, which yielded a remarkable flow; and the large collecting-well was located near it, which presumably receives the water from both valleys.

A retaining gallery, or filter-well was then constructed, thirty-three feet in diameter at the top, and about thirty feet in depth. The ground proved to be clay, here and there slightly mixed with fine gravel and sand.

The progress of the operations was watched with interest by our citizens generally. The excavation was stopped at a depth of twenty-nine feet; and, though a considerable quantity of water was obtained, chiefly from the sides of the well toward the Eastern Valley, it was decided to increase the supply by sinking five tubular wells to enter a stratum of water-bearing gravel, which was believed to be easily within reach, as indicated by the existence of the neighboring springs. These five tubes, of 2½-inch bore, were driven to the further depth of about twenty-four feet, and reached the desired stratum of gravel from which said springs arise. A remarkable and copious flow from these tubular wells was at once established, the jets of water rising to a height of five or six feet above the top of the tubes.

The stand-pipe, located on Powder House Hill, is thirty-five feet in diameter and seventy-five feet in height. It is constructed of the best materials, with iron plates and steel rivets, and in the most thorough manner. It was filled with water for the first time, Feb. 22, 1892, and was found to be practically water-tight.

The pumping station consists of a well-proportioned and convenient building containing the pumping-plant, with coal sheds, and a house for the Superintendent. The pumps were furnished by the Blake Manufacturing Company and are described as duplicate pumping engines of the compound condensing type, twelve-inch stroke.

The pipe-laying included specifications for laying 64,696 feet of pipe, seventy valves and seventy hydrants. The work was begun July 13, 1891, and continued under most favorable weather with little interruption, until Jan. 9, 1892.

A demand for the extension of water mains continued the work of laying pipes in the summer of 1892; with this was combined the work of service-piping. By special arrangement, in accordance with a vote of the town, pipes were laid in many private estates. The net cost of the work to March 1, 1893, was $156,472.33. During the summer of 1893, the demands upon the well were so great that it became evident to the Board

that it was desirable to afford additional vent to the great pressure or head of water seeking to enter through the five two-and-a-half inch tubes which had been sunk in the bottom of the well. Accordingly, awaiting the time of least consumption of the town water, the work of increasing the speed and volume of the supply was begun on December 5. Six tubes, each of four-inch diameter, were driven to about the same depth as the smaller tubes extend; and a considerable quantity of broken stone, and then of coarse Plum Island sand, was deposited over the bottom of the well.

The extremely dry summer of 1894 tested the capacity of the supply and of the works in an unexpected manner, but there was no failure. On July 13, there were pumped 400,190 gallons, the pumps being in operation seventeen hours.[1]

[1] This seems to show that a failure of supply can be caused only by senseless, and from a moral point of view, *criminal* waste.

The Report of 1894 gave the total cost to date as $163,231.42 (exclusive of land damages), embracing 14.4 miles of piping, 120 hydrants, and 381 service-pipe lines. In closing the Report, the Commissioners say:

We feel that our citizens are to be congratulated that, while many other towns have been obliged to increase their water debt over the original bond issues, Manchester has reduced hers under the plan of her series bonds.

The statistics given below are from the Superintendent's Report to the Board of Water Commissioners, March, 1895.

During the year ending March 1, there were pumped 42,030,790 gallons of water as follows:—

March . . . 1,488,420 gal.	September . 4,289,930 gal.
April . . . 1,703,650 "	October . . 2,767,050 "
May . . . . 2,879,770 "	November . 3,074,170 "
June . . . 4,773,800 "	December . 4,289,930 "
July . . . . 7,347,680 "	January . . 2,265,620 "
August . . 5,338,600 "	February . . 1,812,170 "

The water pumped since the works started is as follows:—

For year ending March 1, 1893 . . . . . 20,374,640 gallons.
"   "   "   "   " 1894 36,958,560   "
"   "   "   "   " 1895 42,030,790   "

In their annual Report for 1895, the Commissioners made the following weighty and important suggestions:

It is of the greatest importance that a community should never lose sight of the possibility that it may at some time need more water, and should know where and how it may be obtained, so as to meet the emergency when it comes. The inevitable growth of a town like Manchester will surely repeat the experience of many towns and cities, as shown in the reports of their Water Boards. At first we anticipated a maximum consumption of 200,000 gallons a day, allowing sixty gallons per capita; and yet last summer we reached a maxi-

mum of double that amount. We have fifty-eight more takers
than a year ago; and new houses and larger demands are every
year emphasizing the need of adopting some means of increasing our water supply.

Whether we are obtaining the entire yield in summer of the
subterranean sources of our well, and getting all the underground water available, cannot readily be ascertained without
further testing the area of the water-shed or the adjacent territory by the driving of tubular wells. We believe and ear-
nestly recommend that such tests should be made immediately with a view to obtaining a further supply of ground-
water; and such wells as are found to yield sufficiently should
be connected as far as practicable for the purpose of reënforc-
ing our present collecting-well.

For nine months of the year our present supply is, and may be
always ample. But, for a town whose population and consumption of water are enormously increased during the three summer months, a storage basin may in the end afford the simplest, surest and most economical method of providing an increase of our supply for summer use. Very likely the reën-
forcement of the present supply by a system of connected tubular wells may prove sufficient for some time to come; but
there are uncertainties which it is the part of prudence and
foresight to recognize.

We would recommend, therefore, that the town authorize
its Water Commissioners to have made surveys and maps of
the territory and valley of the water-shed above our well, and
to present a report thereon at some subsequent town meeting;
and that the town appropriate the sum of $1,000 for the pur-
pose and such further sum out of the water rates of the coming year as the Water Board may find necessary for the proper
performance of the work.

Finally, we recommend that in case any petition is presented to the legislature for the right to take water from any
or all of the Chebacco group of ponds, so called, your Water
Commissioners be empowered to appear before the legislature
to obtain such legislation as may be necessary or desirable to
reserve and secure to the town of Manchester the right at any
time to take water from Gravelly Pond in the town of Hamilton.

These recommendations were adopted by the town,
March 19, 1895.

In the summer of 1892, the Water Works being practically completed and in successful operation, it was decided to have a celebration in commemoration of so signal an event. Arrangements were accordingly made to this effect, and carried out under the direction of a large and efficient Committee, of which Charles A. Prince was Chairman, on Thursday, August 18th. The day was one of the most perfect of the season, and the Celebration was in every way a success, worthy of the town and of the great public enterprise of which it was the fitting conclusion. The entire Programme is given below from the beautiful Souvenirs distributed on this occasion.

⊙ OFFICIAL PROGRAMME ⊙

MANCHESTER WATER CELEBRATION,

Thursday, August 18th,

1892.

PARADE.

At 2 o'clock P. M., over the following route:

Procession will start on Masconomo St., at junction of Proctor St., pass through Masconomo to Beach, Beach to Union, Washington and Summer Sts. to the Row Schoolhouse ; countermarch and return through Washington to North and School, as far as Pleasant St.; countermarch through School, Central and Bridge to Bennet, thence to Central through Union, down Beach St. and dismiss at the Station.

Procession composed of Germania Band, Baldwin's Cadet Band, Gloucester Light Infantry and Beverly Light Infantry Companies, under the command of Major Pew, Allen Post,

No. 67, G. A. R., Sons of Veterans, Fire Department, Barges with school children, Magnolia Lodge, No. 149, I. O. O. F., Ladies' Relief Corps, coaches and private carriages decorated with flowers and bunting, and teams of the business men of the town.

CIVIC EXERCISES

Will take place on the Common, at 3.30 o'clock, consisting of the following programme.

C. A. PRINCE, Chairman of the Permanent Committee Presiding.

MUSIC, ...	*By the Bands*
PRAYER, ...	*By Rev. Daniel Marcin*
SINGING—High School March, ...	*By the Children*
OFFERING OF RESOLUTIONS TO THE WATER COMMISSIONERS,	*. Drawn by the Rev. D. F. Lamson*
MOTION TO ADOPT THE RESOLUTIONS,	*. . By H. C. Leach*
MOTION SECONDED, By A. S. Jewett, Chairman Board of Selectmen	
RESPONSE, ...	*By the Water Commissioners*
SINGING—An Original Ode, ...	*By the Children*
ADDRESS, ...	*By R. H. Dana, Esq.*
MUSIC, ...	*By the Band*
ADDRESS, . . By His Excellency, Governor William E. Russell	
MUSIC, ...	*By the Band*
ADDRESS, . By His Honor, Mayor Robert S. Rantoul, of Salem	
SINGING—" Gently Fall the Dews of Eve,"	*. By the Children*
RECITATION—" Our Treasure from the Flowing Springs,"	
. . . .	*By Joseph Proctor*

(Original Ode, by MRS. L. F. ALLEN.)

DOXOLOGY, ... *Sung by the assembly led by the bands*
" Praise God from whom all blessings flow," etc.

EXHIBITION

By the Fire Department, at 4.30 o'clock, on the Common.

Evening.

RIVER CARNIVAL

To commence at 8 o'clock.

Flotilla of Boats, illuminated with lanterns and lights, to start from near the railroad, go down into the harbor and return.

Near the Town Hall will be a temporary fountain which will play during the afternoon, and in the evening the water will be illuminated with colored lights.

BAND CONCERT

During the evening by both bands.

A complete history of the Water Works from their first inception, including Tables of Construction, Cost, Analyses of the Water, etc., is contained in the Reports of the original Committee and those of the Water Commissioners, *seriatim*. For fulness, clearness of arrangement and general style of execution, these Reports are models of their kind, and leave nothing to be desired.

The efficiency of the Water Service has been tested at fires more than once, especially on Nov. 16, 1894, at the burning of the buildings of Roberts and Hoare on North street, a conflagration which threatened most serious consequences; and it has been shown that the service is indispensable to the public safety as well as to health and comfort.

APPENDIX N.

SELECTMEN. 1645–1895.

This list, it will be seen, is defective in the earlier years, owing to the loss of the records.

1645. John Sibley, William Allen, John Norman.
1658. Pasco Foote, John Sibley, Robert Leach.
1660. William Bennett, Robert Leach.
1661. John Pickworth, Samuel Friend, Robert Leach.
1668. Thomas Jones, William Allen, Samuel Friend.
1672. William Bennett, John Sibley, Samuel Friend.
1676. William Bennett, Samuel Allen, Samuel Friend.
1680. Robert Leach, John Lee, Isaac Whitchar.
1684. Robert Leach, John Elithorpe, Thomas West.
1686. Robert Knight, Samuel Leach, John Lee.
1687. John Sibley, John Elithorpe, Robert Leach.
1688. John Sibley, Robert Leach, John Elithorpe.
1689. Aaron Bennett, Thomas Tewksbury.
1690. Samuel Leach, Samuel Allen, John Sibley.
1691. Thomas West, Robert Leach, John Lee.
1692. John Sibley, John Elithorpe, Thomas Tewksbury.
1693. Samuel Allen, Thomas West, Thomas Tewksbury.
1694. John Sibley, Robert Leach, John Lee, John Elithorpe.
1695. Joseph Woodbury, Thomas West, John Sibley.
1696. Robert Leach, John Lee, Isaac Whitchar.
1697. John Sibley, John Lee, James Pittman.
1698. Robert Leach, George Norton, Thomas West.
1699. John Sibley, Thomas West, Richard Walker.
1700. Robert Leach, Samuel Lee, John Knowlton.
1701. John Sibley, Robert Leach, John Lee.
1702. John Lee, Robert Leach, John Allen.

1705. Aaron Bennett, Robert Leach, John Knowlton.
1707. Samuel Leach, Samuel Lee, John Knowlton.
1708. John Sibley, Robert Leach, John Knowlton.
1714. Samuel Lee, Samuel Leach, Benjamin Allen.
1715. William Hilton, Aaron Bennett, Samuel Lee.
1717. Robert Leach, Thomas Pittman, John Lee, Jun.
1718. John Knowlton, Aaron Bennett, John Lee, Jun.
1719. Samuel Lee, Richard Leach, John Lee, Jun.
1720. John Foster, Aaron Bennett, John Lee, Jun.
1721. Benjamin Allen, John Foster, Samuel Lee.
1722. Richard Leach, John Foster, John Lee, Jun.
1723. Samuel Lee, John Foster, John Lee, Jun.
1724. William Hooper, John Foster, Jabez Dodge.
1725. Benjamin Allen, John Foster, John Lee.
1726. Samuel Lee, John Foster, Aaron Bennett.
1727. John Foster, Thomas Lee, Samuel Lee.
1728. John Foster, Nathaniel Marsters, Samuel Lee.
1729. John Foster, Nathaniel Marsters, Samuel Lee.
1730. John Foster, Richard Coy, Samuel Lee.
1731. John Foster, Aaron Bennett, Thomas Lee.
1732. John Foster, Ezekiel Goodell, Thomas Lee.
1733. John Foster, Samuel Lee, Thomas Lee.
1734. Benjamin Allen, Samuel Lee, Richard Coy.
1735. John Foster, Benjamin Allen, Thomas Lee.
1736. John Foster, Samuel Lee, John Lee.
1737. Robert Herrick, Jeremiah Hibbard, Richard Coy.
1738. Richard Coy, John Lee, Robert Herrick.
1739. Richard Coy, John Lee, Samuel Lee.
1740. John Foster, Robert Herrick, Benjamin Presson.
1741. John Lee, Richard Coy, Thomas Lee.
1742. John Lee, Richard Coy, Robert Herrick.
1743. Robert Herrick, John Lee, John Lee, 3d.
1744. Robert Herrick, Jonathan Herrick, John Lee.
1746. Robert Herrick, Jonathan Herrick, John Lee.
1747. Jonathan Herrick, Thomas Lee, John Lee.
1748. Jonathan Herrick, Andrew Hooper, Benjamin Lee.
1749. Jonathan Hooper, Andrew Hooper, John Lee.
1750. Jonathan Herrick, Andrew Hooper, John Lee.
1751. Jonathan Herrick, John Lee, Thomas Lee.
1753. John Lee, Thomas Lee, Samuel Lee, Jonathan Herrick, Samuel Allen.
1754. John Lee, Thomas Lee, Benjamin Lee, Samuel Lee.

1755. John Lee, Benjamin Lee, Jonathan Herrick.
1756. John Lee, John Foster, Jonathan Herrick.
1757. John Lee, John Foster, Jonathan Herrick.
1758. Benjamin Kimball, John Foster, Jonathan Herrick.
1759. Benjamin Kimball, Thomas Lee, John Allen.
1760. Benjamin Kimball, John Foster, John Tewksbury.
1761. Benjamin Kimball, John Foster, John Tewksbury.
1762. Joseph Whipple, Jonathan Herrick, John Allen.
1763. Joseph Whipple, Jonathan Herrick, John Allen.
1764. Joseph Whipple, John Tewksbury, John Allen.
1765. Joseph Whipple, John Tewksbury, John Allen.
1766. Joseph Whipple, John Tewksbury, John Allen.
1767. Jonathan Herrick, John Allen, John Tewksbury.
1768. John Tewksbury, Andrew Woodbury, John Allen.
1769. John Tewksbury, Andrew Woodbury, John Allen.
1770. Aaron Lee, Jonathan Herrick, Benjamin Kimball.
1771. Aaron Lee, Andrew Marsters, Benjamin Kimball.
1772. Jonathan Herrick, Andrew Marsters, Benjamin Kimball.
1773. Aaron Lee, Jacob Hooper, Benjamin Kimball.
1774. Jonathan Herrick, Andrew Woodbury, John Tewks-
        bury.
1775. Andrew Woodbury, Eleazer Crafts, John Tewksbury.
1776. John Cheever, Eleazer Crafts, John Edwards.
1777. John Allen, William Tuck, Jonathan Herrick.
1778. Eleazer Crafts, John Cheever, Jonathan Herrick.
1779. Eleazer Crafts, John Cheever, John Allen.
1780. Eleazer Crafts, Aaron Lee, John Allen.
1781. Eleazer Crafts, Aaron Lee, John Allen.
1782. Isaac Proctor, Aaron Lee, Eleazer Crafts.
1783. Francis Crafts, Aaron Lee, Eleazer Crafts.
1784. Eleazer Crafts, Aaron Lee, Francis Crafts.
1785. Eleazer Crafts, Aaron Lee, Isaac Lee.
1786. William Tuck, John Cheever, Francis Crafts.
1787. William Tuck, John Cheever, Francis Crafts.
1788. William Tuck, John Cheever, Francis Crafts.
1789. William Tuck, Eleazer Crafts, Francis Crafts.
1790. William Tuck, Francis Crafts, Henry Story.
1791. William Tuck, Francis Crafts, Isaac Lee.
1792. William Tuck, Francis Crafts, Isaac Lee.
1793. Ebenezer Tappan, Francis Crafts, Aaron Lee.
1794. Isaac Lee, Aaron Lee, Delucena L. Bingham.
1795. William Tuck, Benjamin Ober, Delucena L. Bingham.

1796. Delucena L. Bingham, Aaron Lee, Benjamin Ober.
1797. Delucena L. Bingham, Aaron Lee, Benjamin Ober.
1798. Delucena L. Bingham, Benjamin Ober, Samuel Bennett.
1799. Henry Story, Aaron Lee, John Knight.
1800. Henry Story, Aaron Lee, Francis Crafts.
1801. Ezekiel Leach, David Colby, Delucena L. Bingham.
1802. Henry Story, Delucena L. Bingham, Benjamin Foster.
1803. Henry Story, Delucena L. Bingham, Benjamin Foster.
1804. Israel Foster, Delucena L. Bingham, William Tuck.
1805. Israel Foster, Delucena L. Bingham, Henry Lee.
1806. Israel Foster, Delucena L. Bingham, Henry Lee.
1807. Delucena L. Bingham, Henry Lee, Ebenezer Tappan.
1808. Israel Foster, Delucena L. Bingham, Henry Story.
1809. Israel Foster, Tyler Parsons, Obed Carter.
1810. Israel Foster, Delucena L. Bingham, Burley Smith.
1811. Delucena L. Bingham, Tyler Parsons, David Crafts.
1812. Israel Foster, Henry Lee, Obed Carter.
1813. Israel Foster, Andrew Marsters, David Crafts.
1814. David Crafts, Tyler Parsons, John Knight.
1815. Israel Foster, Delucena L. Bingham, Henry Lee.
1816. Israel Foster, Delucena L. Bingham, Henry Lee.
1817. Israel Foster, Delucena L. Bingham, Tyler Parsons.
1818. Israel Foster, Tyler Parsons, John Hooper.
1819. Israel Foster, Andrew Marsters, John Cheever.
1820. Israel Foster, John Cheever, David Crafts.
1821. Israel Foster, John Lee, John Cheever.
1822. Israel Foster, Tyler Parsons, John Cheever.
1823. Israel Foster, John Knight, John Cheever.
1824. Israel Foster, John Knight, John Cheever.
1825. Tyler Parsons, Thomas Leach, Richard Allen.
1826. Tyler Parsons, Richard Allen, Andrew Marsters.
1827. Tyler Parsons, Thomas Leach, Andrew Marsters.
1828. Andrew Marsters, Samuel Cheever, John P. Allen.
1829. Andrew Marsters, Samuel Cheever, John P. Allen.
1830. Andrew Marsters, Jonathan Hassam, Samuel Cheever.
1831. Andrew Marsters, Amos Hilton, Israel F. Tappan.
1832. Israel Foster, John W. Allen, Israel F. Tappan.
1833. Israel F. Tappan, John W. Allen, Daniel Leach.
1834. Israel F. Tappan, John W. Allen, Daniel Leach.
1835. John W. Allen, Daniel Leach, Ariel P. Crowell.
1836. Benjamin Leach, Daniel Leach, Samuel Cheever.
1837. John W. Allen, Israel F. Tappan, A. P. Crowell.

1838. Samuel Cheever, Benjamin Leach, 3d., Albert E. Low.
1839. Benjamin Leach, 2d, A. E. Low, A. P. Crowell, John Lee.
1840. Benjamin Leach, 2d, David Crafts, John Lee.
1841. Benjamin Leach, 2d, David Crafts, John Lee.
1842. Benjamin Leach, 2d, Jonathan Hassam, John Lee.
1843. Benjamin Leach, 2d, John Lee, Jonathan Hassam.
1844. Benjamin Leach, 2d, Samuel Cheever, Henry P. Allen.
1845. Benjamin Leach, 2d, Samuel Cheever, Henry P. Allen.
1846. Benjamin Leach, 2d, Henry P. Allen, A. E. Low.
1847. Benjamin Leach, 2d, Henry P. Allen, Isaac S. West.
1848. Benjamin Leach, 2d, Stephen Story, John Girdler, 2d.
1849. John Lee, John Girdler, 2d, Luther Allen.
1850. John Lee, John Girdler, 2d, Luther Allen.
1851. Luther Bingham, Isaac S. West, John C. Long.
1852. John C. Long, Samuel Cheever, Philip C. Wheeler.
1853. John Lee, Philip C. Wheeler, A. E. Low.
1854. John Lee, Samuel Cheever, John W. Allen.
1855. Philip C. Wheeler, A. W. Smith, A. E. Low.
1856. A. E. Low, A. P. Crowell, J. P. Gentlee.
1857. A. E. Low, A. P. Crowell, J. P. Gentlee.
1858. A. E. Low, A. P. Crowell, J. P. Gentlee.
1859. A. E. Low, John Lee, Samuel Crowell.
1860. John Lee, Samuel Crowell, John Price.
1861. John Lee, John Price, Aaron Bennett.
1862. John Price, A. E. Low, Aaron Bennett.
1863. John Price, Aaron Bennett, George F. Allen.
1864. Aaron Bennett, George F. Allen, George F. Rust.
1865. George F. Allen, Aaron Bennett, Albion W. Gilman.
1866. George F. Allen, Aaron Bennett, A. W. Jewett.
1867. George F. Allen, A. E. Low, Aaron Bennett.
1868. John Lee, Aaron Bennett, A. W. Smith.
1869. John Lee, Aaron Bennett, A. W. Smith.
1870. John Lee, John H. Cheever, William A. Stone.
1871. John Lee, John H. Cheever, William A. Stone.
1872. John Lee, John H. Cheever, William A. Stone.
1873. John Lee, John H. Cheever, William A. Stone.
1874. John Lee, Amos F. Bennett, Samuel Knight.
1875. John Lee, Amos F. Bennett, Samuel Knight.
1876. John Lee, William A. Stone, Samuel Knight.
1877. John Lee, Henry T. Bingham, Samuel Knight.
1878. John Lee, John H. Cheever, William A. Stone.

1879. John Lee, William A. Stone, John H. Cheever, Albion W. Gilman.
1880. William A. Stone, J. H. Cheever, Albion W. Gilman.
1881. William A. Stone, J. H. Cheever, Albion W. Gilman.
1882. William A. Stone, J. H. Cheever, Albion W. Gilman.
1883. J. H. Cheever, H. T. Bingham, Daniel W. Friend.
1884. J. H. Cheever, H. T. Bingham, W. A. Stone.
1885. J. H. Cheever, H. T. Bingham, Samuel Knight.
1886. J. H. Cheever, H. T. Bingham, W. A. Stone.
1887. Samuel Knight, Edward A. Lane, N. P. Meldram.
1888. H. T. Bingham, N. P. Meldram, N. C. Marshall.
1889. H. T. Bingham, N. P. Meldram, J. H. Cheever.
1890. A. S. Jewett, W. J. Johnson, B. S. Bullock.
1891. A. S. Jewett, B. S. Bullock, Edward S. Knight.
1892. A. S. Jewett, B. S. Bullock, E. S. Knight.
1893. A. S. Jewett, B. S. Bullock, E. S. Knight.
1894. A. S. Jewett, B. S. Bullock, H. T. Bingham.
1895. A. S. Jewett, H. T. Bingham, Jeffrey T. Stanley.

Town Clerks. 1645-1895.

1645. Robert Leach.
1658. " Goodman " Jones.
1680. Samuel Friend.
1684-91. John Lee.
1692-94. Thos. Tewksbury.
1695-1708. John Lee.
1714. John Knowlton.
1715. John Lee.
1717-23. John Lee, Jr.
1724. Jabez Dodge.
1725-38. Samuel Lee.
1739. John Lee.
1740. Samuel Allen.
1741-46. John Lee, Jr.
1747. Richard Lee.
1748-53. Benjamin Lee.
1754, '55. Jonathan Herrick.
1756. Benjamin Lee.
1757-63. Benjamin Kimball.
1764-66. Joseph Whipple.

1767-69. John Tewksbury.
1770-73. Benjamin Kimball.
1774, '75. John Tewksbury.
1776. Jacob Tewksbury.
1777, '78. John Allen.
1779-1800. Aaron Lee.
1801. Delucena L. Bingham.
1802-06. Aaron Lee.
1807-19. Delucena L. Bingham.
1820. Joseph Hooper.
1821-37. Delucena L. Bingham.
1838-43. John C. Long.
1844-54. John Lee.
1855-57. John Price.
1858. George F. Allen.
1859-61. John Lee.
1862-67. George F. Allen.
1868-79. John Lee.
1880. John Price.
1881-87. William A. Stone.

1888 — A. S. Jewett.

REPRESENTATIVES AND SENATORS. 1665 – 1895.

REPRESENTATIVES.

Thomas West,	1665.	David Crafts,	1839.
Thomas West,	1672.	Arba Burnham,	1840.
Thomas Tewksbury,	1692.	Samuel Cheever,	1841.
Thomas Tewksbury,	1693.	Amos Hill,	1842.
John Sibley,	1701.	Ebenezer Tappan, Jr.,	1843.
Thomas West,	1702.	Albert E. Low,	1844.
John Knowlton,	1717.	John Lee,	1847.
Jonathan Herrick,	1756.	John Lee,	1848.
Eleazer Craft,	1773.	Stephen Story,	1849.
Andrew Woodbury,	1774.	Samuel O. Boardman,	1850.
William Tuck,	1777.	John Girdler,	1851.
Eleazer Craft,	1779.	Daniel W. Friend,	1852.
William Tuck,	1806.	George A. Brown,	1855.
Henry Story,	1808.	Albert E. Low,	1856.
Israel Forster,	1810.	Larkin Woodbury,	1857.
Ebenezer Tappan,	1811.	Luther Allen,	1859.
David Colby,	1812.	Charles W. Reding,	1861.
Delucena L. Bingham,	1824.	Daniel Leach, Jr.,	1863.
John Cheever,	1829.	William W. Hooper,	1865.
Daniel Annable,	1830.	John Lee,	1868.
John Knight,	1832.	Lewis N. Tappan,	1877.
John W. Allen,	1833.	William H. Tappan,	1881.
John E. Bohonon,	1834.	John H. Cheever,	1883.
Benjamin Leach,	1835.	Jeffrey F. Stanley,	1887.
A. P. Crowell,	1836.	Henry T. Bingham,	1891.
Israel Forster,	1837.	Benjamin S. Bullock,	1895.
Joseph Hooper,	1838.		

SENATORS.

Charles Fitz, 1874 and 1875.
William H. Tappan, 1885 and 1886.

One family has been represented in the councils of the State in three generations:

Ebenezer Tappan, 1811.
Ebenezer Tappan, Jr., 1843.
Lewis N. Tappan, 1877.
William H. Tappan, 1881, '85, '86.

SUPPLEMENT.

THE TWO HUNDRED AND FIFTIETH ANNIVERSARY.

JULY 18, 1895.

THE SAME TIDES FLOW.

Song, with Music, composed by Prof. N. B. Sargent.

Sung at the Celebration.

O'er the rugged hills so grand,
 Now to us a joy and pride;
And along the rocky strand,
 Where we watch the rolling tide;
Masconomo, chieftain bold,
 With his arrows and his bow,
Used to wander, we've been told,
 Many years ago.

REFRAIN.

But the same tides flow,
And the same stars glow;
 And the waves sing the same wild glee.
Just the same the seabird's screech,
And the Shining Singing Beach
 Takes the kisses of the same old sea.

But the Indian Hunting Ground
 Has become a garden fair;
Where the wigwam once was found,
 Stands the mansion, rich and rare.
Wealth and skill have brought their power,
 Everywhere their work we see;
Love and beauty grace the bower,
 This is Eden by the sea.

REFRAIN.

Now the school is on the hill,
 And the church is in the vale,
And our homes with light they fill,
 Brightest hopes that cannot fail.
They have been the beacon light
 As the years have passed away,
Brought us from the gloom of night
 To the splendors of the day.

REFRAIN.

THE TWO HUNDRED AND FIFTIETH ANNIVERSARY.

THE following extract from the Colonial Records fixes the birthday of the Town beyond question.

June 18, 1645. Att y⁰ request of y⁰ inhabitants of Jeofferyes Creeke, this Courte doth graunt yᵗ y⁰ said Jeofferyes Creeke henceforward shall be called Manchester.

In the margin is the note "by both Houses." The entry under May 14,

It is ordered, yᵗ Jeffryes Creeke shalbe called Manchester,

does not give the real date, as this records only the action of one branch of the General Court.

As before stated (page 23), this is the only Act of Incorporation of the Town in existence. But the Town's corporate rights are here recognized, and at this date — June 18, 1645 — its history as a Town may be said to begin.

Arrangements for the Celebration of the 250th Anniversary began with the appointment of a General Committee on the Celebration, at the March meeting, 1894.

General Committee.

A. E. Low,
D. L. Bingham,
G. F. Allen,
D. F. Lamson,
Samuel Knight,
T. J. Coolidge, Jr.,
O. T. Roberts,

R. C. Lincoln,
W. H. Allen,
C. C. Dodge,
W. J. Johnson,
Charles O. Lee,
John Baker,
Daniel Leach,
L. F. Allen.

William H. Tappan,
A. S. Jewett,
H. P. Kittfield,
Russell Sturgis,
H. T. Bingham,
F. K. Hooper,
A. F. Bennett,

The following Committees were subsequently appointed by the General Committee :

Executive.

Samuel Knight,
Alfred S. Jewett,
Henry P. Kitfield,
Franklin K. Hooper,

William J. Johnson,
George F. Allen,
Isaac S. West,
Oliver T. Roberts.

Historical.

William H. Tappan,
R. C. Lincoln,

D. F. Lamson,
D. L. Bingham.

A. S. Jewett,

Invitation and Reception.

D. L. Bingham,
H. T. Bingham.
Daniel Leach,

William H. Allen,
C. C. Dodge,
George F. Allen,

F. B. Rust,
B. S. Bullock,
George L. Allen.

Literary Exercises.

H. C. Leach,
T. J. Coolidge,

R. C. Lincoln.
George Wigglesworth.

A. S. Jewett,

Parade.

Russell Sturgis,
H. L. Higginson,
H. W. Cunningham,
F. M. Stanwood,
Gordon Prince,
W. L. Dickson,

T. D. Boardman,
J. T. Stanley,
Enoch Crombie,
E. P. Stanley,
S. L. Wheaton,
Edward Robinson,

Charles S. Hanks.

Gov. Winthrop Party.

Samuel Knight,
John A. Burnham,
Henry S. Grew,

Caleb A. Curtis,
T. J. Coolidge, Jr.,
H. P. Kitfield.

Banquet.

H. T. Bingham,
Gerald Wyman,

G. A. Kitfield,
E. A. Lane,

B. S. Bullock.

Illumination, Fireworks and Salute.

Oliver T. Roberts,　　　　　　C. L. Hoyt,
F. J. Merrill,　　　　　　　　Charles P. Crombie,
C. C. Dodge,　　　　　　　　E. F. Preston,
Ed. S. Knight,　　　　　　　George A. Kitfield,
John W. Marshall,　　　　　　James Hoare

Art and Loan Exhibit.

Mrs. John Baker,　　　　　　Mrs. Charlotte Brown,
Miss Lila G. Goldsmith,　　　Mr. J. F. Rabardy,
Mr. G. W. Jewett,　　　　　Miss Florence G. Lamson,
Miss E. Grace Kitfield,　　　Mr. J. H. Kitfield,
Miss Annie Clarke,　　　　　Miss Hattie P. Knight,
Mr. John Baker,　　　　　　Mr. G. W. Beaman,
Mrs. G. W. Beaman,　　　　Mrs. C. W. Sawyer,
Mrs. J. R. Allen,　　　　　Mrs. C. S. Hanks,
Mr. Andrew Lee, 2d,　　　　Mrs. H. L. Higginson.
Miss Etta L. Rabardy,　　　Miss Mary L. Bullard,
　　　　　Mr. Charles O. Lee.

Musical Exercises.

N. B. Sargent,　　　　　　A. P. Richardson,
A. B. Palmer,　　　　　　A. C. Needham,
F. K. Swett,　　　　　　L. F. Allen.

Bands.

T. W. Long,　　Charles H. Stone,　　　T. C. Rowe.

Tablets.

D. F. Lamson,　　　　　John Baker,
A. E. Low,　　　　　　Charles O. Lee,
D. L. Bingham,　　　　W. H. Tappan.

Decorations.

Edward Robinson,　　　John Scott,
John Allen,　　　　　I. S. West.

Sunday Services.

Rev. D. F. Lamson,　Charles H. Johnson,　D. B. Kimball,
Rev. F. A. Fate,　　T. B. Stone,　　　L. F. Allen.

Indian Tribes.

George S. Sinnicks, I. M. Marshall, Lewis Andrews.
C. L. Hoyt, David E. Butler, Leonard Andrews,
Charles O. Howe.

Reception of the Press.

I. M. Marshall, F. G. Cheever, L. W. Floyd.

Information and Registration.

N. P. Meldram, J. H. Rivers, E. P. Crooker.

Transportation.

Frank P. Knight, E. P. Crooker, William Doogue.

Grand Stand and Doric Columns.

William J. Johnson, E. A. Lane, W. H. Allen.

The opening exercises of the Celebration took place
on Sunday, July 14, in the form of a Commemorative
Service, in the Congregational church, under the direction of the Committee on Sunday Services. Rev. D. F.
Lamson, Chairman of the Committee, presided and made
a brief address; Rev. F. A. Fate, pastor of the church,
read the Scriptures and offered prayer; Rev. L. T.
Chamberlain, D. D., preached the sermon from 1 Sam.
7 : 12. "Then Samuel took a stone, and set it between
Mizpeh and Shen, and called the name of it Eben-ezer,
saying, Hitherto hath the Lord helped us." In the
evening an informal service was held, at which addresses
were made by Dea. A. E. Low, Mr. Henry C. Leach,
Rev. D. F. Lamson and Rev. F. A. Fate; a letter was
also read from Rev. C. W. Reding, a pastor in town from
1856 to 1861, and representative from the town in the
legislature of 1861. The music through the day was
furnished by the choir, with congregational singing.
The attendance was large, and the exercises of an appropriate and impressive character.

Beginning with Monday morning, July 15, the busy note of preparation was heard on every hand. The streets and public buildings were handsomely decorated, as were many stores and residences. The town soon became fairly aflame with the national colors and various appropriate devices. Committees were energetically at work, and the permanent and summer residents vied in public spirit in doing honor to the occasion. On Wednesday evening, a beacon fire blazed on the site of the Old mill, off Beach street, lighting up land and water for miles around.

OFFICIAL PROGRAMME
(abridged)
As carried out July 18, 1895.

Sunrise: Ringing of Bells and Salute.
7 o'clock. Signal Gun calling Indian Tribes.
8 " Band and Vocal Concert at the Arena.
8 to 9 " Gathering of the Indian Tribes.
9 " Good Ship "Arbella" sighted.
9.15 " Governor's Salute.
9.30 " Landing of Gov. Winthrop's Party.

> Reception by the Indian Chief Masconomo and his Tribe.

10.30 " Exercises at the Arena.

> Music by the Band.
> Prayer by Rev. F. A. Fate, Pastor of the Congregational Church.
> Address by the Chairman, Henry C. Leach, Esq.
> Singing, "The Star Spangled Banner," by the School Children.
> Singing, "The Same Tides Flow," words and music by N. B. Sargent. By select chorus.
> Oration by His Honor, the Lieutenant-Governor, Roger Wolcott.
> Singing, "America," by the School Children.
> Music by the Band.

12 " Salute.
12 to 1 " Band Concert.

1 o'clock. Collation in Town Hall.

> Presiding officer, Henry C. Leach, Esq. Address of
> Welcome by Alfred S. Jewett, Esq., Chairman of the
> Board of Selectmen. Addresses by His Honor the
> Lieutenant-Governor; Rev. D. F. Lamson, Historian
> of the Town; Richard H. Dana, Esq.

3   "   Forming of the Floral and Historical Parade,
the Parade moving promptly at 3.30 in the
following order:

> Platoon of Policemen.
> Chief Marshal, Maj. Russell Sturgis.
> Aids.
> Band.
> First Division.
> Marshal, Col. A. P. Rockwell.
> Aids.
> Second Corps of Independent Cadets.
> Allen Post 67 of G. A. R.
> His Honor, the Lieutenant-Governor; and other guests,
> in Carriages.
>
> Second Division.
> Marshal, Charles S. Hanks.
> Aids.
> Band.
> Indians.
> Representative Members of Society of Colonial Wars.
> Continentals.
> Coaches with the Winthrop Party.
> Ladies' Floats.
> The Spinners.
> The Tea Party.
> Indian Float.
> Fisheries.
> Ox Team with School Children.
>
> Third Division.
> Marshal, Gordon Prince.
> Aids.
> Decorated Carriages.
>
> The Route:
> Beach street, Union, Washington, Summer, through
> the Grounds of the Essex County Club, School street,
> Bridge Street to West Manchester; Countermarch by
> Bridge street and Central street, and dismiss.

7.30   "   Band Concert on the Common.
Sunset Gun.

8   "   Illumination and Fireworks.

The general plan and arrangement of the Celebration was under the immediate supervision of the artist, Ross Turner, Esq., of Salem.

The ship "Arbella" was designed and constructed by David M. Little, Esq., of Salem, marine architect. The vessel was intended to be a reproduction of the ship on which John Winthrop sailed from Yarmouth, England, March 20, 1630, reaching these shores June 12. The ship, whose name was originally the "Eagle," was a craft of 350 tons, manned by 52 seamen and carrying 28 pieces of ordnance. The vessel constructed to represent her was the old sloop, "Hard Chance," of Gloucester, built in 1857; such alterations were made in her build above the water-line, including a high poop and forecastle with gun ports, and lateen and bowsprit sails, flags and pennants, as answered to the peculiar shape and rig of Dutch vessels of the seventeenth century. As the vessel entered the harbor (towed by a tug), with the party personating Governor Winthrop and his companions on board, it presented a picturesque appearance, and with the realistic costumes of the period, both English and Aboriginal, helped to carry the imagination back over the intervening centuries.

The reception of Governor Winthrop (R. H. Dana, Esq.), with his secretary (H. W. Skinner, Esq.) and his page (R. H. Dana, Jr.), all descendants of the great Puritan, was at the landing, by Masconomo (Mr. Leonard Andrews) and his "braves." The smoking of the pipe of peace, and the other formalities, including the serving of strawberries in birch bark, was a brilliant scene, witnessed and applauded by the vast throngs in the Arena and on the adjacent grounds. This unique and spectacular feature of the day's exercises, as well as the Procession, was admirably conceived and carried out, and added much to the interest of the occasion.

The day was one of the most delightful of the season, and seemed greatly enjoyed by the immense and orderly crowds (estimated as high as twenty-five thousand) who all day long thronged the streets and held every vantage ground. At a comparatively early hour, the multitudes dispersed and quiet reigned over the ancient town. A favoring Providence smiled upon all from the beginning to the close, evoking from grateful hearts thanksgiving to Him "from whom all blessings flow."

The following features of the Procession are worthy of special notice :

In the first divison was the Manchester G. A. R. Post, led by Commander J. H. Rivers. Behind the column came a carriage, in which were seated four veterans, Julius F. Rabardy, Jacob H. Dow, Samuel Lendall and William H. Hooper. Each of them had lost an arm or a leg in the war. The remainder of the first division comprised the guests of the town, the General Committee of the celebration and the Parade Committee in carriages.

In the second division were the Indians who had taken part in the morning exercises, about one hundred men in all. Two carriages followed them containing Grand Officers of the Red Men's Society. Next in line were two carriages containing representatives of the Society of Colonial Wars. Following them was a body of young Manchester men dressed in the costume of Continentals. The old Governor Eustis coach, which carried Lafayette on his visit in 1824, was in the line. It was followed by the coach of Wellesley Hotel, and both contained the Governor Winthrop party, in the costumes that they wore during the morning exercises.

Next in order was the float of the Colonial spinners, who were seen busy at work at a loom. The representation was perfect in every detail, and was commended highly all along the route. Another float represented a Colonial tea party. It was most artistically decorated, the young people being dressed in costume. A float occupied by a dozen of the Daughters of Pocahontas, was fitted up with spruce boughs as an Indian camp and presented a very picturesque appearance. It furnished considerable amusement. It was followed by a float representing the fisheries. A big dory called the "Nancy" was manned by four grizzled sea dogs in oil-skins and sou'westers. They could be seen busy mending a dilapidated net. The men were Capt. Josiah Dow, George A. Rowe, Thomas Dow and Josiah H. Dow. A float upon which were seated fifty school children brought up the end of the second division; it was drawn by two pairs of oxen.

This made way for the advent of the third division, the floral parade. There were many entries. Three prizes had been offered for the most beautifully decorated carriages in this division. The prizes were: First, a silver loving cup, given by John A. Burnham; second, a carriage clock; third, a carriage whip. The committee awarded the prizes as follows: First, Mrs. Gordon Prince; second, Miss Elvira Bartlett; third, Mr. Schirmer. Honorable mention was accorded Misses Curtis, Misses Wetherbee, Misses Burnham. The colors were distributed before the parade, and the successful competitors were applauded all along the line.

Too much credit cannot be given to the several Committees for the harmonious and efficient manner in which they discharged their duties, which were in many cases onerous and exacting, in coöperation with the Executive Committee, to whom was entrusted the general management of the entire proceedings.

A notable and attractive part of the Celebration was the Art and Loan Exhibit in G. A. Priest School Building, open July 17–19. There were gathered here ancient heirlooms in silver, glass, china, household furnishings, dress, books, manuscripts, coins, pictures, autographs, etc., some of which were of almost priceless value, descended through generations, and in some cases brought from far over seas. The old-fashioned kitchen, with its great fireplace and its fittings, its chairs, tables, loom, spinning-wheels, and other antique furnishings, was a unique and constant attraction to visitors. The whole exhibit was an object lesson that will not soon fade from memory, for the perfect success of which much was due to the public spirit of the people as well as to the energy and good judgment of the Committee.

This Volume fitly closes with the Addresses given on this memorable occasion. The briefer Addresses are given from the excellent stenographic reports of the Boston *Journal*.

ADDRESS

By Henry C. Leach, Esq.,
President of the Day.

Friends and Fellow-Citizens: Manchester is "at home" today. In her name and on behalf of the Committee of Arrangements I welcome most cordially every person within her borders.

For two hundred and fifty years Manchester has lived under a town government as a self-respecting, law-abiding community; holding fast to the principles which brought our fathers to these shores, proud of their Puritan ancestry and all that Puritanism stood for, in the contest between King and Parliament that marked the earlier years of New England's settlement. She has been a loyal daughter of the Commonwealth, responding with patriotic alacrity to any call from the Supreme Executive, the Governor, provided always that the Governor was the choice of a free people and not the representative of royal authority from over the sea.

*   *   *   *   *

The men who settled Manchester were representatives of the sturdy Independents who made the rank and file of Cromwell's army. They were not " forehanded," for the land and sea must yield them a living as the reward of hard work. The records do not disclose any man of special prominence in the learned professions. Law, theology and medicine seem to have been neglected, save as her people obeyed the first, with becoming humility illustrated the second, and accepted the latter as a mysterious dispensation of Providence.

The town has not produced many men with, using the old form, "a liberal education," but she has sent to all parts of the world a class of men highly educated in a "knowledge of men and things." The shipmasters of Manchester were worthy descendants of that class of men who, under Blake and Hawkins, made the navy of England famous.

*   *   *   *   *

Her sons commanded the ships of Derby, of Gray, of Peabody, and of Ropes, and other sons were before the mast as sailors, competing in all ports of the world with the merchants of England.

Manchester men were not wanting in the almost perpetual conflict between the whites and the Indians. You find them along the coast of Maine, pushing their way through the wilderness to the St. Lawrence, where Sergeant Jacob Allen (whose great-grandson, Senator Galloup, sits on this platform) helped plant the flag of the colonies on the walls of Quebec.

The war of the Revolution found prompt and hearty supporters in Manchester, from the first sound of battle at Lexington down to the surrender at Yorktown. Maj. Eleazer Crafts of our town marched with his regiment to the support of Gates at Saratoga, and took part in that decisive conflict. (His grandson, Eleazer Crafts, is present to-day.) But the greater number of men from Manchester in that war were on the sea in the naval and privateer service. Two brothers, Ezekiel and Benjamin Leach, First Lieutenant and sailing master on board a privateer, were captured and spent three long years at Dartmoor, enduring many hardships. There is a tradition that among the men who managed the boat which carried Washington and his fortunes over the Delaware on that stormy night was the late Mr. Daniel Kelham, well known to our older citizens.

*　　*　　*　　*　　*

As the nation enlarged its borders, the energetic and capable young men of our town turned from the dangers and risks of a sailor's life to the equal risk and danger of the new and untried life to be found in the South and West. They were among the first to carry New England thrift and enterprise into the South and the West, beyond the Mississippi, and across the Rocky Mountains. In New Orleans, Memphis, St. Louis, as early as 1830 and 1834, your sons had established themselves in business life. As early as 1846, attached to the Rifle Regiment under Colonel Loring, our fellow-citizen, William H. Tappan, had made the march across the plains and the mountains to Oregon, blazing a trail for the multitudes that have since followed.

Among the earliest emigrants to California were the men of this town. Some of them went on foot from the Missouri River to the Pacific coast, others made the long voyage by sail around Cape Horn. Capt. John Carter, the last survivor of the old ship masters, still living and honored among us to-day, commanded the brig Benjamin L. Allen, owned, officered, equipped and sailed by Manchester men in a voyage from Boston to San Francisco.

Manchester contributed her best blood and brain in the building up of the states of California and Oregon. Among the first organized bands of emigrants from New England to Kansas was one led by Samuel F. Tappan, who did heroic service in the struggle to make Kansas a free state, and won military success in command of the First Colorado Cavalry during the War of the Rebellion.

Other Manchester men were active and prominent in the settlement of Kansas, Colorado, Montana, and other Western States. Many of them, with their descendants, are to-day active in the business and political life of those states.

* * * * *

We recognize the changes which have come over the town. The little village by the sea, with its homogeneous population, has become metropolitan in its habits and cosmopolitan as to population. The primitive has given place to the modern. The "good old times" are only a tradition.

"You may build more stately habitations, but you cannot buy with gold the old associations." Unchanged and unchangeable is our love for the old town and the old associations. Unchanged, also, is "old ocean's wild and solitary waste." "Just as creation's morn beheld her we behold her now."

And so long as the waves of ocean shall "dash themselves to idle foam" upon your rock-bound shore, the sons and daughters of Manchester, at home and abroad, will be true to all that makes for the peace, prosperity, and happiness of this embryo city by the sea.

ADDRESSES AT THE COLLATION.

A. S. JEWETT, ESQ.,
Chairman of the Board of Selectmen.

Mr. President, ladies and gentlemen, and friends: We meet to-day to commemorate an event of great historic importance. In emphasizing this particular day, we claim no special patent. It is a custom, as old as the ages, among all races and conditions of men, to mark the epochs of their history by exercises flattering to their local or national pride. The mind is fond of instituting comparisons, and passing in review the various stages of growth and development.

The life of a town never ceases to interest its true sons and daughters, wherever they may be located, or however situated. Let us picture in our minds William Jeffries, the early explorer, silently threading his way, in his little shallop, down the coast, up the harbor, through the creek to the highest navigable point; thence disembarking, he selects a suitable spot for his habitation. Years roll by; the last trace of the humble cottage has disappeared long since, but upon the site of the lowly fisherman's home there now appears the stately mansion, fit residence for royalty.

Many will recall the appearance of our wharves fifty years or more ago, with all of their bustling activity, as the freighters from the neighboring city discharged their cargoes of assorted wares and brought the news from the outer world. The old stage coach, unfamiliar to the present generation, was once the centre of local news, and its welcome appearance stirred the lethargy of village life. Some of you have also been thinking of the changes that have come to pass in the industries of the place. Years ago we were accustomed to boast of the many famous captains who carried our flag to every foreign shore, but of whom there now remains only a memory.

Others recall the first cabinet shop, located in a distant part of the town, and that it was by the energy of a descendant of one of the first settlers that the town became noted for the excellence of its work. A survey of the past is profitable if it can be used as a stepping stone to the future. It is the ever living present with which we have to deal. In the changed condition of affairs is it not wise to so adjust ourselves that we can make the most of every favorable opportunity? While all about us signs of social discontent are apparent, have we not cause for thankfulness that one of our large-hearted citizens has manifested his interest in the town by the erection of an enduring granite structure, fit memorial of the noble dead, and also a repository of the world's best thought? Ere long upon our Common there will be erected a beautiful fountain, a loving memorial to one whose benefactions were countless.

We welcome you again to the fullest enjoyment of our

matchless scenery and unrivalled rockbound coast. Nature here lavishes her gifts with prodigal hands. "To him who in the love of nature holds communion with her visible forms she speaks a various language." We have here a heritage which cannot be invalidated. Why sigh for title deeds? The truly artistic soul cannot be robbed of the boundless wealth which lavish nature presents to the view. In behalf of this good old town, radiant in its summer glory, I bid you welcome, thrice welcome, and may the memory of this day, with all its hallowed associations, be a helpful influence and an inspiration for good for years to come.

The LIEUTENANT GOVERNOR, the Orator of the Day, on being called upon, made some most felicitous remarks upon the value of celebrations like the present in fostering public spirit, promoting acquaintance and good fellowship, and resulting in a larger life. The speech is omitted for want of room.

REV. D. F. LAMSON,
Historian of the Town.

Mr. President: In view of the lateness of the hour and of the good things which we have already enjoyed, and of the other good things which are yet in store for us, I think I will omit some things that I intended to say at the outset with regard to the spirit of history, and you are at liberty to assume, if you choose, that this would have been the best part of my speech.

No one can rightly understand past times, or interpret rightly public events, who is not acquainted with the way in which people lived, how they dressed and talked, what amusements they had, what books they read, what was the daily atmosphere of their homes. It was with this principle in view, however poorly it may have been acted upon, that the history of the town has been written.

Your historian is reminded on the present occasion of the contrast between the fare of which we have just partaken and that which was served on these shores two hundred and fifty years ago to-day. Whatever may have been the viands upon the tables of our forefathers, it is safe to say that there

was a less elaborate spread; not but that our forefathers had
something to eat usually, even though at times they might
have been fain to suck of the abundance of the seas and of
the treasures hid in the sands, for which they were duly
grateful, and for which, with the self-consciousness of the
age, they were careful duly to record their gratitude.

* * * * *

But our forefathers had no doubt an advantage of us in one
respect. If it be true, as is often implied, that plain living
and high thinking are inseparable, why, then it follows that
our forefathers were better off than we are; for they had plain
living, and, *ergo*, they must have had high thinking, while we
do not have plain living, and, *ergo*, we cannot have high
thinking. If there is any fallacy in this reasoning, Mr. President, I hope you will not be over-critical. The present occasion is not one in which too much should be expected of a
man in the way of strict reasoning.

* * * * *

There is one other thing, that has taken the form of a
query in my mind, and that is whether, after all, the difference
between our modern civilization, on which we so much pride
ourselves, and the civilization of a former age, was not somewhat like the difference between our fare to-day and the fare
of two hundred and fifty years ago; that is, that it consists, in
part at least, in a more elaborate spread. I must confess, Mr.
President, I feel unequal to settle this question. I must leave
it to wiser heads than that of the historian. I have always
found that it is a deal easier to ask questions than to answer
them. But, speaking of the Puritans, whatever they may
have been, with all their limitations, with all their foibles and
their mistakes — and it is easy to exaggerate these things, and
there are persons, I suppose, who find delight in seeing spots on
the face of the sun — we must acknowledge that they were men
of great excellences, of excellences which their small detractors
are not able to appreciate or understand. When we think of
them as clinging to these rugged shores, wresting a subsistence from the stormy seas, planting their dwellings in the
dark and impenetrable forests, carrying on their daily work
under the pressure of constant fear and anxiety and danger,
"one hand on the mason's trowel and one on the soldier's

sword," laying broad the foundations on which those who were to come after them were to build, sowing the seeds of harvests which other men were to reap, we cannot withhold from them the tribute of a sincere admiration and reverence.

*   *   *   *   *

RICHARD H. DANA, ESQ.

Mr. Chairman, and Ladies and Gentlemen:

*   *   *   *   *

It is perhaps a peculiar coincidence that my grandfather, who was the first summer resident, as it is called here, happens to be a descendant of no less than six of the summer residents on board the "Arbella," who one pleasant summer morning stayed here for an hour or two on their way to Salem, including among them Thomas Dudley, and one or two others of the distinguished persons who were on board of that vessel, Mr. Simon Bradstreet among the others.

But to come down to the fifty-one or fifty-two years ago when my grandfather was the first here, it seems a simple enough thing for us who are used to it to think of the condition of a New England town, but it is something so unique in the world at large that it might be worth while pausing for a moment to ask, What would be an English farming town of the size of Manchester in 1844 or 1845 ? Why, it would be a collection of tenant farms. This was a collection of land owners, owning their premises in fee simple, self-respecting, self-ruling men, educated, and composed largely of farmers and sea captains, and just beginning manufactures. Among them, as the pastor of the church — there was only one then, the Congregational Church — was Rev. Oliver A. Taylor, a man whose reputation spread far beyond this town, and my grandfather made a trip all the way from the end of the Cape, at Pigeon Cove, where he was then staying, to see Mr. Taylor; and it was Mr. Taylor, during the four or five years that my grandfather stayed at Pigeon Cove, that suggested his coming to this beautiful town and staying here. My grandfather then drove up and down, and hearing the sound of the surf, he said, "There must be a beach," and following up an old wood road he came to the spot which he afterwards selected.

*   *   *   *   *

I think it has been one of the fortunate occasions that we have had now this two hundred and fiftieth anniversary, that we have all been brought together and to meet each other and to know each other and to form friendships, and may these friendships, as I will end by saying, may these friendships which we are forming here to-day always remain firm in this most beautiful spot on earth.

The PRESIDENT then announced that the hour had arrived for the Procession to start, and he would ask those speakers whom it was impossible to hear from at this time, to reserve their remarks until the next two hundred and fiftieth anniversary. At the suggestion of a gentleman in the Hall, these gentlemen were given "leave to print."

SERMON

By Rev. L. T. Chamberlain, D. D.

1 Sam. 7:12. "Then Samuel took a stone, and set it between Mizpeh and Shen, and called the name of it Eben-ezer,
saying, Hitherto hath the Lord helped us."

It was thus that public gratitude found expression, in
the far-off days of Israel's struggling life. As you
doubtless recall, there had been a hard-fought battle.
The hazard had included the lives and fortunes of the
chosen people. The national safety, the national existence, had been at stake. Defeat would have appeared
as the reversal of Jehovah's promise and the overthrow
of Jehovah's decree. Yet, for a moment, as the battle
was joined, suspense took the place of assurance. To
mortal sight, the decisive issue trembled in the balance.
Then came a divine assistance. God thundered from
His holy height. The tide of hostile assault was turned
back. Pursuing the discomfited enemy, the men of
Israel went forth from Mizpeh in triumph.

What wonder that, following a victory so great, in
view of a deliverance so signal, the memorial stone was
set between Mizpeh and Shen, or, in terms of our language, between the watch-tower and the crag! How
natural that the ascription of praise should be to Him
who had so manifestly given success!

Good friends, I trust that in our hearts, this morning,
gratitude to God not only rises but also reigns. Surely,
in the midst of these historic scenes, under a just sense
of our indebtedness for mercies already vouchsafed, it is
wholly fitting that we should ascribe our blessings to
Him who is still a strong deliverer.

*　　*　　*　　*　　*

As, accordingly, the stone of thanksgiving is now set

between our Mizpeh and our Shen, let it be understood
that we thereby distinctly recognize that in the usual
and lesser events of our history, as truly as in the greater
and more unusual, in the quiet orderings of our lives, as
veritably as in the more disturbed, an infinite power has
both upheld and blessed.

And, by that token, what other people have such
abundant cause for thanks! How long the period whose
close we celebrate to-day! How romantic the interest
of its early years! Yet the record bears faithful witness.
When this town was settled in 1645,— the inhabitants
in that year, in memory of ancestral Manchester in
England, having successfully petitioned that the name
be changed from Jeffries' Creek,— the story of Plymouth
across the Bay, was still passing from lip to lip. How, of
the Pilgrim company landing there, almost half, including
their loved and trusted leader, died within the first hundred
days; six between the 31st of December and New
Year's Day; eight in January, seventeen in February,
thirteen in March; yet how, when the Mayflower returned on the 5th of April, not one of the colonists took
passage homeward! John Endicott, with his Puritan
associates, had been but seventeen years in Salem. John
Winthrop, having first landed at Manchester, had begun
his colonial service only fifteen years before. It was not
long after the Pequot War, whose devastations had sent
terror into every New England home. Boston was only
fifteen years old. The settlements in Connecticut were
all recent, and their union in an independent colonial
government, was of only eight years' standing. To the
southward, Jamestown, the first English colony in America, was less than forty years old, and the tyranny of King
James in turning Virginia into an appanage of the Crown,
had occurred only a score of years before.

In those days, the slow ships that came with English

news, brought word of the doings of the Long Parliament; of the battles of Edgehill, and Marston Moor, and Naseby; of Oliver Cromwell as Dictator, and of Charles I, beheaded at Whitehall. The tidings from France told of Louis XIII, and that Cardinal Richelieu, author, courtier, politician, who made French unity the incarnation of tyranny, and who built French glory on the quicksands of material conquest and religious fraud. In Sweden, the mourning for the great Gustavus Adolphus was comparatively recent. In Spain, ruled the ambitious Philip IV. In Central Europe, the Thirty Years' War was drawing to its close, imperious Wallenstein having fallen by the assassin's hand.

*   *   *   *   *

Far from easy is it to reproduce, even in imagination, the external features of those primitive days. The situation seems meagre and harsh, when compared with the affluence of our own possessions. The contrast is like that between "the wicker hut and thatched roof" of Romulus, and the magnificence of the later Roman Empire; like that between the wandering Israel that crossed the Jordan with Joshua, and the nation which afterwards built Jerusalem's Temple, and held sway from the desert to the sea.

Yet the later magnificence is, in itself, a constant witness to the sagacity and fidelity with which our forefathers planned and wrought. Let due allowance be made for the conditions which, in any case, would have favored the gathering of a vast population on these western shores: the spirit of adventure which was everywhere abroad; the reaching out of the Old World after new dependencies; the general fertility of our soil; the variety of our climate; the commercial possibilities of our coast-line, our rivers, and our lakes; our exhaustless mineral resources, awaiting their discoverer; put all these into relationship with each other, and into the matchless combination which, united, they form; add thereto the essential qualities of the Anglo-Saxon race, so that one may aver that if the early settlers had failed in meeting the issue, others of their kin would in time have repaired the loss; yet it still remains not the less, but rather the more, manifest, that the early New Englanders performed their part with large and exceptional wisdom.

Certainly, in whatever else they failed, they were nobly successful in maintaining their faith in God, and in preserving their reverence for the Bible as God's holy word. In saying this, however, I am not asserting that the men of our early history were altogether, or even prevailingly, of the saintly type. It is evident that they had a prudent eye for thrift, and the record shows that they were far from being non-resistants. If the rod of Moses, which aforetime had budded and blossomed, seemed unavailing, they were more than ready, in a just cause, to wield the sword of Joshua or of Gideon. They believed in the God of battles. They sometimes proceeded to extremes in the repression, and in the punishment, of what to them seemed unscriptural and harmful. In their hands, the Church and the State were for a time, brought into perilous identity. The freedom which, at great price, they had purchased for themselves, they were not always ready to accord to those who actively opposed them. Could they have said from the heart, —

" Think not that that which seemeth right to thee,
Must needs be so to all men. Thou canst see
Footprints of light upon the world's highway,
Left there by Him who had not where to lay
His lowly head,— the plainest nearest thee.
There may be footprints which thou canst not see.
Made plain by heaven's light to other men, —
Jesus went many ways into Jerusalem,"—

could they have said that sincerely, a still higher grace would have been conferred on both their practice and their faith. Yet they kept firm hold on many a divine and eternal reality. Their religion was to them a source of both purity and power.

*   *   *   *   *

This, at least, may safely be affirmed; take out of the early history of this town, take out of the early history of New England, the distinctively religious element, the personal faith in God and the Bible, and you take out the force, the verve, the very life, of what is grandest in both achievement and ideal.

Along that line, accordingly, comes one of the serious lessons for us who celebrate the completion of our two hundred and fifty years.

*   *   *   *   *

But again, our forefathers held fast to the great doctrine of the political rights of the individual, and of the corresponding duties of the individual to the government which affords a just protection. As we have already inferred, the founding of the New England colonies was from an inspiration at once religious and civic. Read the open record, and there will be no room for doubt. The persecutions to the death, under bloody Mary; the tyrannical proceedings of the Star Chamber and Court of High Commission, under cruel Elizabeth; the unrelenting intolerance of James I, and his advisers — all these were aimed at both religious and civil freedom.

*   *   *   *   *

What an ample condition-precedent for the genesis, by revolt, of civil as well as religious independence!

*   *   *   *   *

That our fathers were not always consistent with

their political ideal, as they were not always consistent with their religious ideal, must be admitted. The stress of the situation; the almost infinite sacrifice at which they had purchased their own freedom; the bitter resentments of which human nature is always capable; these considerations and forces sometimes carried them beyond the *placidam quietem*, — the peaceful, stable repose, — which their motto declared that they constantly sought. But, for all that, it remains that, in sincere reverence, they laid the foundation of whatever "liberty under law" we of to-day enjoy. There is not an element of truth, and scarce an expression of conviction, in the immortal Declaration of Independence itself, which had not been announced beforehand, in colonial constitutions and bills of rights.

* * * * *

Once more, in our commemoration of the two hundred and fifty years which have now passed, we may not overlook the support given by our forefathers to the cause of public education and popular intelligence. Wellnigh pathetic is the record of their sacrifices for that great end. In these times of well ordered, fruitful peace, it seems but natural that wide and generous attention should be given to mental training. It accords with our physical progress, that vast fortunes should now be bestowed on institutions of the higher learning. In the modern expansion of Christendom; the inter-relations of advancing peoples; the reflections and counter reflections of literary achievement and scientific discovery; it were hardly possible not to feel a virtually constraining impulse toward the fostering of both public and private education. In the days of our colonial history, the circumstances were largely reversed.

* * * * *

And yet, along with the assiduous toil, in the midst of the incessant tumult, in spite of the desperate conflict, our ancestors established the public school and founded the classical college.

* * * * *

They believed that education was the ally of religion, and that the two were like the pillars of brass which upheld the Temple's porch, whereof the one was named Jachin, "He shall establish," and the other Boaz, "It is strength."

* * * * *

Finally, our commemoration will be incomplete, our memorial will be but partially significant, unless, in loyal remembrance of those who have gone before — those who, in the main, dealt humanely with the Indian, and were pioneers in the abolition of colonial Negro slavery — we resolve that we will, henceforth, the more revere the brotherhood of man, and the more devote ourselves to Society's noblest welfare. There is a blessedness which is not wholly included, on the one hand, in the good fortune of government, and does not merely consist, on the other hand, in the embodying of religion and culture in the private individual. The state may flourish, and the prosperity of persons may be realized, yet the common-weal be far from perfect. There is a social well-being which comprehends both state and individual, as the multiple includes its factors, or as the circle is made up of circumference and centre. To secure that largest good, individual rights may well be modified. To achieve that highest felicity, government itself may be among us "as one who serves." For Humanity is more than the units that compose it. Philanthropy is greater than domestic or patriotic devotion.

And we stand, my friends, to-day, where circumstances

make urgent the call for this social good-will. To us there comes with special force, the summons to remember that each soul is sacred and, at the same time, to realize the just preëminence of the collective well-being. The rush and resound of our outward progress, the very radiance and richness of our cherished civilization, tend to make us insensible to the finer and more fundamental issues. Things are now to the fore. They crowd the scene. They claim the primacy. They demand of us that we pay obeisance. And thus it is, I add, that class estrangements, class antagonisms, now find place and power. Instead of the choice of those immaterial treasures — piety, wisdom, virtue, magnanimity — which are ever increased to him who imparts them, the majority are chiefly anxious for the objects, of which, if one has more, another is likely to have less.

Still further, into our social state, thus restless, thus unstable, there are ever coming the insurgent hosts of other lands and other climes. Situate as we are in the very confluence, the very vortex, of the world's migrations, the problem of life is made for us the more appalling, by reason of the diversity of our tribes and tongues. In the days of our fathers, the social order was more sane and simple. Their communities were homogeneous in race and language. To them it was clear that the life was more than meat, even as the body was more than raiment. Their very presence on these wild shores, fugitives from civil and religious oppression, testified to themselves and the world, that it were well to lose all else, if so the higher interests were saved from harm. The common struggle for the common end, warmed the heart, even as it stirred the mind and trained the hand. At such a time, it was but natural to think of the community's welfare as foremost, since, unless the community throve, no individual might keep either fortune or life.

By some means, we must win back, we must preserve,
the old-time zeal for the common welfare. Custom must
reinforce its sanction of disinterested good-will. Law
must put its full protection around the humblest. Government must find its warrant, in the well-being of the
people. The Church must discern her noblest mission,
in making universal the kingdom of God on earth.
When that day dawns, when by the setting up of such
a memorial we show our grateful love, then will the
keeper of Israel be our keeper, and His presence be our
refuge and defence.

Grateful, therefore, for the recorded past; gladly owning the inspiration of an example illustrious with religious
faith, political fidelity, enthusiasm for learning, and a rare
devotion to the common well-being; we turn to the
future. At the close of another two hundred and fifty
years, when the half of a millennium has been reached,
there will be, I trust, another and still grander celebration
on this increasingly memorable spot. The celebrants will
have changed. Many an outward condition will have
been transformed. Dwellings will have become still more
beautiful, and temples more grand. The pliant forces of
nature will have yielded themselves to new uses. Home
industry will have fashioned fairer products. Commerce
will have brought hither rarer treasures.

But as surely as these steadfast hills will keep their
place; this rock-bound shore preserve its trend; the wide
ocean roll its tides; and, skyward, the constellations gleam;
the principles of worthy living will remain as they are
to-day. They share in the divine permanence. Reverence, worship, prayer, praise, intended purity of heart,
repentance for sin, faith in the atoning love, toil for the
Kingdom's coming — these, toward God; gentleness,
good will, the bearing of one another's burdens, the up-
holding of justice, the spread of enlightenment, the honor-

ing of the universal brotherhood — these, toward man; the whole merged, in reality, into the one glory in which God and Humanity alike rejoice; such is the abiding truth, such the changeless lesson. God grant that while we yet linger, we may be faithful to the heavenly vision, and be cheered by the fulfilment of the gracious promise!

ADDRESS

BY HIS HONOR, THE LIEUTENANT-GOVERNOR.

Two hundred and fifty years form no insignificant period in that portion of the history of the human race which is written in books. Not yet have eight such periods passed since the shores of Galilee were trodden by the feet of Him that brought glad tidings, that published peace.

If we glance at the intellectual product of the period just preceding that the completion of which you to-day commemorate, we are amazed at its splendid vigor and achievement. Across the dark firmament of the Middle Ages had flashed the radiance of mighty spirits, whose potent rays are still undimmed in the growing daylight of our own time. In the hands of Michael Angelo and Raphael chisel and brush had produced forms of beauty and majesty which no succeeding century has equalled. Columbus had brought a new world to the knowledge of Europe, and from his lonely watch-tower Galileo had read the story of the stars. By the sturdy blows with which Martin Luther nailed his theses to the door of the church at Wittenberg, he had shivered the domination over men's minds of religious tyranny, and had aroused liberty of conscience from its almost unbroken slumber. In his immortal novel, Cervantes had "smiled Spain's chivalry away." The lofty wisdom of Bacon had taught the stately dignity of the English tongue. Shakespeare had shown the infinite capabilities of the human intellect, and to the ear of Protestant England the verse of Milton had echoed the sonorous tramp of armies.

Such a heritage from the recent past did those bring with them who settled the shores of Massachusetts in

410

the early part of the seventeenth century. Marston Moor and Naseby were contemporaneous with the birth of your town, and a few years later the news of the grim execution at Whitehall must have caused a shudder even in those who believed that the hapless Charles had deserved his fate. In "The Beginnings of New England" John Fiske has clearly shown that this migration of English Puritans to seize and occupy a new continent, insignificant though it was in the numbers engaged, meant nothing less than the ultimate "transfer of the world's political centre of gravity from the Tiber and the Rhine to the Thames and the Mississippi." He, however, must have had clear vision who should discern this high destiny from the deck of the Mayflower landing her little company in Plymouth Bay, or from that of the Arbella as she skirted along your beautiful coast, affording opportunity to those who went on shore to note "the strawberries, gooseberries and sweet single roses," and to be entertained by still earlier settlers on "good venison and beer."

John Winthrop was born in the memorable year of the Spanish Armada. Even before his time, the supremacy of the world had left the Mediterranean, and was travelling westward. Since then the destiny of the English-speaking race has marched apace, and though in some far future time God may raise up another race to the leadership of mankind, it seems now probable that for centuries the history of the world will be what the men of our race shall make it. England, with her colonies dotting the globe, whether destined to continue as dependent offshoots or to become independent or federated nations ; America, holding a continent with a population which in the lifetime of some before me will number two hundred millions, — if these two mighty nations escape the corrosion of vice and the rot of lux-

ury, and remain true to their fundamental beliefs in
education, freedom of conscience and popular government, it is no empty boast to say that the sceptre of
dominion will remain for untold ages in their grasp.
We need not seek to ask too curiously which shall pre-
dominate, for the star of empire still holds its westward
way, and its rays of promise, already gleaming from the
East, will one day bathe our broad land in their vertical
splendor. Yet no nation can continue powerful unless
virtue, education and energy are the common possessions
of her sons.

How little have the physical features of your town
changed since the day of its first settlement. The forest has in part given way to the ploughed field or pasture land; the thickly-strewn stones by patient toil have
been heaped into walls which mark the boundaries of
estates; human dwellings have multiplied in number
and become more and more elaborate and costly; the
railway and the electric car force themselves upon
notice; but all else how unchanged! As of old the
cool, salt breath of the ocean is wafted inland to meet
the hot, resinous fragrance of the pine forests which
still clothe the rocky ridges to which the shore slopes
upward. The magnolia and dogwood still throw out
their blossom-laden branches over the bayberry and
ferns beneath. On the surface of peaceful pool or slug-
gish brook the pond-lily opens its exquisite chalice, and
with the falling dusk of evening folds again its petals,
while the whip-poor-will hurriedly reiterates his monot-
onous plaint from the neighboring thicket. Otter and
beaver, it is true, have sought refuge in Canadian
brooks, and bear and wolf are no longer a menace to the
farmer's flocks. But the little sandpiper tiptoes just in
advance of the rippling wave, and perhaps wonders as
he did two hundred and fifty years ago at the weird

music of the Singing Beach. In autumn the wild-fowl
pierce with their wedge-shaped flight the regions of the
upper air, or circle downward to some wood-fringed
lake to rest on their southward journey. When the
storms of winter rage and the sea mingles its driven
spray with the rack of the lowering clouds, the sea gulls
wheel and eddy with the gusts of the tempest, and their
lamenting cries, accordant with the moaning of the gale,
seem fit requiem to the drowned on Norman's Woe. In
her long struggle with man, Nature gives way but slowly,
and contests every foot of vantage-ground she is forced
to yield.

But with man how mighty the changes which two
and one-half centuries have witnessed! I shall not
attempt to repeat in detail the history of your town,
for that duty has been assigned to other and abler
hands. Save for some conspicuous incident or char-
acteristic which lends local color to the narrative, there
is, as might be expected, a marked similarity in the
history of most of our New England towns, which is
saved from dullness by its intense human interest.
Those who first settled these towns were men of the same
race, religion and purpose; the obstacles and dangers
they were called upon to overcome were the same;
they were similarly affected by the great events of
national importance of which they were a part, and,
except in the ratio of increasing population, influenced
by location and other causes, their growth and development ran upon parallel lines.

The peculiar feature in the history of Manchester
which differentiates it from that of many of her sister
towns lies in her proximity to the ocean. The whisper
of the sea caught the willing ear of her youth and
wooed them to its breast. In these towns of old Essex
the sea-captain has been a familiar and venerated figure

from the earliest days. In time of war the deck of the
privateer knew the sturdy tread of the men of Essex
as did the fishing-smack and merchantman in time of
peace. Hardy and vigorous, they knew the dangers
of the deep and feared them not. Fearless they faced
disaster and death, nor were they appalled even by
that mysterious tragedy of the sea, the total disappearance from the ken of man of some vessel which had left
port, well manned and tight, with the sunshine bright
upon its straining canvas, the waves laughing in its
wake, and the following breeze freighted with the
prayers of women and the God-speed of men. No
record, however brief, of these coastwise towns of New
England can fail to lay weighty emphasis upon the
controlling influence which the neighboring sea exerted
upon the lives and characters of their inhabitants.
They smacked of the salt as does the breeze that blows
over seaweed-covered rocks at low tide.

The early settler in Manchester, like his fellow-pio-
neer elsewhere in the Colony, made timely provision
for a saw mill, in order that he might be saved some of
the labor necessary to produce the roughly fashioned
timbers of his house and fishing-boat. He held out
special inducements to tempt some townsman to set up
a grist mill for the grinding of his corn. He toiled
unremittingly with imperfect tools in felling the forest
and preparing the ground for his rough husbandry.
He took much pains that his children should receive
such education as was then obtainable, and built a
primitive meeting-house to which he not only went
himself but compelled the attendance of others.

And yet it may well be doubted whether the lot of
teacher or minister was an altogether pleasant one. The
nominal salary was small, and was not always promptly
paid ; the fire-wood which was included in the pay was

either not forthcoming or seemed to have concentrated in itself the sap of the forest. In 1681, a schoolmaster in an older and richer town than Manchester complains as follows: "Of inconveniences, I shall instance no other, than that of the school house, the confused and shattered and nastie posture that it is in, not fitting to reside in ; the glass broken and thereupon very raw and cold, the floor very much broken and torn up to kindle fires, the hearth spoiled, the seats, some burnt and others out of kilter, so that one had as well nigh as goods keep school in a hog stie as in it." It is feared that a similar lament might have gone up from many a town had the poor pedagogues possessed an equal power of vigorous expression.

Our Manchester settler heard but little news from the outer world and read few books. He knew well his Bible, which he read with a stern but exalted faith; he may have had access to the grim theology of Michael Wigglesworth's " Day of Doom," or the glowing visions of Johnson's " Wonder-working Providence," and from these he may have turned to the more pleasing allegory of Bunyan's " Pilgrim's Progress." Let us hope that the golden light from the Delectable Mountains illuminated his life of incessant hardship and privation.

He stamped his character upon his descendants, and the generations that succeeded him were like him. His sons marched with Captain Lothrop and the " Flower of Essex " to meet an ambushed death at Bloody Brook. When the early winter twilight seemed to liberate all evil spirits that ride the night wind, they told in awed whispers, as they clustered about the glowing hearth, the ghostly tale of the strange happenings at Salem, and shudderingly prayed that the affliction might pass their children by.

The overthrow and imprisonment of Andros early

taught a lesson of resistance to irresponsible tyranny which was held in retentive memory for future use. The men of Manchester sat down with Pepperell before Louisburg, and the capture by raw Colonial levies of this famous fortress, the Gibraltar of America, defended by the veteran troops of France, planted a seed of self-reliant confidence in the breasts of the Colonists, which was to bear ruddy fruit at Concord Bridge and in the redoubt on Bunker Hill.

Events now crowded thick and fast that were to precipitate the war of the Revolution. With what impatience must the tardy news from Boston have been awaited, when every rider might bring the message that the smouldering fire had burst into flame!

In the long and dubious struggle that was now ushered in, amphibious old Essex played well her part. On land her blood tinged many a battle-field, but it was on the sea that her fame was won. The splendid seamanship, the cool courage, the intelligence fertile in expedient to meet any peril — these were the qualities shown by her sons wherever American privateer and English war-vessel grappled upon the deep. They were no accidental inheritance. They were bred in the bone of these men of Essex; they were transmitted from sires, who had spent their lives in sailing their fishing boats through tempest and darkness over the storm-driven Banks of Newfoundland and along the rock-bound and unbuoyed shores of New England, to sons whose earliest instinct had bidden them embark upon floating plank and seek the main.

With the other colonies they shared the sufferings and discouragements as well as the triumphs of the long years that closed with Yorktown. With some misgivings they adopted the Constitution, and slowly thereafter came to see that from the mighty birth-throe of the

Revolution a nation had been born. They were hard hit by the Embargo Act of 1808, and endured the consequent distress with commendable but not entire patience.

In the War of 1812 the young nation won little glory on land save in the belated battle of New Orleans, but on ocean and lake the mighty sea-power of England found its match, and again and again her flag was struck to vessels of smaller tonnage and less armament than her own. Of this renown no small part is the heritage of Essex County.

Then followed the period of marvellously swift national expansion. The Louisiana Purchase had ceded the vast territory of the Mississippi Valley, and had given an outlet on the Pacific. Florida was bought of Spain; Texas and California were forcibly taken from Mexico after a war which added something to our military fame, but brought no new glory to our political history. To people these new and limitless tracts the men of New England went out by thousands, and joining the hosts from the Middle States and the tide that now set towards our shores from Europe, felled forests, ploughed prairies, built cities and created those mighty commonwealths over whose area the centre of national population from decade to decade slowly shifts westward. In 1849 the discovery of gold in California renewed those eager dreams of El Dorado which had been fading since the early Spanish occupancy of Central and South America, and caused a new exodus from the Atlantic to the Pacific. All these great movements the generations of your townsfolk beheld, and in them they had their share.

During the whole of this period the horizon, otherwise fair, was ominously clouded by slavery. From this fateful institution the politics of the nation seemed to take direction and form; it involved us in war with a foreign power; new states were admitted only as it willed; if ever the Scriptural image of the enemy sowing tares amid the good grain was realized, it was in the accursed crop of hatred and distrust which slavery sowed between North and South.

Manchester was not slow to read the signs of the times and to throw its influence on the side of freedom. In 1853 its citizens in town meeting recorded their indignant protest against the repeal of the Missouri Compromise, and in 1856 the Free Soil Party found here earnest support for its candidate for the presidency, John C. Frémont.

Soon burst the terrific hurricane of civil war, and the stately edifice which had been reared on the foundations laid by our fathers was rocked to its base, but, thank God! the structure held. Blood and treasure were poured out with lavish hand, and the sacrifice was accepted. Lincoln died, scores of thousands of the best and noblest youth of the land gave gladly their lives, and from that awful stress the nation rose mightier, purer, more worthy of man's devotion and God's favor. In the War of the Rebellion Manchester sent to the front nearly one in ten of its entire population.

These great political events which have illustrated the last two centuries and a half, and which I have briefly sketched, stand out with startling distinctness on history's page and are known of all men. We are not so apt to realize how recent is the origin of the vast changes wrought by applied science in many of the most familiar aspects of our social life. For over one hundred and fifty years from the first settlement of New England the daily life of its people underwent but trifling change. Population had increased, the fear of the lurking savage had passed away, there was doubtless a gradual amelioration in the stern conditions of hardship and suffering which

environed the earlier generations, but at the beginning of
the present century the life of the New England farmer
or fisherman varied but little from that of his ancestor.
Luxury was scarcely known, and few even were the comforts in his home.   His journeys were for business and
not for pleasure, and were made in the saddle over wellnigh impassable roads.   Not before 1804 was there a
daily stage from your town to Boston, and regular trains
were not running until 1847.   Steamers began to cross
the Atlantic in 1819, but bore but a remote resemblance
in speed or accommodation to the great liners of to-day.

As a boy in his native town my father used to bear to
the meeting-house on Sabbath mornings the foot-stove,
filled with live embers, which yielded some little warmth
to the mother at the further end of the family pew, while
father and children shivered on hard board seats, and
gave what attention they could to lengthy sermons which
were not wanting in lurid glow.   The first church stove
in Manchester was set up in 1821, and had been long
opposed as smacking too much of effeminate luxury.

The electric telegraph has been in operation but fifty
years, and the telephone but half that time.   The application of electricity as a motive power, which seems
destined to revolutionize transportation, is confined to a
decade, and for the illumination of our streets and houses,
oil, tallow and gas are but now yielding to the incandes-
cent light.   Machinery, driven by water or steam, has
within the memory of those now living multiplied in
infinite ratio the efficiency and product of man's labor.
In the history of New England towns the recurring visi-
tations of small-pox find frequent mention: immunity
from this dread disease was not obtained until the present
century was well advanced.   Modern bacteriology holds
out the hope that other terrors which have ravaged the
world unchecked for centuries may be abated.

Such are a few of the instances which show how recent and how marvellously swift has been the march of material progress. I see no reason to believe that in the future its pace will be retarded. Rather must we look for a constant acceleration, as man's dominion over the forces of nature becomes more complete with each new discovery and achievement. And what is to be the result? Is man to be "chained to the wheel of the world, blind with the dust of its speed," or is his gaze to be more and more lifted to the sun-lit heights where dwell enlightenment, virtue and knowledge? Happy is it for man that it is not given to him to draw aside the veil of the future. We may study the past, we may observe the present, and from that study and observation we may draw some general inference as to what the years that are to come may have in store.

I am not of those who find cause for discouragement or dismay. Upon each generation of men God wisely imposes a condition of struggle and effort, but he must have a strange conception of the Divine purpose who believes that mankind is hastening to destruction. Never before were all elevating and refining influences so strong and so accessible to the masses of the people as here in America to-day. Religion is becoming broader and more Christ-like, and its hold upon the consciences of men is not relaxed, nor are its fervor and sacred enthusiasm dead. Education is more widely diffused than ever before in the history of the world, and nowhere is there so vast a population of eager and intelligent readers as here. Gentle charity has grown more wise in its methods and far more efficacious in its results. Social immorality is still a menace in our great cities, but is powerless to contaminate the life of the great body of self-respecting, God-fearing men and women who constitute the mass of our American population. As never before intemperance is stamped as vice and degradation, and is no longer regarded as a humorous incident of sociability.

The easy optimism which believed that in instituting here free self-government based upon universal suffrage, our fathers had established a machine of perpetual motion which would grind out its beneficent results without vigilance or effort on the part of later generations, has given place to a higher conception of citizenship. I know of no more encouraging sign in American politics than the activity in nearly all of our great cities of organizations of men of high and honest aims, who are pledged to rescue our municipal governments from the misrule which has grown to be our chief national disgrace. In New York and elsewhere these Good Government Clubs have shown that honesty and intelligence can always win if they will. Blind Milton saw clearly when he wrote: "I cannot praise a fugitive and cloistered virtue, unexercised and unbreathed, that never sallies out and sees her adversary, but slinks out of the race, where that immortal garland is to be run for not without dust and heat." Least of all in a republic has such virtue place. In his recent final retirement from political life the venerable and illustrious English statesman thus wrote to his Midlothian constituents, who for so many years have loyally supported him at the polls: "It is beyond question that the century now expiring has exhibited since the close of its first quarter a period of unexampled activity, the changes of which taken in the mass have been in the direction of true and beneficial progress." I think that the verdict of history will hold this a just and moderate estimate. But that this progress may be continuous and not diverted from its present upward path, we of this generation must be true to the past and read aright its lessons of struggle

and achievement; we must be faithful to the present
with its mighty responsibilities and opportunities; so
shall we march full-fronted to the beckoning future, and
not as cowards and poltroons with trailing banners and
lowered crest.

The social and economic problems, which now con-
found us with their complexity and difficulty, must find
their just solution at our hands. The savage strife
which through their mutual fault too often breaks out
between the employer and the employed must cease.
The rights of both must be more clearly defined by
law, and enforced by the collective sense of the community. It is much that the appalling wastefulness of
strikes is already recognized, and that through arbitra-
tion or by other means just causes of complaint and
motives of action are more likely than heretofore to receive fair hearing. How best to reduce to their mini-
mum the colossal evils of intemperance and of other
vices demands the wisest legislation, carried into effective operation by officers of the law whose absolute integrity must be assured by whatever safeguards of organization and discipline experience and vigilance can
devise. Constant warfare must be waged against those
influences of squalor, ignorance and vice which breed
crime, and constant effort exerted to make its punishment such as to give opportunity for reformation.
That poverty which through lack of energy and efficiency ever tends to produce pauperism must be so
touched by the hand of charity as to be stimulated to
self-respect and industry.

The standard of decency and comfort in the lives and
homes of our toiling people must not be lowered. The
amazing power of assimilation which American civilization has displayed must not be overtaxed. When
entire families of those alien in speech, in habit and in

thought, are content to kennel within the bare walls of
reeking tenement or contractor's shanty, and to live
upon what our own people discard, wholly untouched
by the influences which produce the American citizen,
they constitute a menace to the community. The rills
of immigration which, properly distributed, serve to
irrigate and fructify our broad territory, must not be
permitted to become a flood that shall swamp the land
or sweep it bare of the accumulated soil of centuries.
America will ever be hospitable to the immigrant, whatever his nationality, who brings with him intelligence
and industry, and who possesses the capacity and determination to become in very truth an American citizen. But in my opinion the time is come when such
restrictions must be placed upon immigration as shall
not only exclude the felon, the insane and the actual or
prospective pauper, but shall limit the admission of
those who show a racial inability to assimilate with our
people. Our land is broad, but the stars and stripes
alone must cover every foot of its limitless area, and the
supremacy of that flag must be unquestioned and complete. Beneath its rule the anarchist, the oath-bound
assassin and he who gives expression to his prejudices
or passions by the violence of mobs have no place.

We must be exacting and yet just in our judgments
of those who hold public office. Corruption, dishonesty
and cowardice should be sternly dealt with; but gross
injustice is often wrought by embittered partisan abuse
and the reckless imputation of unworthy motives for
acts of which the error at most may be one of judgment
only.

A living and active faith in the great truths of religion is a force for righteousness in a nation, and this
faith is not likely to wane in vitality so long as it con-
forms itself more and more closely to the teachings and

life of Christ. Public education must be ever broadened
in its aims and improved in its methods and results. Forever free from sectarianism, our schools must make
luminous to the eye of the young the page of American
history, so that even the child of the most recent immigrant may early learn that he has become a citizen
of no mean country. If on leaving the school the child
carries with him the hunger for further knowledge —
and this is the true test of the success of any system of
education — he should find in our colleges the way
made easy for character and ability, and in our public
libraries he should find rich storehouse of the best
thought of all lands and all times. Art and music
should bring their refining and elevating influences
within the reach of all; free lectures should hold out
their lure to enter the magic realms of literature and
science, and the weary worker should find rest and
peace with wife and child in those great tracts where
nature is at her fairest which have already been reserved for his use.

These are among the agencies which are hastening the
day when shall be realized the fundamental idea of
American citizenship, that all men shall enter upon the
competition of life upon equal terms of social rights,
obligations and opportunities. The study of history has
caused Mr. Lecky to speak as follows of the prosperity
of nations and the causes that contribute thereto: "Its
foundation is laid in pure domestic life, in commercial
integrity, in a high standard of moral worth and of public spirit, in simple habits, in courage, uprightness and a
certain soundness and moderation of judgment which
springs quite as much from character as from intellect.
If you would form a wise judgment of the future of a
nation, observe carefully whether these qualities are increasing or decaying. Observe especially what qualities

count for the most in public life. Is character becoming
of greater or less importance? Are the men who obtain
the highest posts in the nation, men of whom in private
life and irrespective of party competent judges speak
with genuine respect? Are they of sincere convictions,
consistent lives, indisputable integrity? . . . It is by
observing this moral current that you can best cast the
horoscope of a nation."

If by the test so applied we would read in that horoscope the promise of future greatness and stability, as I
think we may, the nation must not cease to produce the
highest type of citizen known the world over. In this
high service let there be a generous emulation among
the sister states. Shall our own dear state give backward step from the forefront where she has ever proudly
stood in all the long years since your town had its birth?
O stern and rugged cliffs that guard the shores of
Massachusetts Bay and hurl back unshaken the surges of
the Atlantic! O waving forests that clothe the hills and
clasp in their embrace the embosomed lakes! O broad
and fair domain of the Old Bay State, stretching from
beautiful Berkshire, past peaceful village and prosperous
city, to the glistening sands of Barnstable, and on to
historic Nantucket nursed on ocean's breast — thy breed
of men has never failed thee yet. May they continue
to spring from thy loins as we have known them in the
past, sturdy, virtuous and heroic; so for all time may
the prayer go up, not in cringing terror nor pusillani-
mous supplication, but in the full, strong voice of
manly self-reliance, "God save the Commonwealth of
Massachusetts!"

INDEX.

INDEX.

A.

Adams, John, quotation from, 71, 81.
"Agassiz' Rock," 11.
Agawams, Gosnold's description of, 6.
"Age of Homespun," 47.
Aix-la-Chapelle, treaty of, 64.
Alarm in 1746, 63.
Allen family, name and home of, 343; some oldtime members
    of, 323.
Allen, John Perry, 146, 147, 334.
Allen, "Sailmaker," 326.
Allen, William, first of the name, 323; will of, 323, 324.
Andrews, Captain W. A., 341.
Andros, Sir Edmund, 58.
Anti-slavery enthusiasm, 170, 172; prayer-meetings, 171;
    period, an education, 174.
"Arbella," the, arrival of, 17.

B.

Babcock, "Goodman," 325.
Baptist church, the, 246–250.
Baptists, early, character and treatment of, 262, n.
"Barrington," privateer, loss of, 85.
"Bay horse," the, 71.
Beliefs and misbeliefs, 91.
Benjamite, a left-handed, 324.
Bible, oldest in town, 317.
Bingham, Dea. D. L., 153, 303, 332.
"Biskuitt" and "Barbels," 109.
Blockade-running, bold, 131, 132.
Bloody Brook, Manchester men at, 55.
"Blue Laws," 36, n.

iii

R.

S.

U.

V.

Lightning Source UK Ltd.
Milton Keynes UK
UKHW040807040520
362748UK00001B/146